HORIZONS IN ENVIRONMENTAL ECONOMICS

al **Editors:** Wallace E. Oates, *Professor of Economics, University of nd, USA* and Henk Folmer, *Professor of General Economics, Wageningen sity and Professor of Environmental Economics, Tilburg University, The lands*

mportant series is designed to make a significant contribution to the pment of the principles and practices of environmental economics. It es both theoretical and empirical work. International in scope, it addresses of current and future concern in both East and West and in developed and ping countries.

main purpose of the series is to create a forum for the publication of high work and to show how economic analysis can make a contribution to tanding and resolving the environmental problems confronting the world in enty-first century.

ent titles in the series include:

Negotiating Environmental Qua

NE

Gen
Mar
Univ
Neth

This
deve
inclu
issue
deve

T
qual
unde
the t
R

Eco
A T
Fran

The
Achi

Prin
A G
Seco
Edite

Desi
Ince
Cars

Spat
The
Char

Ecor
Cars

Neg
Polic
Marl

Gam
Mich

Susta
Soci
Edite

Envi
Sele
Robe

Inter
Seba

Negotiating Environmental Quality

Policy Implementation in Germany and the United States

Markus A. Lehmann

Post-doctoral Research Fellow,
Max-Planck Project Group 'The Law of Common Goods',
Bonn, Germany

NEW HORIZONS IN ENVIRONMENTAL ECONOMICS

Edward Elgar

Cheltenham, UK • Northampton, MA, USA

Published by
Edward Elgar Publishing Limited
Glensanda House
Montpellier Parade
Cheltenham
Glos GL50 1UA
UK

Edward Elgar Publishing, Inc.
136 West Street
Suite 202
Northampton
Massachusetts 01060
USA

A catalogue record for this book
is available from the British Library

Library of Congress Cataloguing in Publication Data

Lehmann, Markus A., 1965–
    Negotiating environmental quality : policy implementation in Germany and
the United States / Markus A. Lehmann.
        (New horizons in environmental economics)
    Includes bibliographical references and index.
        1. Environmental policy—Germany—Evaluation. 2. Environmental policy—
United States—Evaluation. 3. Game theory. I. Title. II. Series.

GE190.G3 L44 2000
    363.7'056'0943—dc21

                                                                    00–037609

D188
ISBN 1 85898 976 0
Printed and bound in Great Britain by MPG Books Ltd, Bodmin, Cornwall

Contents

Figures

Legal Abbreviations

APA	Administrative Procedures Act
BNatSchG	Bundesnaturschutzgesetz (Federal Nature Conservation Act)
BImSchG	Bundesimmissionschutzgesetz (Federal Pollution Control Act)
CAA	Clean Air Act
CWA	Clean Water Act
ECJ	European Court of Justice
EPA	Environmental Protection Agency
ESA	Endangered Species Act
FOIA	Freedom of Information Act
FStrG	Fernstraßengesetz (Highway Planning Act)
KrW/AbfG	Kreislaufwirtschafts- und Abfallgesetz (Waste Recycling and Disposal Act)
UIG	Umweltinformationgesetz (Environmental Information Act)
U.S.	United States Reports
U.S.C.	United States Code
U.S.C.A.	United States Code Annotated
S.Ct.	Supreme Court Reporter
T.R.O.	Temporary Restraining Order (einstweilige Verfügung)
VwGO	Verwaltungsgerichtsordnung (Administrative Courts Ordinance)
VwVfG	Verwaltungsverfahrensgesetz (Administrative Procedures Act)
WaStrG	Wasserstraßengesetz (Navigable Water Act)

1. Introduction

1.1 THE TOPIC

This book uses game theory to analyze environmental policy implementation. It focuses on the regulation of individual economic projects generating environmental externalities and argues that the licensing procedures for such projects involve bargaining when regulating agencies are given leeway in decision-making. The institutional setting in which these negotiations occur, that is, the specific norms based on national administrative and environmental law, will lead to different regulatory outcomes. Here the system of judicial review of discretionary administrative actions is of great importance. The book will provide a welfare analysis of judicial review. In particular, it addresses the role of the so-called legal standing to sue, that is, the extent to which externality victims, who may be represented by an environmental group, are allowed to take intended regulation to the courts. The theoretical approach is underpinned by an institutional comparison of German and US administrative and environmental law; indeed, as will be explained, legal doctrines with respect to standing differ significantly between these countries.

That bargaining within environmental regulation is a relevant phenomenon is underlined by the large amount of US literature on *environmental dispute resolution* and the German debate on informal administrative action (*informales Verwaltungshandeln*). This contrasts with the conventional economic view, which perceives environmental negotiations below the transnational level as rare exceptions. This divergence stems from the fact that the predominant economists' perspective on such environmental bargaining is strongly shaped by the Coasean tradition, according to which bargaining between the private parties (the facility operator and the externality victims) takes place under well-defined private rights pertaining to the environment and low or absent transaction costs. Private bargaining may then lead to the efficient internalization of environmental externalities, as if due to the direct intervention by a benevolent regulator having a certain public property right.

1

As an example of the view that such negotiations are irrelevant, a well-known and widely-used textbook in environmental economics states:

> [W]e are probably all rather hard-pressed to think of real-world examples of such bargains taking place. It is true that some electricity-generating authorities 'bargain' with the local population to accept nuclear power stations or waste disposal facilities, perhaps offering cash compensation or a contribution to local facilities. ... But ... externality is likely to be pervasive because of the material balance principle. We should therefore be able to point out to many such bargains rather than to isolated examples. The fact that we do not observe many examples of the bargains taking place suggests that there are either obstacles to them, or that the Coase theorem is not rooted in real-world economics. (Pearce and Turner 1990, 74)

When it comes to policy recommendations, this tradition interprets bargaining over environmental quality as an *alternative* policy means to public regulation. Then the usual caveats are enumerated: For many environmental assets, it is technically not possible to define complete property rights. Because of large numbers of externality victims, transaction costs are prohibitively high. Also, strategic incentives to execute inefficient threats or to conceal private information may prevent successful bargaining. In conclusion, the Coasean analysis is characterized as being of restricted practical interest. Its value rests in serving as a benchmark case to legitimate direct governmental regulation:

> The Coase theorem is important in forcing advocates of environmental regulation to define their terms and justify their case more carefully that they may otherwise have done. But there are many reasons why bargains do not, and cannot, occur. An investigation of those reasons may help to explain why government regulation is the norm in pollution contexts. (Pearce and Turner 1990, 78)

The present work does not deny that complete private property rights on environmental assets are – to say the least – very difficult to define. Nor will it dispute the important role governmental agencies and other state institutions have to play within environmental regulation. However, it is argued here that, even when taking these observations as granted, environmental negotiations are not a closed matter. In reality, the clear-cut dichotomy often made between (private) bargaining and (public) direct regulation is blurred.

When agencies are given leeway in regulation, but are sometimes overruled by courts, rights are insecure as long as no legal decision is issued. Lawmakers, in turn, may have to grant agency discretion for complex regulatory problems, that is, for problems for which they cannot consider every contingency when drafting a bill. Environmental bargaining will be shown to just emerge in such a setting, that is, when public rights are insecure due to regulatory complexity and the division of powers in democratic societies. In consequence, legislative bodies cannot prevent bargaining incentives to emerge on the implementation level. What they can do, however, is to change the institutional framework in which the bargaining occurs.

The institutional pattern investigated here is the system of judicial review of administrative actions, involving the political option of a more expansive or a more restrictive standing doctrine. When standing is more than mere formalism (meaning that the court would always dismiss the legal complaint), changing the standing doctrine changes the mixture of (insecure) rights. Standing against administrative actions can be interpreted as an attenuated private property right. The analysis contained herein will explore two impacts on welfare of relaxing standing barriers for organized environmental interests:

- First, administrators having regulatory leeway may have incentives to collude with those whom they are supposed to regulate. Bargaining will happen over the terms of the collusive agreement, for example, over the extent of the transfer to be paid by the regulatee for less stringent regulation. The legal empowerment of environmental groups allows them to play the role of a watchdog organization, which may trigger judicial review of the corresponding administrative decision. Courts overruling agency decisions, in addition to direct control, will also have a deterring effect on administrators open to collusive behavior. This argument will be analyzed in detail in Chapter 3.
- Second, legal standing itself can be analyzed as a means to gain bargaining power. It is usually granted to those subjected to regulation, to protect them against administrators acting in an arbitrary or capricious way. When the court outcome is uncertain and facility operators have a chance to get the level of prescribed environmental safeguards lowered by the courts, negotiations between the agency and the facility operator will result even when the agency is not open to collusion. Legal standing for environmental groups, besides opening the possibility to actually file suit, may also empower them to enter the negotiations as a bargaining party. Here, the group, representing the interests of externality victims, may

influence the bargained regulatory outcome. This line of reasoning will be the topic of the Chapters 4 to 6.

Consequently, the analysis presented in this book differs in several respects from the Coasean tradition:

- Bargaining may not only happen between private actors, but also involve the regulating agency itself.
- By identifying a class of projects for which benevolent legislators may prefer to grant discretion to regulating agencies instead of intervening directly, a regulatory framework involving environmental bargaining will be presented as a *complementary*, not as an alternative, policy means.
- Secure property rights will be shown not to be a prerequisite for the existence or efficiency of private environmental bargaining.
- The Coasean tradition may overestimate the costs of organizing externality victims, as environmental groups may represent environmental interests in the negotiations.

In contrast to the large literature on the Coasean analysis, comparatively few contributions analyze real-world environmental bargaining, and those which do so use alternative models seemingly incompatible with the Coasean setting. This book, by referring to both strands of the literature, will characterize Coasean bargaining between private parties under secure rights as a special case of the bargaining model presented here.

The two impacts of a more expansive standing doctrine described above provide the rationale for the further organization of the book.

1.2   ORGANIZATION OF THE BOOK

The objectives of the next chapter are twofold. First, it gives a thorough introduction into the problem. It will elaborate on what is meant by regulatory complexity and, hence, will give a rationale as to why agencies may be granted discretion in decision-making. It will then spell out possible abuses of discretionary power and, by thus identifying possible sources of welfare inefficiencies, will present the conceptional entry points for the analyses of the following chapters. Second, as far as necessary to illustrate the general argument and in order to be prepared for the subsequent, more detailed analyses, it presents information on the legal and institutional setting for environmental policy implementation in Germany and the United States. Hence, this overview will not be comprehensive; more detailed institutional information will be given when appropriate within the following theoretical investigations.

Chapter 3 analyzes legislators' decisions whether or not to grant the agency leeway in regulation. Agency discretion, in addition, may be combined with a more or less expansive standing doctrine. It presents a collusion model where the investor has private information on variables relevant for efficient regulation. Agencies, due to a collaborative relationship with industry, gain access to the private information, which they may use for collusion if granted regulatory discretion. An uninformed environmental group may implicitly detect collusion by engaging in costly research on the investor's private information. Research only imperfectly reveals the investor's information. Standing for the environmental group means that they are entitled to present the found evidence in court and plead against planned regulation. Courts will overrule regulatory decisions when the quality of the evidence exceeds a specific threshold level, which represents the strength of the group's standing. It is shown that granting the agency discretion, in combination with a substantial legal standing regime, is, for some distributions of unknown investor types, the welfare-superior solution. By presenting a variant where the court is allowed to decide autonomously on the basis of updated beliefs, a rationale for the court's commitment to the simple decision rule is also given. Furthermore, in addition to the welfare analysis, it is also shown that the number of suits filed in equilibrium is possibly lower under a lower standing barrier, which qualifies the often-raised skepticism that liberalizing standing would increase the courts' caseload.

In contrast to the analysis of Chapter 3, which explicitly addresses the decision of the legislature, the following chapters take regulatory discretion as given and present a model focusing on the bargaining incentives under a stochastic court outcome. Chapter 4 presents the basic setting. It then proceeds to analyze a constellation in which the environmental organization does not have standing. Negotiations over the permit conditions between the facility operator and the regulating agency take place even while monitoring and enforcement costs are not taken into consideration, and the agency is not open for collusive behavior. According to the literature on informal administrative action, which is briefly reviewed in this chapter, negotiations that occur between investors and regulating agencies are the typical bargaining constellation in Germany.

The analysis addresses several issues. First, bargaining over the permit conditions for planned and for existing facilities are distinguished. Intuition suggests that operators of existing facilities should profit from their more favorable bargaining position, because, as long as the negotiations are ongoing, regulation would not apply. This intuition, which gives a rationale for the grandfathering of existing facilities within negotiations over the conditions of regulation, will be confirmed, but only to a limited extent.

Second, the analysis addresses another characteristic of the German constellation, namely, that environmental bargaining occurs informally and, hence, agreements must be self-enforcing. Specific features developed within German administrative practice will be considered:

- the introduction of offset duties in nature conservation,
- the toleration of temporary permit violations, and
- the practice of grading permits within the licensing of large projects.

All are shown to make sense under the specific German bargaining constellation. These features improve the welfare efficiency of the bargaining outcome and facilitate self-enforcement of the informal agreement between the regulating agency and the project operator.

Chapter 5 introduces standing for the environmental organization into the bargaining framework and, hence, changes the mixture of insecure rights. Some background information is given on the institutional situation in the United States, where standing barriers are lower, and where environmental organizations play a more important role in negotiations. Expected welfare from trial is modeled to decrease by this balancing of standing rights between industry and environmental groups. Even then, efficiency of the bargaining outcome is shown to improve.

The chapter also considers the citizen suit provisions prevalent in the United States. These are a means of private enforcement: in the United States, a citizen can act as a private attorney-general when operators are not in compliance with environmental regulations. Citizen suits will be shown to decrease the possibility for self-enforcement of informal agreements between project operators and agencies.

The analyses of Chapters 4 and 5 assume that the bargaining parties are completely informed. Consequently, bargaining will always be successful as long as incentives to negotiate exist. Relaxing this assumption opens up the possibility that bargaining breaks down in equilibrium. To investigate this scenario, Chapter 6 reconsiders the bargaining framework under incomplete information.

First, a setting will be considered in which the project operator is privately informed. An inefficient equilibrium will be derived, in which the case goes to trial with positive probability. This result is used to address the possibility of improving inefficient bargaining outcomes by the intervention of a mediator. Under the heading of alternative dispute resolution, mediation is now an accepted practice within US administrative procedures. In the nineties, it was hotly debated in Germany whether this concept might also be applied to German environmental regulation. The theoretical analysis, however, shows that, given incomplete information, non-assisted negotiations generate the most efficient possible outcome under the presented bargaining model. Hence, mediation is no panacea when inefficiencies in bargaining arise because of information asymmetries.

Second, it is assumed that the environmental group is privately informed on environmental damages. It is shown that, when the court outcome features private values, the environmental group's incentive to strategically misrepresent its private information may vanish for every distribution of types, and the bargaining outcome may be first-best efficient even under one-sided asymmetric information. The result of Chapter 5 with respect to standing is further strengthened in this setting.

The concluding Chapter 7 summarizes the main results and then focuses on possible policy conclusions. It explores the limits of the theoretical investigation with respect to the lessons to be learned for environmental policy, by discussing the lessons of the book in the light of often-raised concerns and objections against a more expansive standing regime for environmental groups.

1.3   LITERATURE AND METHODOLOGY

Related Literature. With respect to the institutional comparison, this work resembles Rose-Ackerman's (1995) study of German and US environmental policy implementation. Her analysis relies on economic reasoning, but does not use game-theoretical tools. While also stressing the importance of the regime of judicial review, her approach differs in several crucial respects:

- Rose-Ackerman does not explore the bargaining incentives emerging from a given system of judicial review. In not doing so, her reasoning resembles the setting presented in Chapter 3, where the environmental organization's watchdog function implies that suits are actually filed.

- Whereas the present analysis focuses on policy implementation at the project level, she mainly addresses administrative rulemaking relevant for entire industries. However, at this level, incentives to fight environmental regulation, which frame possible bargaining incentives, will crucially hinge on the regulatory instrument. This issue will be considered in brief in Chapter 5.

With respect to the institutional environment and real-world bargaining, the investigation will refer to some non-economic literature:

- the German debate on informal administrative action and policy implementation, which underlines the prevalence of negotiations between agencies and regulatees,
- the US literature on environmental dispute resolution, and
- the recent German debate on the applicability of these dispute resolution techniques to the German regulatory setting.

As most of these contributions deal with questions of limited economic interest, their presentation will be concise and selective. The objective of the review will be to point out the empirical relevance of environmental bargaining, and to extract important peculiarities to be addressed by the subsequent theoretical analyses. These, in turn, will refer to the following works of literature:

- Spurred by the seminal contributions from McCubbins and Schwarz (1984) and McCubbins et al. (1987), several authors have addressed the topic of overseeing agencies having discretionary power by watchdog organizations. An introduction into the main argument will be given in Chapter 2. Chapter 3, whose analysis is strongly connected with this literature, will give a more extensive overview.
- Bargaining incentives emerging in private liability disputes under uncertain legal outcomes were extensively analyzed by the literature on settlement bargaining. The older strand of this literature assumes complete information and will be referred to at the beginning of Chapter 4. Newer contributions use models of incomplete information and will be reviewed in Chapter 6.

- By presenting the Coasean world of private bargaining under secure rights as a benchmark case, the analyses of Chapters 5 and 6 also consider several issues addressed by contributions arguing within the Coasean context. Specifically, going back to Mumey (1971), some recent contributions have investigated how parties, in private bargaining under complete information, could commit themselves at a pre-bargaining stage to extract additional rents. This 'extortion' literature will be referred to in Chapter 5. Moreover, in a setting of incomplete information, several authors compared the welfare performance of private bargaining and of second-best centralized regulation in the tradition of Farrell (1987). This literature will be reviewed in Chapter 6.
- Dispersed recent contributions addressing environmental negotiations within a non-Coasean context will also be discussed in Chapters 4 to 6.

Excluded Questions. In focusing on project-specific regulation and the role of environmental groups in the corresponding negotiations, the analysis will leave aside some questions:

- The emergence of environmental groups will not be addressed. As taking action against an environmentally harmful project is a public good from the viewpoint of persons affected by negative externalities, the formation of environmental groups could be analyzed within a framework of private provision of public goods, on which an extensive literature exists.[1] The present investigation, however, begins with the observation that collective environmental actors are empirically relevant. Hence, within the theoretical analysis, the existence of environmental groups will be presupposed. As positive (albeit inefficiently low) contribution levels are a typical result in the theoretical literature, this assumption can also be defended on theoretical grounds.
- Throughout the book, the environmental group is treated as a single player. Consequently, possibly diverging interests between the group's leadership, its members and its external constituency, which could be addressed within a principal–agent framework, will be excluded from the analysis.

---

[1]The classical contribution is Olson (1965). See also Palfrey and Rosenthal (1984), Nitzan and Romano (1990), Gradstein (1992) for models of binary choice of contributions, and Bergstrom et al. (1986), Fershtman and Nitzan (1991), Varian (1994), Buchholz and Konrad (1995) for models of continuous choice. Cornes and Sandler (1996, 144–59) present an elementary non-cooperative model.

- Even while considering some issues usually addressed within a monitoring and enforcement framework, the investigation will generally not use such a framework. Throughout the book, it will be assumed that monitoring and enforcement costs are nil; consequently, the corresponding literature will mostly be ignored.[2]

Methodology. Numerous bargaining models are presented in strategic as well as in axiomatic game theory. Except for Chapter 3, the present work will use the Rubinstein (1985) bargaining protocol where parties alternate offers until agreement is reached or one party quits. The parties' possibility to quit the bargaining table and search for a judicial decision will be depicted as an outside option within the bargaining game. The analysis will apply the outside option principle formulated by Binmore et al. (1986). The choice of this procedure can be defended on several grounds:

- In contrast to procedures whereby all offers are assumed to be submitted exclusively by one party, depicting bargaining as a sequence of alternating offers comes closer to real-world bargaining situations. Furthermore, the alternation of offers may also result from strategic considerations of the parties. As was recently shown by McKelvey and Palfrey (1997) in a setting of bilateral asymmetric information, to alternate offers may be the unique Nash equilibrium in a bargaining game where the parties, in each period, decide simultaneously whether or not to submit an offer.
- For exogenously given gains from trade, welfare does not hinge on the specific division of the surplus, as long as negotiations lead to an agreement. Then, simpler bargaining procedures can be used without loss of insight. For this reason, the model of Chapter 3 will use a simpler procedure, where one party simply submits a take-it-or-leave-it offer. However, in the setting considered in later chapters, welfare levels will crucially depend on the bargained agreement.
- In contrast to these other procedures, the credibility of a threat to quit the bargaining table by taking the outside option can be derived endogenously within the Rubinstein bargaining model. This feature is crucial for some results and, hence, shows the limitations of simpler procedures.

---

[2]See, for example, Deily and Gray (1991), Segerson and Tietenberg (1992), Malik (1993) on monitoring and enforcement, and Ricketts and Peacock (1986), Fenn and Veljanovski (1988) on emerging bargaining incentives in such a setting.

- For the time elapsing between offers being very short, the bargaining outcome can be approximated by Nash's axiomatic bargaining solution, which allows for a compact presentation of the results.

All strategic models use well-established solution concepts. Chapters 3 and 6 present dynamic games of incomplete information and derive Bayesian perfect equilibria. To ensure the uniqueness of the bargaining outcome, Chapter 6 introduces an additional refinement coming close to Cho and Kreps' (1987) intuitive criterion. Chapters 4 and 5 consider dynamic games of complete information and apply Shaked and Sutton's (1984) technique to solve the bargaining models for perfect equilibria.

1.4 ACKNOWLEDGEMENTS

This book was written while I was with the department of economics at Free University of Berlin and with the Max-Planck Project Group 'Law of Common Goods' (Bonn); it was accepted as an *Inauguraldissertation* by the former institution. Many people from Berlin's three university departments of economics were helpful in preventing analytical shortcomings, suggesting additional issues for investigation and clarifying the presentation of my thoughts. Among these, Helmut Bester, Anette Boom, Uwe Dulleck, Carsten Helm, Franz Hubert, Roman Inderst, Kai A. Konrad, Christoph Kühleis, Georg Meran, Kay Mitusch, Reimund Schwarze, Roland Strausz and Dietrich Winterhager particularly deserve to be mentioned; Georg Meran and Dietrich Winterhager acted as my PhD supervisors. In the last stages of the work, comments from Christoph Engel, Christian Geiger and Katharina Holzinger (all Max-Planck Project Group) helped to improve the interaction between the theoretical models and their legal background. The usual disclaimer applies.

Paper versions of several chapters were presented at the 1997 Conference of the European Association of Environmental and Resource Economists (EAERE) in Tilburg (The Netherlands), the 1998 World Conference of Environmental and Resource Economists (AERE, EAERE, FEEM) in Venice (Italy), the 1998 Conference of the *Verein für Socialpolitik* in Rostock (Germany) and the 2000 Annual Meeting of the European Public Choice Society in Siena (Italy). I have to thank Dieter Balkenborg (University of Southampton), Andreas Wagener (University of Siegen) and Bouwe Dijkstra (Interdisciplinary Institute for Environmental Economics Heidelberg), who served as discussants in Tilburg, Rostock and Siena, and gave valuable comments. Beneficial suggestions also came from two anonymous referees.

Research on the United States' real-world environmental negotiations and their legal underpinnings was made possible through a grant from the German Marshall Fund of the United States (No. A-0316-33) as well as through the hospitality of Lance Taylor and the department of economics of the New School University (New York City), and of the Cardozo School of Law (New York City). Furthermore, discussions with US practicioners in environmental negotiations and dispute resolution were very useful in keeping model-building rooted in the real world. Especially helpful were Gail Bingham (RESOLVE, Washington, DC), Richard Collins (University of Virginia), Michael Elliott (Georgia Institute of Technology), Deborah Dalton (Federal Environmental Protection Agency), Peter Lehner (Natural Resources Defense Council), Patricia McKay (1000 Friends of Florida), Larry Morgan (State of Florida Department of Environmental Protection), Suzi Ruhl (Legal Environmental Assistance Foundation, Florida) and Thomas Taylor (Florida Growth Management and Conflict Resolution Consortium).

2. Discretion, Agency Control and Judicial Review in Germany and the United States

2.1 COMPLEXITY AND AGENCY DISCRETION

It is a common feature of both Germany and the United States that environmental acts only vaguely state the objectives and means of environmental regulation.[1] As a result, regulating agencies possess leeway in the interpretation of a statute and, hence, discretion in policy implementation. Two approaches to explain this phenomenon can be found in the literature.

First, it is argued that it is '[t]he complex, highly technical nature of environmental problems [that] deters legislators from resolving all issues in the text of statutes. Wide areas of policy space are left to be filled in by public administrators.' (Rose-Ackerman (1995, 7). This view is normative: legislators, acting as a collective entity, have good intentions (that is, are welfare-maximizing), but technical or scientific complexity hinders them from issuing complete (and efficient) regulations. As the present work aims to derive policy conclusions for implementing statutes, it will adopt this normative perspective. Before more extensively exploring this line of reasoning, consider shortly the second explanation.

According to this view, environmental acts are often vaguely formulated because the political process is deficient. Hence, the underlying problem is not complex, and could in principle be regulated more completely by the legislature. In this sense, environmental law is often just bad law. Air pollution through homogenous pollutants is the classic example, whereby traditional command-and-control policy (implemented by agencies) can, in

---

[1]This feature is frequently stressed in the literature. As examples, see Jarass and DiMento (1993, 53, 69); Rose-Ackerman (1995, 7). In Germany, legal scholars coined the expression of 'indeterminate legal expressions' (*unbestimmte Rechtsbegriffe*) for poorly specified statements in the statutes which give rise to agency discretion. It is regularly underlined that these are abundant in environmental law (see, for example, Eberle 1984, 452; Kloepfer 1998, 139–40; Rose-Ackerman 1995, 58).

principle, easily be substituted by taxation or permit systems, under which the role of implementing agencies would be more restricted.

A positive analysis of legislative decision-making is necessary to fully explore the mechanisms responsible for these deficits. As an example, consider the following argument forwarded in the literature. Those to be regulated, while not being able to prevent the passage of regulatory legislation, may try to obtain broad delegation of power to agencies, which can then be captured during the implementation phase. When voters, due to high monitoring costs of observing actual administrative practice, care more about the passage of environmental legislation than about its degree of actual implementation, lawmakers may be ready to engage in legislation apparently effective in its rhetoric, but poorly implemented.[2]

For the reason given above, this work will provide no further elaboration on this or similar analyses. However, with the exception of Chapter 3, which explicitly use the assumption of a welfare-maximizing legislature, the formal analyses are open for a positive interpretation of the legislative process.

Return now to the complexity argument. Following Laffont and Tirole (1993, 2–4), two interpretations are possible with respect to the constraints of the (welfare-maximizing) legislature:

- *Information constraints.* Legislators are only incompletely informed in regard to relevant decision parameters in the regulation of specific projects. In contrast, agencies implementing a statute will gain superior knowledge during the process of actual regulation and, ideally, may then be able to issue detailed prescriptions in the spirit of the underlying environmental act. Agencies may be able to observe the value of relevant variables unobservable to the lawmakers.
- *Transactional constraints.* It may be prohibitively costly to consider all future contingencies of actual regulation when drafting the bill. Such costs may be interpreted as transaction costs, along the lines of Coase (1937) and Williamson (1975). Analogous to an incomplete contract within a firm-theoretical setting, environmental law will necessarily be incomplete.

---

[2]See Komesar (1990), Rubin (1991). Farber and Frickey (1991, 80–85), and Farber (1992, 62–7) offer a summary and a critique of this and other positive theories of environmental policy formulation. Farber's critique is that this theory depends on voter myopia: '[rational voters] should predict that delegations will result in unfavorable administrative decisions [and] ... hence, ... should not be fooled by congressional delegations.' (Farber 1992, 64). However, when information asymmetries exist between voters and lawmakers as to assess the complexity of regulatory problems, it may be suspected that even rational voters could be ready to accept legislators sometimes exploiting their lack of knowledge by symbolic politics.

The legislature may wish to additionally establish a specific governance structure by delegating power of decision-making to implementing agencies.[3]

At first glance, these two points bear strong similarities. The difference is that under the first argument, legislators cannot observe the values of some variables important for the regulatory outcome. However, they could still condition the law on all observable variables whose values are verifiable by a court (that is, contingent prescriptions that could be enforced). In this sense, the environmental law would still be complete. Under the second argument, some variables or some values of a given variable may be perfectly observable during the specific regulatory context; however, it is too costly to foresee the relevance of those variables or of those values of a given variable when drafting the bill.

To illustrate the first point, consider again air pollution. Assume that the legislature knows the aggregate damage function stemming from a given homogenous pollutant with ubiquitous diffusion (agencies may not have superior knowledge at least in this respect). However, in contrast to implementing agencies, it does not know the specific abatement costs of the firm planning construction of a facility. Still, delegation of power is not the necessary conclusion. The legislature could tax the pollutant or issue tradable permits. Then, lawmakers would not have to know the firms' specific marginal abatement costs when drafting the corresponding bill.

The analysis presented here will focus on externalities where economic instruments like taxes or tradable permit systems cannot be applied, because it is not possible to define a formal tax base. In the case where environmental damage results from homogenous pollutants like sulfur dioxide, a formal base can easily be defined. In contrast, the aesthetic harm of a facility on neighbors cannot be internalized through taxation, because it is not possible to define a formal tax base for what is called 'landscape consumption' in Germany (*Landschaftsverbrauch*). The regulatory situation is unique with respect to the site and the aesthetic impact of the planned facility and, hence, requires a case-by-case approach.

Irrespective of whether the externality can be solved by taxation or not, the question is whether it needs to be addressed by centralized intervention in the

---

[3]Within a firm-theoretical context, the role of the governance structure, specifically, the delegation of power to fill unspecified contingencies is stressed by Williamson (1975) and Grossman and Hart (1986). See Tirole (1988), 29–34, for a summary and Schweizer (1992) for an basic application of this approach to political economy.

first place. Consider the latter example: Where there is a single neighbor, or, at least, the number of neighbors affected by the facility is small and well-defined, internalization is not a public good and Coasean bargaining is, in principle, possible.

However, many projects generating non-taxable externalities affect more persons than just immediate neighbors. This is particularly so when the environmental impact involves issues of nature preservation. Again, problems of landscape protection or of habitat preservation of endangered species cannot be solved via taxation. Pristine nature also generates use values for persons who, while not being neighbors, use the area under consideration for recreational purposes. Furthermore, nature preservation typically generates substantial existence values accruing to persons living elsewhere. Hence, even when no immediate neighbor exists, developments degrading nature or threatening endangered species will generate substantial external losses, borne by persons who are not neighbors.

These considerations make it possible to formulate a classification of environmental externalities generated by a single project as given by the matrix of Figure 2.1. In Figure 2.1, the rows depict the range of environmental externalities' possible scope with respect to the group of affected persons, whereas the columns indicate whether a formal tax base exists or not. Typical examples are given in the corresponding cells.

The first column represents the class of externalities accessible, in principle, by Pigovian taxation,[4] whereas the 'single neighbor' end within the rows gives problems which could be solved via Coasean bargaining. Hence, taxable cases to be classified within or near this 'single neighbor' category represent the contested area within the classic Coase–Pigou controversy in environmental economics. For the class of problems in the second column, legislators cannot use taxation or tradable permits, but have to rely on other regulatory instruments. It is for these problems that the delegation of power to agencies becomes a relevant alternative. Therefore, the present study will focus on such problems.

For problems falling within or near the 'single neighbor' category in column two, Coasean bargaining was often favored over direct regulation. However, Farrell (1987) showed that under asymmetric information, the relative welfare performance of direct regulation by the agency (the

---

[4]Note that the figure assumes the ubiquitous diffusion of pollution within the scope under consideration. When pollutants are diffused only on a regional level and the corresponding damage functions largely differ between regions, a system of regionally differentiated tax rates will be appropriate (Peltzman and Tiedeman 1972).

'bumbling bureaucrat') and of Coasean bargaining between the private parties depends on the type distributions: second-best regulation by an uninformed agency may perform better than private bargaining under asymmetric information. Farrell's analysis will explicitly be reconsidered in Chapter 6. Its thrust, however, will also appear in Chapter 3, which analyses the decision of a welfare-maximizing, but uninformed legislature as to whether to issue direct regulation, or whether to delegate power in decision-making to a set of interacting institutions and actors.

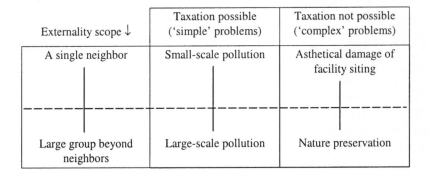

Externality scope ↓	Taxation possible ('simple' problems)	Taxation not possible ('complex' problems)
A single neighbor	Small-scale pollution	Asthetical damage of facility siting
Large group beyond neighbors	Large-scale pollution	Nature preservation

Figure 2.1 A taxonomy of environmental externalities

The book will focus on non-taxable problems which involve a larger group of externality victims, beyond immediate neighbors. As will become clear in a moment, this focus is made to analyze the differences between the US and the German standing doctrines. Problems of nature conservation are particularly compelling examples for such externalities, as the above considerations made clear. For this reason, the institutional setting and the specific cases given to illustrate the following theoretical analysis will have a special focus on nature conservation issues.[5]

For such problems, the following Chapter 3 explicitly addresses the choice of an informationally constrained legislature as to whether to delegate regulative power to agencies. In contrast, the subsequent Chapters 4 to 6 will take wide regulatory discretion as given and, hence, assume that no

---

[5]In Germany, the relevant acts are the Federal and State Nature Conservation Acts. In the United States, nature conservation law encompasses the Endangered Species Act and other statutes or ordinances focusing on specific issues of nature conservation. Among these, the so-called wetland ordinances will be addressed in more detail in Chapter 4.

instruments of direct regulation exist. The legislature is transactionally constrained; the analysis follows the approach of incomplete contracting and exogenously assumes an incomplete environmental law.

As a next step, consider how agency discretion is exercised in practice in the United States and in Germany.

2.2 LEVELS OF ADMINISTRATIVE DECISION-MAKING

In both countries, agency discretion in policy implementation is exercised on three stylized levels:

- First, agencies specify environmental acts by issuing rules or regulations to be applied on the level of whole industries. In Germany, such rules are promulgated by higher bureaucracies under the heading of *Verwaltungsverordnungen* (executive ordinances), with quasi-legal power, and *Durchführungsvorschriften*, which are internal administrative guidelines (Arndt and Rudolf 1992, 73–5).
- Second, even under comparatively detailed industry-wide rules, agencies may still have discretion in issuing regulation for individual large projects or facilities, when those generate complex externalities in the sense described above. On this level, permit systems play an important role, especially in Germany. This point will be more fully explored in the next section.
- Third, due to limited budgets for monitoring and enforcement, agencies usually have leeway in ensuring compliance of firms with the requirements of the rules or permits. This enforcement discretion appears in different characteristic features. In Germany, agencies are often ready to informally tolerate permit violations (this is the so-called *Duldung*[6]). In the United States, operators who are detected to not be in compliance can often negotiate the type and amount of the penalty with the supervising agency (Lawrence 1996).

As pointed out in the introduction, the analyses of the following chapter will have no special focus on enforcement discretion. It will be assumed that, once permits are issued, the agency can always ensure compliance without costs.

At first glance, industry-wide rules and facility-specific prescriptions seem to be mutually substitutive: More detailed general regulations would rather

---

[6]See Randelzhofer and Wilke (1981), Hermes and Wieland (1988), Kloepfer (1998, 293).

preclude discretionary decisions at the level of specific facilities, and *vice versa*. However, when environmental problems are complex, industry-wide regulation cannot cover every site-specific peculiarity due to informational or transactional constraints, and the above reasoning applies accordingly to the formulation of rules. As an important difference to the promulgation of environmental acts by the legislature, agencies, when formulating the respective rules, usually have no leeway as to which policy instrument to apply. For instance, traditional pollution policy prescribes command-and-control in the respective acts, while it often leaves to the administration the process of formulating the corresponding set of standards with which industry has to comply.[7]

In reality, both legislators and higher bureaucracies often try to cover as many peculiarities as possible when formulating the law and, subsequently, the corresponding executive ordinance. The mere quantity of environmental law, that is, the bundle of specific bills and corresponding rules issued by executive agencies, is emphasized by German and US authors (Jarass and DiMento 1993, 53, 69f.). Jarass and DiMento also point out that US environmental statutes are even more detailed than their German counterparts (ibid., 53). By referring to German voices claiming that German environmental protection seriously suffers from an excessive amount of regulation,[8] they ironically note that '[o]ne may not readily agree with this assessment, ... when comparing the quantity of German law to the enormous volume and diversity of federal and state environmental law in the United States' (ibid., 69f., see also Jarass 1993a, 53).

The quantity of administrative rules may provide major obstacles to implementation (Jarass and DiMento 1993, 70). In reaction, it was discussed in the United States to circumvent application of the existing set of regulations and to use instead an 'alternative regulatory pathway' (Aspen Institute 1996). One result of this discussion is the so-called 'Program XL' of the Federal EPA. Under this programme, the agency does not apply its own rules, but uses its discretion for more flexible regulation within the permit processes. One example of such greater flexibility is the ability to grant an overall permit for a plant, instead of implementing the whole set of detailed rules covering specific technical appliances and production processes. As the specific requirements of such a permit are supposed to be determined by a

---

[7]The US Acid Rain Programme, which uses a system of tradable permits, was also introduced at the legislative level, through the 1990 amendment of the Clean Air Act. See Rose-Ackerman (1995, 25).

[8]See for example Brohm (1986, 1987).

collaborative approach, such regulation is more negotiation-inclined, where the existing set of rules is used as a default, should negotiations fail (see Caldart and Ashford 1999, 182–85).

Even without such an explicit program, it could be argued that the high degree of specificity of environmental rules does not necessarily restrict agency discretion at the actual implementation level, that is, when regulating specific facilities. As is argued in the German case by several authors,[9] the mere quantity of formal requirements laid down in executive ordinances and technical and administrative guidelines is well beyond the information-processing capacities of the typical agency. Moreover, increased regulatory specificity means increased risk of inconsistent rules. In consequence, the regulating bureaucrats will apply discretion *de facto* when deciding which subset of rules to learn and, in the case of inconsistencies, which rule to apply in a specific regulatory case. Thus, even while a more detailed regulation may formally restrict agency discretion, it may not do so in reality, where an agency's restrictions in computing regulatory information are high. Instead, a highly specified and internally inconsistent environmental law may increase the opportunities to challenge agency decisions for those having legal standing to sue. As a stylized example, an investor who is not satisfied with the requirements upon her project may try to find a rule open for an interpretation of less stringent requirements or even exemption from regulation, which the bureaucrat did not apply for the reasons given above. When finding such a rule, the investor could hope that a court will not follow the agency's interpretation of the statute.

The incentives to negotiate the authority's prescriptions resulting in such a setting will be the topic of Chapters 4 to 6. Thus, the analysis presented in this work will concentrate on the question as to how environmental acts are implemented on the level of specific sources of environmental harms. Several important differences to the formulation of industry-wide regulations will be discussed at the end of the fourth chapter. Some aspects relating to the issue of enforcement discretion will also be addressed in Chapter 4.

2.3 THE ROLE OF LICENSING PROCEDURES

In Germany, the compliance of specific projects with environmental statutes and regulations is ensured by the use of permit or licensing systems. The

---

[9]For example, Benz (1992), Brohm (1986), Dose (1997) and Lahl (1993).

responsibility for issuing the permit for a project is usually granted to a specific agency which, in turn, may solicit comments from other – specialized – authorities within the permit procedure.[10] Because of this 'concentration' of responsibilities (*Konzentrationswirkung* of the licensing procedure, see Kloepfer (1998, 225f.), the permit that is finally issued is comprehensive; it encompasses all relevant areas of environmental law (ibid.).

The licensing procedures (*Genehmigungsverfahren*) are differentiated in accordance with the procedural rights of third parties. For large projects, the environmental acts call for so-called *Planfeststellungsverfahren*, as defined by §§72 ff. VwVfG, the German Administrative Procedures Act.[11] This procedure requires a public announcement of the project, public access to the written permit application and related records, the possibility, for those affected, to raise objections within a given period of time, and a public hearing (*Anhörung*). Agencies are obliged to comment on the objections. Jurisdiction explicitly recognizes that agency decision-making is discretionary under this procedure (see Kloepfer 1998, 209).

For other projects, the less formal procedure of *Plangenehmigung* is required, where these procedural specifications do not apply (Kloepfer 1998, 210–11). Recent legislation extended the applicability of this simplified procedure. The main objective was to speed up licensing procedures.[12] Also, the Federal Pollution Control Act requires only a 'simplified permit procedure' for project types specified in an annexed list, where the aforementioned procedural requirements are also dropped (§19 BImSchG, see Kloepfer 1998, 964). Furthermore, even under the formal licensing procedure of the Pollution Control Act, the above participatory rights are unequivocally granted only for the licensing of new projects, whereas changes of existing facilities (*Änderungsgenehmigung*) may be exempted from these requirements (Burmeister and Winter 1990, 94; Kloepfer 1998, 234). Most

---

[10]Which agency is granted this responsibility will depend on the specific regulatory case and is spelled out in the so-called *Zuständigkeitsverordnungen* at the Länder level. This is why one uses the general term of *Genehmigungsbehörde* (the licensing agency) in the related legal literature.

[11]For example, §31 KrW/AbfG (Waste and Recycling Act), §17 FStrG (Highway Planning Act), §14 WaStrG (Navigable Waters Act), §10 BImSchG (Federal Pollution Control Act). See Kloepfer (1998, 228ff., 234ff.). The statutes do not use this expression consistently: for instance, §4 BImSchG speaks of *förmliches Genehmigungsverfahren* even if the procedural requirements are very similar to the procedure of a *Planfeststellung* (ibid., 235, 961).

[12]The act implementing this reform was named *Genehmigungsverfahrensbeschleunigungsgesetz*, meaning 'Act to Speed up Licensing Procedures' (Kloepfer 1998, 211).

permits   issued   under   the   Pollution   Control   Act   are   such
Änderungsgenehmigungen.[13]

The use of permit systems is said to be less pertinent in the United States,
albeit of growing importance (Jarass and DiMento 1993, 67; Jarass 1993b,
197). For instance, in Clean Air Regulation, a permit system was first
introduced by the amendments of the Clean Air Act (CAA) in 1990. In
general, procedural requirements for granting permits are low (Pedersen
1999, 4.14–5). Furthermore, facility operators often have to gather different
permits for specific areas of environmental protection issued by the respective
specialized agencies. There is no general permitting procedure comparable
with a German *Planfeststellungsverfahren* with respect to the procedural
requirements and the bundling of responsibilities (Jarass 1993b, 197)[14].

There still is, however, a 'reasonably' uniform set of procedural
regulations for some permit systems (see Novick and Percival 1999, 46–7).
An example is the permit system under section 404 of the Clean Water Act,
which establishes that the US Army Corps of Engineers must issue permits
for the discharge of dredged or fill materials into waters of the United States
(Rodgers 1994, 320ff.). While restricted to this issue, the program is relevant,
for instance, for development projects within wetlands or the construction of
dams, and thus has a clear impact on nature conservation objectives.[15] This
procedure also has to meet the 'notice-and-comment' standard used for
rulemaking: prior to its decision, the agency has to give notice of its intended
regulation and solicit comments[16] from the interested public within a public
hearing (Rodgers 1994, 326). Because of these procedural requirements, the
404 program comes closer to the typical German licensing procedure.

---

[13]Burmeister and Winter (1990, 94) guess that, because of this exemption, 72 percent of all
pollution control permits are issued without public participation, even while the formal
procedure of the Pollution Control Act requires such a participation in principle.

[14]See the discussion on EPA's 'consolidated permit regulations', which were ultimately defeated
in 1983. See Novick and Percival (1999, 46).

[15]Consistent with the relevance of nature conservation objectives, Rodgers (1994, 324)
underlines that decision-making under this program is highly complex.

[16]For instance, the Corps, by consulting with the U.S. Fish and Wildlife Service, must ensure
that the project meets the requirements of the Endangered Species Act. When an endangered
species is jeopardized, the permit may be refused or mitigation measures ordered.

2.4   AGENCY CONTROL

2.4.1   Administrators' Objectives

If implementing public administrators were simply be diligent prosecutors of the law, it should not create a problem to give them regulatory power in project licensing by granting them discretion on the interpretation of statutes. On the contrary, administrators could use their superior knowledge[17] gained within a specific licensing procedure to implement the will of the legislature in the best possible way. An additional control of agency decisions would not be necessary.

In reality, administrators may have their own agenda. Moe (1989, 271) states that

> [e]xperts have their own interests – in career, in autonomy – that may conflict with those of [legislators]. And, due largely to experts' specialized knowledge and the often intangible nature of their outputs, [Congress] cannot know exactly what its experts are doing or why. These are problems of conflict and asymmetric information, and they are unavoidable. Because of them, control will be imperfect.

Thus, it is the conjunction of information asymmetries between the legislature and agencies and their diverging objectives that yields a non-trivial problem of agency control with respect to the efficiency of environmental regulation, which can be analyzed within a principal–agent framework. Administrators' interests may diverge in different ways from those of legislators':

- When administrators derive utility from the size of their office's (time and monetary) budget, in the tradition of Niskanen and others,[18] and are better informed than legislators, they will have incentives to hide parameters of the regulatory case that are relevant for their budget, for example, administrative effort necessary for regulation. First, by overstating the effort necessary for regulation, they may strategically influence the amount of appropriations assigned by the legislature. This incentive alone does not

---

[17]The insight that delegation may be an attractive alternative means to direct regulation when the legislature is incompletely informed was also formulated in Germany's political science research on policy implementation. See Mayntz (1987, 195). A formal comparison between delegation and direct regulation will be undertaken in Chapter 3.

[18]Niskanen (1971, 1973), Migue and Belanger (1974) (where bureaucracies maximize discretionary budgets) and Bernholz and Breyer (1984) (where chief bureaucrats maximize staff numbers). See Holzinger (1987) and Horbach (1992, 1996) for applications with respect to the German bureaucracy's role in environmental policy.

necessarily influence the quality of the actual regulation. Second, however, agencies will also try to minimize unobservable effort, which may have a negative impact on the quality of regulation (Schweizer 1992, 1993). Legislators who have to condition appropriations on observable variables may only be able to implement second-best allocations, where bureaucrats gain informational rents.

- Furthermore, the 'slack' (Kalt and Supan 1984, 282–4) between the general polity and the administrator can be used to favor special interests (see also Levine and Forrence 1990, 176ff.). Agencies' decision-making can be captured by those affected by the regulation. Bureaucrats may be interested in receiving personal transfers. Then, agencies could collude with industry by implementing, in exchange for a transfer, lenient regulation which is welfare-inferior, but cheaper to comply with.[19] When externality victims are represented by an environmental interest group possessing sufficient funds, a transfer, in principle, could also happen in exchange for overly strict regulation. Typically, however, their funds do not compare with the resources available to investors executing large projects (Farber 1992, 61, 64).

  Besides personal bribes, additional interpretations of transfers are possible.[20] As a point more relevant to the United States, administrators may hope for future employment opportunities with the regulated firm. Furthermore, personal relationships with the investor may create incentives for generous treatment within the regulation.

  When the agency's preferences are geographically biased, another possible reading is given by the economic theory of federalism. The size of jurisdictions usually diverges from the geographical scope of environmental externalities, which leads to benefit spillovers of externality regulation. When a facility is to be regulated, under federal or state law, by a local or regional agency (the usual case in Germany), administrators, while formally required to consider overall welfare, may be biased in favor of the community or region in which the project will be sited. Then, the bureaucrat may be ready to execute a more lenient regulation in exchange for additional spending by the investor on community purposes. If the environmental damage resulting from the project were borne exclusively

---

[19] In contrast to collusion, agencies open for transfers may also engage in extortion by threatening investors with welfare-inferior strict regulation. When such a threat is credible, investors may be ready to pay a transfer in exchange for adequate regulation. The issue will be discussed in Chapter 3.

[20] See, for example, Levine and Forrence (1990, 169–70), Laffont and Tirole (1993, 476).

by the community (meaning that no spillover exists), such an arrangement could be an example of efficiency-improving compensation in kind. When, however, the bulk of environmental externalities is borne by community outsiders, benefit spillovers from regulating these externalities are substantial. Then, the agency could be ready to trade additional community income for out-of-community damage that is inefficiently high.[21]

- Even if such transfers are ruled out, administrators possess personal values. The prosecution of the legislature's will may thus be distorted by bureaucrats being biased towards special interests.[22]

2.4.2   Bargaining Incentives

The option to exchange more lenient regulation for a transfer may create bargaining incentives. Indeed, negotiations between operators and regulating agencies frequently happen in Germany; they were intensely debated under the heading of 'informal administrative action' (*informales Verwaltungs-handeln*), an expression coined by Bohne (1981, 1984).[23] As is stressed by Novick and Percival (1999, 47), such negotiations may also happen in the US within the context of licensing procedures.

Note that such negotiations do not necessarily happen on account of collusion. In the model presented in Chapter 4, incentives to negotiate will emerge because of the possibility of systematic court errors. Within German emissions control policy, Greve points to other important reasons, which, however, generate a similar result:

> [B]ecause formal enforcement proceedings entail delay through litigation, high costs, and the risk of losing cases, the bureaucracy usually seeks to implement environmental law through informal bargaining with applicant-firms. The resulting

---

[21]Hence, the regulation of externalities can be analyzed analogous to the provision of a local public good, for which the described phenomenon leads to fiscal nonequivalence (Olson 1969, Oates and Schwab 1988). Typically, underprovision by local authorities results when benefit spillovers are positive (see Cornes and Sandler 1996, 32–3, 363–9).

[22]For instance, Ricketts and Peacock (1986), Fenn and Veljanowski (1988), Mohr (1990) or Amacher and Malik (1996) analyze the impact of a regulator having 'green' preferences regarding the regulatory outcome. Ricketts and Peacock (1986) and Fenn and Veljanowskl (1988) argue within an enforcement context and, by not using a game-theoretical bargaining model, only derive the set of possible agreements. Therefore, in contrast to Mohr (1990) and Amacher and Malik (1996), their contributions will not be considered in the later analyses.

[23]See, for example, Bohne (1990), Breuer (1990), Eberle (1984), Hennecke (1991), Ossenbühl (1987), Tomerius (1995). Peacock (1984, 133–54) gives an English synopsis. Kloepfer (1998, 292–9) gives a concise summary. A review of the insights of this literature, as far as they are important for the present analysis, will be given in Section 4.3. The literature stresses that third parties do not play an active role within this process of informal bargaining.

agreements, such as an extension of statutory deadlines, solicitation of a promise to clean up an old plant in exchange for a license for a new one, and installation of workable (as opposed to the 'best available') pollution control technology, often fall short of what the letter of law demands (Greve 1989, 203–4).

Within project licensing, such negotiations occur before the beginning of the formal licensing procedure; one speaks of 'pre-bargaining' (*Vorverhandlungen*) or 'arrangements' (*Absprachen*) (Eberle 1984). It is because of this collaborative, negotiation-oriented relationship between the agency and the investor developing before and within the licensing procedure that agencies may gain a superior knowledge of information held by investors, when compared with the legislature or other parties (Eberle 1984, 442). While this may not extend to market-specific data (determining the profitability of the project), it may cover information relevant to environmental regulation, that is, technical opportunities to avoid environmental damages and the associated costs. In the following analyses, it will therefore be assumed that the administrator learns the privately held investor information with respect to avoidance opportunities.

2.4.3 Oversight and Judicial Review

Less-informed legislators thus face a tradeoff: delegation may improve welfare, because of the agencies' superior knowledge about the specific regulatory case. But delegation may also decrease welfare, because of agencies' possible abuse of discretionary power. Clearly, to issue simpler regulation which does not need discretionary decisions is then a relevant policy alternative.[24]

When deciding to grant discretion, legislators may, as a first step, introduce a general rule that administrators have to use their leeway in the best possible way. In Germany, such a general rule is the requirement that agencies must weigh up competing public and private interests in their decision-making (*Abwägungsgebot*[25]). For instance, the Federal Conservation Act, as a general rule, states that 'objectives of nature conservation have to be weighted against each other and against other demands of society on nature

---

[24]The question to what extent it is permissible to grant discretion to executive agencies has a long legal history in the US, under the heading of the constitutional delegation doctrine. See Farber and Frickey (1991, 78–85) for a summary and a discussion from a public choice perspective.

[25]Kloepfer (1998, 189–90). This *Abwägungsgebot* is a specific application of the general *Verhältnismässigkeitsprinzip* (proportionality principle) important in German administrative law and practice. See Rose-Ackerman (1995, 75f.) for a discussion from a US perspective.

demands of society on nature and landscape' (§1, (3) BNatSchG[26]). In the United States, a similar requirement exists within the regulations of the Army Corps of Engineers on how to issue a dredge-and-fill permit under section 404 CWA, relevant within conservation issues.[27]

Lawmakers have several instruments at hand to oversee agency behavior with respect to this requirement. In principle, they may engage themselves in monitoring agencies and punishing misbehavior. However, high monitoring costs put limits to such a direct system of 'police-patrol' oversight by congressional committees (McCubbins et al. 1987, 248–53). As an alternative, lawmakers could also establish an indirect system of 'fire alarm' oversight, that is, in the words of McCubbins and Schwarz (1984, 166),

> a system of rules, procedures, and informal practices that enable individual citizens and organized interest groups to examine administrative decisions, ... to charge executive agencies with violating congressional goals, and to seek remedies from agencies, courts or Congress itself.

With respect to congressional oversight, the political systems of both countries differ: while congressional oversight of executive agencies plays an important role in the United States (McCubbins et al. 1987, 250), this is not so in Germany. Jarass and DiMento (1993, 51) write:

> [T]he executive agencies in the United States are much more influenced by Congress than are the agencies by Parliament in Germany. For example, congressional oversight of the Environmental Protection Agency regarding budgets and compliance with policies is foreign to the Parliament. In general, Parliament's committees do not exercise a great deal of supervision over the federal executive. ... As a result, the parliamentary system does not entail the separation of powers between the legislative power and the executive power, as found in the United States.

However, the court system is an alternative monitoring institution which becomes active only as a reaction to legal complaints and thus forms a system of fire alarm oversight. When political actors seek to rely on the decentralized enforcement of environmental acts, 'courts are indeed the key' (McCubbins et al. 1987, 255). Courts play an important role in shaping environmental policy in both the United States and Germany (Jarass and DiMento 1993, 57);

---

[26]'Die sich ... ergebenden Anforderungen [des Naturschutzes] sind untereinander und gegen die sonstigen Anforderungen der Allgemeinheit an Natur und Landschaft abzuwägen.'
[27]'Corps regulations require that the decision to issue a permit requires a "careful weighting" of the benefits that "reasonably may be expected to accrue" against the "reasonably foreseeable detriments"'. (Rodgers 1994, 341).

however, it is with respect to the rules and procedures of administrative law, constituting judicial review as a system of fire-alarm oversight, that implementation of environmental law differs. The analysis presented in this book will focus on these differences.

At this stage, an important theoretical aside can be made. Judicial review of administrative acts is trivial when the relevant information is verifiable: the court could just subpoena the parties to reveal the privately held information which possibly gave rise to agency misbehavior. When the information itself is not verifiable, the court will have to rely on evidence presented by plaintiffs and defendants. Evidence, almost by definition, is verifiable, but may only imperfectly represent the true state of the world. Such a setting will be explicitly modeled in Chapter 3 and implicitly assumed in Chapters 4 to 6. Thus, the analyses will assume non-verifiable information.

In both the United States and Germany, the respective administrative law recognizes that some administrative actions must be discretionary and may thus be unreviewable (5 U.S.C.A. §701 (a)(2); §40 VwVfG). It defines specific conditions under which courts are empowered to review these actions (5 U.S.C.A. §706; §114 VwGO).[28] Under both German and US administrative law, the direct subjects of regulation are entitled to let agency decisions be scrutinized by a court. However, it is with respect to legal standing for parties affected by environmental externalities and their information rights that environmental law differs between the two countries. Standing and information rights for these parties are more restrictive in Germany than in the United States.[29]

The theoretical analyses of the following chapters, which focus on problems affecting more persons than a few neighbors, assume that the interests of these parties can be represented by an environmental group. The group may play the role of a watchdog organization to control agencies' decision-making (Farber 1992). Most of the theoretical analyses will abstract from possible differences between small local or regional environmental

---

[28]US courts can review discretionary action which is 'arbitrary, capricious [or] an abuse of discretion', or was 'made without gathering all substantive evidence' (5 U.S.C.A. §706 (2) (A), (E), see Aman and Mayton 1998, 437ff. for further information). In Germany, courts ascertain whether agencies committed errors in applying discretion (*Ermessensfehler*), either by going beyond the limits of discretion (*Ermessensüberschreitung*) or by abuse (*Ermessensmißbrauch*) (§114 VwGO, see also Arndt and Rudolf 1992, 228).

[29]Greve (1989, 230) points to the differing legal traditions and political systems to explain this phenomenon. The US system, by stressing the separation of powers 'which locks the legislature in a persistent struggle for power', creates strong incentives for the legislature to implement mechanisms for controlling the executive. Such incentives are weaker in a system where the executive is elected and can be dismissed by the legislature.

groups and major environmental organizations important at the national level.[30] This point will become an issue in Chapter 6.

Empirically, US environmental organizations are major players[31] in environmental litigation (Farber 1992, 72f.; Russell 1993, 10669f.). O'Leary's (1993) study on how the legal system influences policy implementation of the federal Environmental Protection Agency (EPA) cites 115 important court cases, out of which 47 were filed by environmental organizations, or 41 percent (227–32).[32] For reasons that will become clear in the following paragraphs, the legal activities of environmental groups in Germany, albeit existent to some extent, are more modest.[33]

2.5 STANDING

2.5.1   Standing in Germany[34]

In Germany, the principle overarching the standing issue is that of protecting individual rights, where the term *individual* refers to persons in a legal sense and also covers companies and formal organizations. A plaintiff has to demonstrate that an administrative decision possibly violates his or her individual rights to be allowed to sue the agency (§42 Abs. 2 VwGO). The most important objective of this rule is to exclude the so-called *Popularklage* (Arndt and Rudolf 1992, 224; Kloepfer 1998, 510): in Germany, citizens merely arguing with the public, general interest beyond their individual rights

---

[30]These major organizations are usually organized along regional chapters or offices.

[31]Two of the largest environmental organizations in the United States heavily engaged in litigation, the Natural Resources Defense Council (NRDC) and the Environmental Defense Fund (EDF) had annual budgets, in 1997, of $27.4m and $23.5m, respectively. The EDF had a staff of 160 in 1997. See McSpadden Wenner (1990), Openchowski (1990) or Russell (1993) for older, but more comprehensive information on other major US organizations like the Sierra Club or the National Wildlife Federation. The most important German organization, the Bund für Umwelt und Naturschutz Deutschland (BUND), has an annual budget, in 1997, of DM22.5m, or approx. $11m.

[32] Forty-three of which were filed by the three most important organizations at federal level: The Environmental Defense Fund (EDF), the Natural Resources Defense Council (NRDC) and the Sierra Club Legal Defense Fund (now Earthjustice Legal Defense Fund). O'Leary's study covers only cases within the Federal Court system.

[33]Ormond (1991, 86f.) gives an overview of cases brought by environmental groups based on their limited options to initiate legal action.

[34]Greve (1989) offers a summary of the history of environmental litigation and legislation in Germany with respect to standing for affected parties. In this paragraph, only the recent situation will be presented.

do not gain standing. Unlike in the US, citizens are not supposed to play the role of a 'private attorney-general'.

The precondition of possibly violated private rights is clearly fulfilled for the subjects of environmental regulation. It will also be fulfilled for some externality victims. For instance, neighbors[35] of an environmentally harmful project usually have standing because of possible losses in property values. However, other utility losses caused by environmental harm will not be covered by individual rights. Take again the above example of a project to be sited within a specific area. The utility losses of those who use the area for recreational purposes, but are not neighbors of the project, will not be covered. Also, existence values of the natural assets in this area will not necessarily be related to property or other rights.

The principle of individual rights' protection is somewhat mollified under the procedural rights of the *Planfeststellungsverfahren*. Here, every 'affected person' (*Betroffene*) is entitled to raise objections and, consequently, to participate in the hearing (§73 Abs. 4 VwVfG). It is not necessary to be legally affected in the sense of a potential violation of a specific right. Under the formal procedure of the Federal Emissions Control Act, anybody – affected or not – can raise objections (§10 Abs. 3 BImSchG; see Kloepfer 1998, 962). However, the right to voice concerns and participate in a hearing *within* the licensing process is distinct from the right to appeal to an outside institution designed to control the administration.

To have standing after the issuance of the permit, neighbors of the project must raise objections within the formal licensing procedure. It is because of this requirement that investors are said to better protected when the permit was issued after a formal procedure (Kloepfer 1998, 234): neighbors cannot keep silent during the licensing process and then try to delay the project by taking legal action against the permit afterwards.

To some extent, German nature conservation law departs from the principle of individual rights' protection. Procedural rights are granted by the Federal Nature Conservation Act to formally recognized environmental organizations (§29 Abs. 1 BNatSchG). When a planned project is licensed

---

[35]Legal practice is not so restrictive as to grant standing only to immediate neighbors. Still, the definition is restrictive. The German Federal Administrative Court (Bundesverwaltungsgericht), the highest court for administrative law, requires from a potential plaintiff a 'special relationship to the project in the sense of a close spatial and temporal connection', when compared to the general public (see Kloepfer 1998, 517). If this is the case, it may be suspected that individual rights are violated. Close temporal relationship means that the plaintiff has to live near the project, using the siting area only sometimes, for example, for recreational purposes, is not covered by this definition (ibid., 515–19).

under a *Planfeststellungsverfahren* and constitutes a 'major and enduring interference with nature and landscape' (§8 BNatSchG[36]), environmental associations have a right to comment and to examine experts' written opinions (Kloepfer 1998, 231, 747).[37] They can sue when these procedural rights were violated during the permit process (ibid., 749). Similar provisions exist in the Conservation Acts at the *Länder* level.

More interestingly, some *Länder* Conservation Acts also grant standing to environmental associations not only on procedural, but also on substantive issues. This departure from individual rights' protection, under the so-called associational standing (*Verbandsklage*[38]), however, is restricted:

- First, such provisions exist only in some *Länder* (Berlin, Brandenburg, Bremen, Hamburg, Hessen, Saarland, Sachsen-Anhalt, Sachsen, Thüringen).
- Second, a general associational standing against any administrative act affecting nature conservation exists only in a few *Länder* (Berlin, Brandenburg, Bremen, Saarland, Sachsen-Anhalt). In other *Länder*, standing is more restricted; specifically, it may not apply under the licensing procedures of *Planfeststellung*[39] (see Kloepfer 1998, 582, 750).
- Third, standing is restricted to nature conservation: when the project does not interfere with nature, or when the impact is not a 'major and enduring' one (which clearly leaves leeway for interpretation), environmental associations do not have standing.
- Fourth, the *Länder* conservation acts do not apply for projects under the supervision of federal agencies (for instance, the construction of highways and railroads) (Kloepfer 1998, 749–50).

Recent lawmaking activities present a mixed picture concerning standing. On the one hand, some new *Länder* of the former German Democratic Republic

---

[36]The is the so-called *Eingriffsregelung*, which prescribes to avoid harm and offset unavoidable harm. This prescription will be analyzed in greater detail in Chapter 4, Section 3.3. The formulation of *erheblicher und nachhaltiger Eingriff in Natur und Landschaft* is a good example for an indeterminate legal expression (*unbestimmter Rechtbegriff*) mentioned above.

[37]Similar procedural rights exist for environmental organizations when local or regional nature conservation agencies issue administrative ordinances (Kloepfer 1998, 747).

[38]The debate whether to introduce standing for environmental groups beyond the doctrine of individual right's violation (*Verbandsklagerecht*) has a long tradition in Germany. Rehbinder (1972) is the paradigmatical contribution. See Kloepfer (1998, 520–23), Greve (1989) or Wolf (1994) for summaries of the discussion.

[39]For instance, Hessen restricts standing to *Planfeststellungsverfahren* and to administrative waivers from specific nature conservation requirements under the respective act. Hamburg does not even cover *Planfeststellungsverfahren* (Kloepfer 1998, 521).

introduced liberal standing requirements for environmental groups within their conservation acts (Brandenburg and Sachsen-Anhalt). On the other hand, however, new federal legislation, by extending the applicability of the simplified procedure of *Plangenehmigung*, reduced the importance of the *Planfeststellungsverfahren* within project licensing.[40] Thus, this reform not only restricts the procedural rights of environmental organizations under the Federal Nature Conservation Act, but also the right to sue on the merits under some *Länder* Acts, as far as those are also linked to the special procedure of *Planfeststellung*.

Environmental groups may also find other ways to legally challenge the project, under the so-called *unechte Verbandsklage* or 'improper' associational standing. First, they may support individual neighbors filing suit against a project's permit, by financing attorney's and other legal fees (Greve 1989, 209; Kloepfer 1998, 521). However, 'the courts' clinging to the ideology of private rights makes such legal actions dependent on the circumstances and whims of the individual plaintiff' (Ormond 1991, 82). Second, the organization may acquire land near the project (a so-called *Sperrgrundstück*). As an owner of land whose property value may be affected by the project, the organization will then have standing (Ormond 1991, 83). However, the merit of the case will also be restricted to this – possibly violated – right. Furthermore, when economic activities induce problems of nature conservation, it may not be possible to acquire a plot which is situated near enough to the project. An example for such a setting is given in Section 5.7.

2.5.2   Standing in the United States

Standing to sue agency decisions in environmental regulation is handled less restrictively in the United States. There are two entry points for legal action to be brought by environmental groups:

- the general review provisions within the Federal Administrative Procedure Acts (Sec. 702 APA), and
- the Citizen Suit provisions within the major environmental acts.[41]

---

[40]See footnote 13.
[41]Citizen Suit provisions exist in the Clean Water Act (sec. 505, 33 U.S.C. §1365), the Clean Air Act (sec. 304, 42 U.S.C. §7604), the Resource Conservation and Recovery Act (which implements waste disposal policy, sec. 7003, 42 U.S.C. §6972) and the Comprehensive Environmental Response, Compensation and Liability Act (addressing hazardous waste cleanups, sec. 113, 42 U.S.C. §9659). See Garrett (1991) or Rodgers (1994) for overviews.

Citizen Suits. These latter provisions are especially important for the enforcement of environmental regulation. Albeit varying in detail, the general feature is that every citizen may sue 'any person' alleged to be in violation of an 'emission standard or limitation' or an order issued by the administrator or the state with respect to such a standard or limitation. The formulation includes permit violations by industry. Violations of 'nondiscretionary duties' of the administrator may also be subjected to court review (quotations are from CAA, subs. 304(f)). A person has to notify the EPA, the state, and the alleged violator 60 days before commencing suit; he or she is barred from instituting action if the EPA is 'diligently prosecuting' an enforcement action. The citizen may seek for injunction (the polluter has to stop the pollution, the agency has to correct its action) and, in enforcement cases, for civil penalties payable to the government. Furthermore, citizen suits permit the recovery of counsel fees and fees for expert witnesses, when the citizen bringing the suit demonstrates at least some probability of success on its merits. This 'fee-shifting' provision is a major departure from the standard rule in US lawsuits that every party bears its own attorney fees and other legal expenses, and comes close to the usual rule applied in Germany, where the loser of the case has to bear the legal costs (see Rodgers 1994, 154, 177).

This kind of legislation gives citizens a role as private attorney generals in enforcement cases. As they can sue only on alleged violations, for example, of a permit, citizens seemingly do not have an influence on the actual permit requirements. However, it will be shown in Chapter 5 that standing under these provisions may also have a substantial impact when the permit conditions are the object of informal negotiations between industry and the agency.

Despite the language of the provisions focusing on 'citizens', it is almost exclusively environmental organizations that file these suits, because of the necessary backing in money and expertise (Greve 1990). Moreover, unlike the expression 'every citizen' may suggest, it is not everyone in a literal sense who may file suit under these provisions. Instead, he or she must have 'an interest which is or may be adversely affected' (CWA, sec. 505(g)). In contrast to Germany, however, this definition is not restricted to *legal* interests.

The Case Law. Two decisions by the Federal Supreme Court established a liberal standing doctrine relevant not only for Citizen Suits, but also for the general review provisions under the APA. In *Association of Data Processing Organizations v. Camp* (397 U.S. 150 (1970)), the Supreme Court departed from the 'legal interest' or 'legal injury' doctrine applied before: a plaintiff no longer needed to show a violation of legal interests established by the respective law. Instead, the court ruled that anyone who could show 'injury in fact, economic or otherwise' should be granted standing; this test, however, is barely related to the underlying law (Sunstein 1992, 185).

In *Sierra Club v. Morton*, the Supreme Court issued a ruling especially important for associational standing (405 U.S. 727 (1972)). In this case, the Sierra Club wanted to push through a 'real' standing for environmental organizations (in the sense of the German *Popularklage*). The Supreme Court, however, insisted on the injury-in-fact test: the plaintiff should suffer from the administrative decision in order to obtain standing. Even while doing so, the Court allowed environmental organizations to sue *on behalf* of their members, if they could prove that at least one of their members had an injury-in-fact.

The standard developed by the court after this decision was low: in order to obtain standing, environmental organizations were required to include, by affidavits, allegations by individual members that they use the affected resources and were injured by defendants' conduct. In a conservation case, their alleged using of an area for recreational purposes was generally accepted by the courts as a proof of an injury-in-fact (Rodgers 1994, 102).

At the beginning of the nineties, the Supreme Court again tightened the standing requirements in two widely-discussed[42] rulings: the 1990s decision *Lujan v. National Wildlife Corporation* (497 U.S. 871) and the decision in *Lujan v. Defenders of Wildlife* (112 S.Ct. 2130), in 1992. To prove an injury-in-fact after these rulings, plaintiff's counsel 'must establish "concreteness" at a place certain and "actuality" or "imminence" at a time certain. To satisfy the courts' majority in *Defenders*, affidavits must give 'concrete plans' to return to observe, collect, and/or recreate at a specific time and place where the injury will be suffered.' (McElfish 1993, 100026–27). Thus, it seems that mere existence values of environmental assets are more difficult to cover under the tightened injury-in-fact test. Even after these rulings, the broad injury definition still captures aesthetic, conservation, or recreational interests (Babich 1995, 10146).

Most standing requirements on the state level are more liberal than on the federal level (McGrath et al. (1991), 608–14, 648). McGrath et al. (1991, 604) also observe that, 'although state courts often apply the federal doctrine, they rarely pick up on the more restrictive trends emanating from recent

---

[42]See, for example, Burt (1994), Mansfield (1993), McElfish (1993), Sheldon (1993) and Sunstein (1992).

Supreme Court decisions.' Only a few states, like, for example, Pennsylvania, are consistent with or even more conservative than the federal practice (ibid., 608–14).

2.6 INFORMATION RIGHTS

Information rights shape the scope of agency control in different respects.

Sunshine Legislature. The US Government in the Sunshine Act requires that 'every portion of every meeting of an agency shall be open to public observation' (5 U.S.C.A. §552b(b)). Even while exemptions are specified,[43] collusive transfers may be more difficult to arrange under this so-called sunshine legislature. Similar acts at the state level also provide for public access to meetings between regulators and the subject of regulation. For instance, the corresponding statute in Florida provides that

> all meetings of any board of any state agency or authority or of any agency or authority of any county, municipal corporation, or political subdivision ..., at which official acts are to be taken are declared to be public meetings open to the public at all times, and no restriction, rule, or formal action shall be considered binding except as taken or made at such meeting. The minutes of a meeting of any such board or commission ... shall be promptly recorded, and such records shall be open to public inspection (chap. 286.011 Florida Statutes (1989), cit. McSwain 1991, 311).

To the knowledge of the author, no comparable legislation exists in Germany.

Information Access. Access to information held by the administration is another prerequisite to controlling agencies' behavior. It may be only this possibility that actually enables interested parties to find evidence of agency misbehavior that is presentable in court; a more liberal access to information would at least lower the costs of gathering such evidence. Two aspects can be distinguished:

- First, the agency's duty to actively deliver information, that is, without preceding request. In the present context, this especially concerns the

---

[43]They roughly correspond to the exemptions from FOIA, which are discussed below. See also Aman and Mayton (1998, 693–702).

agency's duty to give notice of an intended project and the subsequent beginning of the licensing procedure.

- Second, the actual access to the records held by the agency, which comprise the relevant data of this specific regulatory case.

In the United States, agencies must give notice of intended regulation when issuing a dredge-and-fill permit under section 404 of the Clean Water Act. In general, however, procedural requirements within licensing procedures are rather low. Access to the agency's records, as a general rule, is guaranteed by the federal Freedom of Information Act (FOIA). FOIA permits 'any person' to obtain access to all federal[44] agency records; there is no limitation with respect to the status of the person or to specific types of procedures.

The act specifies nine exemptions from this general rule of public access, one of which is the trade secrets of companies. Jurisdiction and environmental law has put restrictions on the applicability of this exemption.

- Information about a 'plan, formula, process, or device' is a trade secret (and thereby protected from public access) only if there is a clear relation to the production of commodities (Gurlit 1990, 528–9).
- Under the Clean Air Act and the Clean Water Act, emission or effluent data must be revealed even if this 'would divulge methods or process entitled to protection as trade secrets' (Gurlit 1990, 541).

It is because of this latter provision that citizen suits gain bite in pollution control. Under both acts, industries are required to report their emissions on a regular basis to the EPA, by the so-called discharge monitoring reports, which are publicly accessible under this proviso. As a result, environmental groups can compare factual emissions reported in the discharge monitoring reports with the standard set in the respective permit. In the 1980s, environmental organizations were thus able to effectively enforce permits under the Clean Water Act (CWA) by using the citizen suit provisions.

In Germany, agencies have to give notice under the procedure of the *Planfeststellungsverfahren*, where, in emissions control, this provision only applies to the construction of new projects. Public access to the records is also guaranteed under this procedure. However, it used to be restricted to this procedure. No provision for public participation and for related access to information existed under the normal licensing procedures in the

---

[44]Similar freedom-of-information provisions exist at the state level. See Gurlit (1990, 517); Senate Committee on the Judiciary (1978).

environmental acts. Then, the general rule of the German Administrative Procedure Act applied. It restricts access to information to parties (*'Beteiligte'*) of the procedure, whose definition relies again on a potential violation of rights (§§13, 29 VwVfG, Kloepfer 1998, 276).

Like in the US, trade secrets are exempted from disclosure. Information can be declared a trade secret by the agency upon application by the investor. Judicial review of this decision, however, was limited: under § 44a VwGO, it is not possible to take action against a procedural decision without taking action against the substantive decision to be made under the procedure. Thus, courts dismissed complaints on procedure while the said procedure was still ongoing and the decision not yet made (Burmeister and Winter 1990, 120).[45]

Recently, Germany was forced by the European Union to adopt a more liberal policy of environmental information disclosure. A directive issued by the EU in 1990 provided for this liberalization of informational rights, closer to the US practice. It was incorporated into German law in 1994 by the *Umweltinformationsgesetz* (Environmental Information Act), which grants access to information for any private person irrespective of legal injury (Kloepfer 1998, 277ff.). However, the rule governing protection of trade secrets (§8, 1 UIG) is only vaguely formulated and still gives considerable leeway to administrators (Kloepfer 1998, 280). Furthermore, the act still contained an exemption provision for ongoing administrative procedures (ibid., 279), which, however, was declared as violating the EU directive by the European Court of Justice (ECJ C-321/96).

2.7 THE COSTS OF JUDICIAL REVIEW

After this short synopsis of real-world systems of judicial review, we come now back to the theoretical reasoning. Section 2.5 argued that the introduction of judicial review as a system of fire-alarm oversight may have advantages for agency control. However, it will also raise regulatory costs (Asimov 1994, 133–4).

- *Legal costs.* Obviously, it will be costly to run the actual court system. Private parties deciding to use it will be summoned to (partly) finance the system by legal fees. Additionally, however, they will have to pay attorney's fees. Gathering evidence presentable in court will also be costly.

---

[45]Führ's (1989) study presents anecdotal evidence suggesting accommodating behavior of agencies concerning such applications for confidentiality. See also Führ (1990, 135–6).

- *Delay.* Due to the limited resources of the court system, legal adversaries usually have to wait for trial. The trial itself is also time-consuming. When the project's realization is postponed as long as the case is pending, costs of delay will result. Private parties have different incentives in this respect: while victims of environmental externalities want to hamper a project whose environmental impact can only be reduced, but not completely be avoided, the interests of investors lie in a fast realization.
- *Legal errors.* When relevant information is non-verifiable, legal errors may decrease the quality of regulation. The (verifiable) evidence presented in court may not depict the actual technical or ecological reality. Even if this were be the case, judges may misinterpret the evidence. Consequently, they may overrule or remand an agency's regulatory decision even if it was the efficient one.

In the German discussion whether to lower the standing barriers for environmental organisations, it was often argued that such a legal reform would lead to an explosion of filed suits in a situation where court already complain about their caseload.[46] Environmental groups, by filing suit, could delay the realization of economic projects generating environmental externalities (Greve 1989, 203). They could even hope that investors will ultimately cancel the project because of delay and additional legal costs. In this respect, the 'litigious' US society could be interpreted as an awful example pointing to the dangers of too low requirements for access to the judicial system. It will be explored in Chapter 3 whether a more liberal standing regime necessarily leads to an increased caseload.

2.8   AN OUTLOOK ON FURTHER PROCEEDINGS

Within a welfare analysis, the potential improvement in quality of environmental regulation by the introduction or extension of judicial review has to be weighted against the enumerated costs. The following chapters will deliver such an analysis. While doing so, they will elucidate two mechanisms to reduce or avoid the costs of review:

---

[46]See Weyreuther (1975) for a summary; see also Greve (1989, 223) and Bizer et al. (1990, 55ff.).

- *Deterrence.* The mere threat of having regulation overruled by a court may deter agencies from abuses of discretion, even when no suit is actually filed. Chapter 3 addresses this issue.
- *Bargaining.* Standing may create bargaining power for the respective private party, and will thus shape the bargaining constellation and its outcome. Several authors, whose works are reviewed at the beginning of Chapter 4, point to the large empirical difference between the number of filed suits and those actually decided by courts. It is just high legal fees which create incentives to bargain an out-of-court settlement. This 'most cases settle' -paradigm will indeed form an important empirical underpinning of the chapters following Chapter 3. When environmental groups have standing, a suit does not actually need to be filed, as it is the threat to sue which lets the environmental group enter the bargaining game.

Overregulation. While thus possibly avoiding the costs enumerated above, the introduction or extension of standing for environmental advocacy groups may also have an additional negative impact because of possible overregulation. These organizations, with their bias towards environmental objectives, only focus on the environmental harms economic projects generate, but do not take into account their social benefits. In the following chapters, overregulation will be addressed under both the deterrence and the bargaining framework. When the probability to prevail in court is high for an environmental group, and when lost cases are related to substantial sanctions for the agency, the latter may be deterred from issuing correct regulation which would trigger a suit filed by the environmental group. Within the bargaining framework, too much power for environmental interests may lead the other parties to (reluctantly) agree on too strict regulation.

The analyses presented in the next chapter and the subsequent ones are complementary with respect to the modeling detail of legal decision-making and of the bargaining process. Within the deterrence analysis of Chapter 3, the court's ruling is modeled in more detail, as an evaluation of evidence presented by the plaintiff. The strength of associational standing is depicted by the standard of evidence required by the court to overrule the agency's decision. Court errors may occur, because the presented evidence, even while meeting the standard of evidence, may not represent the true state of the world. While thus elaborating on the legal process, the collusion negotiations between the investor and the agency are stylized by a simple bargaining procedure. Moreover, it is exogenously ruled out that the environmental group can become a bargaining party. In contrast, the subsequent chapters will explore the bargaining situation in more detail and use instead a simpler model of legal decision-making and possibly resultant legal errors.

3. Standing, Collusion and Collusion Deterrence

3.1 INTRODUCTION

This chapter will present an analysis of the legislature's decision as to whether to grant discretion to regulating agencies, and whether to combine this discretion with legal standing for environmental advocacy groups.

The model depicts a licensing procedure for a planned, indivisible economic project. One may especially have in mind the realization of a major water-related project, like the construction of a dam. Such a project would trigger a 404-permit procedure in the United States and a *Planfeststellungsverfahren* in Germany. Procedural requirements of 'notice and comment' are then similar.

Investors seeking a project permit are assumed to have private information concerning the technical means of avoiding environmental damage and the associated costs. Investors differ by their avoidance technologies and associated costs; in consequence, optimal regulation would have to prescribe type-specific avoidance levels. Taxation is ruled out for the reasons given in Chapter 2 (remember that this assumption is realistic for conservationist cases; again, the construction of a dam is a typical example).

The legislature is uninformed and aims to choose a welfare-superior regulatory regime. It may grant discretionary power to an agency responsible for the implementation of the law, that is, for issuing optimal type-specific regulation when licensing the specific project. The agency will learn the private information during the permit procedure, from which welfare-oriented lawmakers may wish to profit. The administrator, however, has an incentive to collude by not obeying the law and offering false regulation more cheaply for the investor, in exchange for a bribe (remember that this expression is not to be taken literally). This potential for the abuse of regulatory discretion may be mitigated by the legislature: it may additionally introduce standing for environmental groups which enables them to bring in the legal system and thus play a watchdog role.

Even while the investor's private information is observed only by the agency, the uninformed environmental organization can engage, at positive costs, in research activities to overcome its information deficits. When agencies have discretion, they are obliged to give public notice of any intended regulation. Consequently, the environmental group, by engaging in research, may find evidence indicating whether the announced regulation is (type-specifically) optimal or not. This evidence, in turn, is verifiable, but will only imperfectly reveal the private information. The model analyses the efficiency implications of a simple legal rule, where courts are compelled to decide in accordance with the presented evidence, when its quality exceeds an exogenously set threshold representing the strength of the legal standing of the environmental group.

As an alternative to this regulatory solution, the legislature may issue a uniform standard with which investors must comply irrespective of their type, that is, irrespective of their specific technology. Then, giving the agency leeway in decision-making is not necessary.

When deciding whether to grant agency discretion or not, lawmakers face a tradeoff between the superior knowledge of implementing agencies and their incentive to collude. This incentive may be mitigated at least to some extent by the introduction of associational standing and, hence, the use of the court system. This, however, will generate other inefficiencies described in the preceding chapter: legal and research costs, delay, and inefficient regulation due to court errors. Except for delay costs, the corresponding efficiency losses will be incorporated into the formal analysis presented now. The issue of delay will be reiterated shortly in the concluding part; a more comprehensive analysis is postponed to Chapter 4.

The following analysis will derive several results.

- When legislators decide to grant agency discretion, they will always combine it with a substantial legal standing for the environmental group. Lowering standing barriers may have beneficial welfare effects.
- For some type distributions, the introduction of agency discretion and a substantial standing for organized environmental interests will yield higher welfare than uniform regulation.
- Furthermore, a rationale for the court's commitment to the simple decision-making rule used in the model will be given. Generally, an institutional regulatory regime where the court is allowed to update its beliefs in a Bayesian way and decide accordingly will perform worse.

- Moreover, it will also be shown that, contrary to the concerns raised in the legal discussion, a more expansive standing regime may lead to a decline in legal battles.

The intuition behind these results is that such an extension of standing, in addition to raising the opportunity to actually sue, also deters the agency from collusion. When, however, the agency decides correctly, the environmental group, in turn, may decide not to undertake research and, eventually, go to court.

Literature. The general framework relates to the principal–agent literature analyzing the principal's problem in three-tier hierarchies: the principal, to control the agent, may introduce another agent as a supervisor, who, however, may have incentives to collude (Tirole 1986, 1992). The supervisor's report, in turn, may be double-checked by hiring another supervisor (Khalil and Lawarrée 1995, 1996; Kofman and Lawarrée 1993). In the present model, this role of the second supervisor is taken by an environmental watchdog and a court, which, while not open for collusion, have other imperfections from the principal's viewpoint.

Within political economy, oversight models relying on additional information by third parties were presented by several authors (Banks and Weingast 1992, Laffont and Tirole 1990, 1993, Lupia and McCubbins 1994, Epstein and O'Halloran 1995). Except for Laffont and Tirole (1990, 1993), these authors present models of direct, congressional oversight of administrative decision-making: watchdogs who report directly to the legislature, and where courts do not play a role. Furthermore, and in contrast to the present analysis, these contributions treat agency discretion exogenously and, hence, do not investigate whether it is efficient in the first place to give administrators leeway in decision-making.

In Boyer and Laffont (1999), the choice whether to delegate regulatory power is endogenous, but made at the constitutional level. It is a (welfare-maximizing) constitutional assembly which may grant discretion to a legislative body with respect to the use of specific regulatory instruments. Within the legislature, better informed politicians have incentives to depart from efficiency, in order to serve the private agenda of the constituency holding the majority in the legislature. In this model, neither the legal system nor potential watchdog organizations play a role.

In the following analysis, the timing of the subgame under agency discretion is inspired by Laffont and Tirole (1990, 1993). In their model, however, the quality of the watchdog's research result is perfect (that is, when undertaking research, the group always finds verifiable, precise information on the firm's type), whereas the following analysis models the verifiable research results as signals of imperfect quality over the true state of the world. Such an approach is frequently used in the literature;[1] however, the model used here differs from these contributions in that is assumes that the quality of the information gathered is learned only after spending funds on research. For example, in Che and Earnhart (1997), the quality of the information gathered is known from the beginning, and courts are modeled to always accept the presented evidence, irrespective of its quality. Even evidence unfavorable to the plaintiff will be revealed to the court, whereas in the present analysis, the environmental group may decide not to reveal the evidence found. The court cannot infer anything from the fact that no evidence is revealed (like in Lewis and Poitevin 1997), for the simple reason that the court is only brought into the game when the environmental group presents favorable evidence.

Depicting research results as verifiable, but imperfect signals allows us to model a required minimum quality of evidence as a policy variable and to analyse the efficiency implications of parametric variations of this standard of evidence.[2] A somewhat similar setting is used by Lewis and Poitevin (1997); in their model, however, it is the regulated party which reveals the 'noisy' evidence to the (welfare-maximizing) regulator. Consequently, the regulator, who has prior beliefs on the regulated party's type, can update beliefs contingent on the regulated party's decision as to whether to reveal (possibly unfavorable) evidence. The standard of evidence is then set endogenously by a cost-benefit calculus of the regulator on the basis of these updated beliefs. Such a setting will be discussed shortly in Section 3.5.

This chapter is organized as follows. Section 3.2 describes the general framework, the actors and the timing of the game. The following Section 3.3 analyses the strategic interaction of the regulatory agency and the environmental group under agency discretion and legal standing, describes the possible equilibrium constellations and states expected welfare contingent on the exogenous standard of evidence required to overrule the agency's decision. This section also elaborates on extortion incentives of the agency and on possible overregulation. Section 3.4 analyses regulation without discretion and shows that it is, for some type distributions, optimal for a

---

[1]For example, by Shavell 1985, Kofman and Lawarrée 1993, Khalil and Lawarrée 1995, Froeb and Kobayashi 1996, Che and Earnhart 1997 and Lewis and Poitevin 1997.
[2]This standard differs from the one used by Priest and Klein (1984), where the court's threshold is a critical level of the defendant's fault.

welfare-maximizing legislature to introduce agency discretion and a substantial legal standing. Section 3.5 discusses the role of the legal decision-making rule. Section 3.6 concentrates on the issue as to whether an extension of standing necessarily raises the number of filed suits. Section 3.7 presents a simplified version of the model and addresses the possibility to collude with environmental groups. Section 3.8 summarizes and draws some conclusions concerning overregulation, the recovery of legal costs, the role of informational rights, and delay.

3.2 THE MODEL

The model presents a three-tier governance structure (legislature, a regulating agency and a court). There are also investors and an environmental group. All actors are assumed to be risk-neutral.

Technology. Consider a set of N indivisible private projects which are identical insofar as they yield profit Π_0 for the investor and consumer surplus Cs for society; moreover, each project generates a monetary environmental damage D_0. In order to focus on the different legal situation prevailing in Germany and the United States, assume that D_0 represents environmental damage which is not protected by individual rights. For instance, D_0 may represent the utility loss of those persons who use the pertinent area for recreational purposes, but who are not neighbors of the project. Consequently, externality victims represented by the environmental group would not have standing under the German principle of individual rights' protection, while they would have standing under the more liberal *injury-in-fact* standard applied in the United States.

Because of the harmful effects on the environment, investors are obliged to apply for a – possibly conditional – permit from a regulating agency before executing the project. The following analysis will investigate the procedure of licensing a specific project. The individual investor's spending on protective activities S reduces environmental damage. The spending level related to a specific damage level is given by the decreasing, strictly convex function $S = S(D)$, where $S(D_0) = 0$. The amount of damage reduction per monetary unit spent depends on the technical abatement opportunities the investor has at hand. Assume that the projects differ in the effectiveness of abatement opportunities at hand: $S(.) \in \{S_l(.), S_h(.)\}$. As the example below will make clear, l stands for low marginal abatement costs. For every damage level D, $S_l(D) < S_h(D)$: $S_l(.)$ represents the more effective abatement technology.

The actual technology is privately known to investors. When the game starts, other actors know only the potential types and q, which is the fraction of investors having less effective technology; hence, q is the uninformed actors' prior belief that the investor applying for a permit is of type $S_h(.)$. such an investor will also be called the 'high' type. Consider Figure 3.1 for a graphical illustration.

An example. Note that $S(D)$ maps monetary environmental damage into (monetary) spending on avoidance. By not explicitly considering physical variables generating physical environmental damage, this formulation reflects the assumption that a formal tax base is impossible to define. To see how privately known information on avoidance technology shapes $S(D)$, consider now a specification where damages and spending depend on a homogenous physical variable E ('emissions'). Assume the corresponding damage function to be quadratic (and, hence, strictly convex) and the avoidance function to be

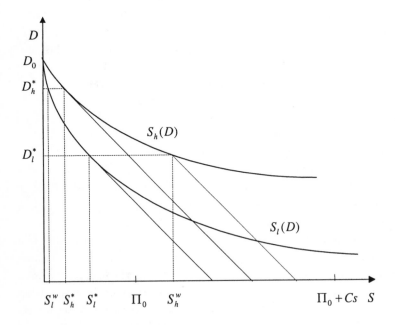

Figure 3.1 Type-specific efficient regulation

linear:

$$D(E) = E^2,$$
$$S(E) = s(E_0 - E),$$

where E_0 stands for the emissions level corresponding to D_0 and s are the privately known marginal abatement costs with respect to E: $s \in \{s_l, s_h\}$. Substituting yields

$$S(D) = sE_0 - sD^{0.5},$$

which satisfies the assumptions that $D(S)$ is decreasing and strictly convex. Generally, these assumptions will be satisfied for both functions being convex and at least one strictly convex.

Thus, q represents the share of investors with high marginal avoidance costs with respect to D:

$$S_l'(D) < S_h'(D) \tag{3.1}$$

for every D. Efficient levels of environmental damage are thus type-contingent; denote the respective levels by D_l^*, D_h^*, and $\Delta D = D_l^* - D_h^*$. Assume an interior solution exists for both types: $D_i^* \notin \{0, D_0\}$. Denote social benefits of the project under marginally efficient regulation by

$$V_i^* = Cs + \Pi_0 - S_i(D_i^*) - D_i^*, \; i \in \{l, h\}.$$

There is no interaction between the damage level and the consumer surplus because projects are indivisible. Conditions for efficient spending levels are

$$S_i'(D_i^*) = -1, \tag{3.2}$$
$$V_i^* > 0. \tag{3.3}$$

Condition (3.3) is met by assumption. Denote $S_i^* = S_i(D_i^*)$. Because of (3.1), $S_l^* > S_h^*$: as her technology is more effective, a low-type investor, in the optimum, has to spend more.[3] Because of $S_l(D) < S_h(D)$, $D_l^* < D_h^*$. Furthermore, denote $V_0 = Cs + \Pi_0 - D_0$. To avoid corner solutions, assume

---

[3]Adverse selection problems may result as long as $S_l^* \neq S_h^*$.

$V_0 > 0$. Assume also both project types to be privately profitable, when regulated correctly:

$$\Pi_0 - S_i^* > 0. \tag{3.4}$$

The legislature. Lawmakers are welfare-maximizing, but have limited knowledge. They only know the potential investor types and q. In designing the environmental law, they face a trade-off: by granting discretion to a regulating agency, they may profit from the agency's superior knowledge, but simultaneously risk collusion. Therefore, they may either empower environmental organisations parties to let agency decisions be scrutinized by a court, or decide not to grant discretion in the first place. In the latter case, the legislature prescribes a uniform standard, and fails to gain from the agency's superior information.

When lawmakers decide to grant discretion, they will prescribe type-specific regulation and give the agency discretion to decide which standard to apply in permitting the specific project. This setting thus depicts a stylized regime of differentiated standards. The legislature will then introduce, as a general rule, a weighting obligation like the German *Abwägungsgebot* which requires agencies to use discretion efficiently. Legislators will empower the environmental organisation by fixing a parameter $\overline{\theta}$, which will be explained in detail below, when considering the court's ruling.

For a given q, the welfare-maximizing legislature will derive the optimal set of differentiated standards and the optimal $\overline{\theta}$ and compare the resulting welfare performance of this solution with the welfare level under an optimal uniform standard. For the purpose of this chapter, however, such a derivation is not necessary (moreover, it requires numerical specifications of the variables presented above). To show that the discretion–cum–standing solution will, for some type distributions, perform better than an optimal uniform standard, it is sufficient to show this property for a specific $\overline{\theta}$ and the set of optimal type-specific damage levels D_l^*, D_h^*. When the legislature then chooses to introduce discretion and standing under these type distributions, it indeed chooses the optimal regulatory regime, irrespective of the fact that it could further improve welfare by fine-tuning the relevant policy variables.

The agency. Information on the investor type applying for a permit is observable by the agency. However, the information is not verifiable: it cannot credibly be communicated to the court. Therefore, a court cannot subpoena the agency or the investor to present information on the latter's true type. This formulation depicts the observation, often made in environmental economics, that technical avoidance opportunities and, hence, avoidance costs, are the intrinsic information of the firm's management. Regulating agencies may have the opportunity to overcome this problem at least to a certain extent, due to the collaborative, intimate relationship with the investor that evolves during the permitting procedure; for other parties, however, this problem may remain a serious one, the more so when informational rights are weak.

When the agency does not have discretion, it must simply apply the law and prescribe the uniform standard.[4] When it has discretion, the agency, in principle, is free to decide which standard to apply. It is here that the agency objective is crucial for possible collusion incentives. Clearly, when the agency is welfare-maximizing, such an incentive does not exist. Therefore, in models on agency oversight and control, bureaucracy is often assumed to maximize a monetary income, stemming either from legislative appropriations, extortion or from collusion.

In the setting considered here, the bureaucrat may offer to regulate according to the standard preferred by the investor, in exchange for a side-payment P. Using the superscript w for wrong regulation and $i, j \in \{l, h\}, i \neq j$, the respective spending levels under standards D_l^*, D_h^* are given by

$$S_i^w = S_i(D_j^*).$$

Observations

3.1: As $D_l^* < D_h^*$ and $S_i(.)$ is decreasing in D, $S_l^* < S_l^i$ and $S_h^w > S_h^*$.

3.2: For $S(D)$ being strictly convex, $S_l^* - S_l^w < \Delta D < |S_h^* - S_h^w|$.

Consider Figure 3.1 for a graphical depiction of these observations. Denote by V_i^w the gain for society from realization of the project under false regulation:

$$V_i^w = Cs + \Pi_0 - S_i^w - D_j^*,$$

---

[4]In the model, there is actually no function left for an agency with no discretionary power. In reality, the introduction of specialized bodies may save administrative costs of implementing non-discretionary regulation, an issue not considered here.

where $i, j \in \{l, h\}, i \neq j$. Again, to avoid corner solutions, assume $V_i^w > 0$ and $\Pi_0 - S_h^w > 0$: the high-type investor still executes the project under incorrect regulation.

As the present model does not intend to analyse direct congressional oversight of agency behavior, the appropriations process and related opportunities of control will not be considered. However, a somewhat related consideration enters the agency's decision-making process in regard to the possibility of legal costs. The bureaucrat may prefer regulation cheaper for his office, meaning that he has an incentive to avoid costly legal battles, insofar as related costs C^a have to be borne by his office. Utility of the agency is given by $A(C^a, P)$, where, denoting the transfer level in the bargaining equilibrium by P^B and the amount of trial costs by C^c,

$$C^a = \begin{cases} C^c & \text{when } V_i \text{ is enforced by the court,} \\ 0 & \text{else,} \end{cases}$$

and

$$P = \begin{cases} P^B & \text{when } V_i \text{ is based on collusion and not overruled,} \\ 0 & \text{else.} \end{cases}$$

The specification of legal costs presupposes application of the British cost recovery rule: the agency must bear all legal costs when the intended regulation is overruled by the court. As transfers are assumed to take place at the end of the game, that is, after unsuccessful research by the group, the agency either gets the transfer or must bear the legal costs. Normalize the agency's utility to zero under correct regulation, and $A(C^c) < 0 < A(P^B)$. Denote by b the probability that the bureaucrat agrees on a bribe for wrong regulation. Allow for mixed strategies: $b \in [0,1]$.

Recall from the introductory Chapter 2 that the transfer P is not necessarily to be interpreted as a personal bribe for the bureaucrat handling the regulatory case. For instance, the implementing authority may also be biased towards local interests. When substantial negative spillovers exist, meaning that the bulk of environmental damage is borne by community outsiders, the agency could trade additional community income for inefficient high out-of-community damages. Then, the setting formalized above would also apply.

The investor. It is only in the case of agency discretion that the investor faces a relevant decision-problem: it then has to decide whether to pay a side-payment or not. It maximizes the net private profit of the project. Because of $S_l^w < S_l^*$ and $S_h^w > S_h^*$, it is only the low-type investor who has an incentive to pay for more lenient regulation.

Side-payments. Incentives to arrange a side-payment will also depend on the environmental group's decision whether to investigate and, eventually, whether to file suit. When such incentives exist, the payment level agreed upon, by assumption, will be the result of a simple bargaining procedure, where the agency offers a side-contract and the investor can just accept or reject it. Thus, the agency is assumed to have all the bargaining power and to reap the gains from trade. This assumption is made for presentational convenience. The results are not substantially altered when bargaining gives rise to other divisions of the gains from trade (for example within Nash bargaining).

The environmental group. The public will be given notice of the intended regulation, which is possibly the result of an informal agreement between the investor and the agency described above. This amounts to the agency announcing that the investor is of a specific type. Denote this announced type by S_i^a. Remember that is the low investor type who may be interested in being regulated according to the more lenient standard D_h^*, in exchange for a side-payment. Therefore, when the agency announces S_h^a, the group may suspect that the investor is not accurately regulated, and can then decide to engage in research, at cost C^r, to detect the true investor type. The group is interested in minimizing environmental damage; therefore, when the agency announces S_l^a and thus intends to regulate according to the stricter standard D_l^*, the group does not have an incentive to undertake research.

Let $k \in [0,1]$ be the probability that the group engages in research after an announcement S_h^a. Notice that the group does not have to find evidence on actual collusion, but on the actual technical avoidance opportunities. Research is modeled in the following way: the group must randomly choose a specific type of evidence or 'test' out of a given set of evidence types or 'tests' of differing quality. The chosen evidence or 'test', in turn, gives a specific result. Thus, as a research result, the group receives

- a signal $s \in \{S_l, S_h\}$ indicating whether the investor is of the high or the low type, and

- a parameter θ representing the quality of the signal, that is, the correlation of the signal found with the actual type: after research, $\theta = \text{prob}[s = S_i | S = S_i], i = l, h$.

θ is distributed on the interval $[0.5, 1]$ with distribution $F(\theta)$ and strictly positive density $f(\theta)$, which is common knowledge. When $\theta = 0.5$, the type of evidence would be uninformative; when $\theta = 1$, the signal would be perfectly informative. Both the signal s and θ are verifiable: once learnt by the environmental group, they can credibly be communicated within a trial.

In the literature, it is usually assumed that the quality of the research result is known before undertaking the research. Here, in assuming that θ is learnt only during the investigation, a situation is depicted where the group does not know beforehand which type of evidence will be found. For instance, in the perception of the court, technical experts' opinions on the technical abatement opportunities of a facility, may be more reliable when their expertise is based on additional technical blueprints. However, it will not be known whether these blueprints are available or not without expending funds on research.

When the group, upon announcement of a type S_h^a, receives a signal $s = S_l$, evidence points to wrong regulation. The group's only decision is then whether to file suit or not: a non-collaborative relationship between the agency and the environmental organization is assumed. Specifically, the group cannot communicate the result of the research before trial. If this were the case, the group, by presenting the evidence gathered, could possibly convince the agency to reverse intended regulation and avoid a costly trial. Hence, possibly emerging incentives to bargain 'in the shadow of the law' are excluded at this stage, to focus on the impact of lower standing barriers *within* the legal system.

The court.   The judge has to base its decision on verifiable information. First, given that discretion is limited, it will (and has to) overrule any regulation not consistent with the underlying standard, that is, leading to damage levels different from D_l^*, D_h^*.[5] Second, upon action taken by the environmental group against intended regulation, that is, the agency's announcement S_h^a, implying regulation D_h^*, the court will overrule the agency if and only if the group presents a signal $s = S_l$, and the quality of the signal θ is equal or

---

[5]It may be objected that the court will only intervene when a plaintiff files suit. However, one may imagine that there will always be an obedient citizen suing the agency when observing intended regulation different from D_l^*, D_h^*. Intended regulation that is publicly announced is clearly verifiable; in consequence, the citizen has to spend neither research nor court costs.

higher than a threshold level $\bar{\theta}$, which is the standard of evidence set by legislators.

By assumption, the court must apply the British cost recovery rule: legal costs are borne by the loser of the case. No further sanction is imposed by the court. Remember that the evidence may only indicate a wrong investor type, but not the actual side-payment arrangement (the agency may thus always argue that it misperceived the actual type).

Denote by $p(\bar{\theta})$ the probability, before research, that the signal's quality is higher than the standard of evidence:

$$p(\bar{\theta}) = \text{prob}[\theta \geq \bar{\theta}] = 1 - F(\bar{\theta}).$$

Note that $p(1) = 0$. Hence, $\bar{\theta} = 1$ depicts a situation where the court would always dismiss the group's complaint, which amounts to the group not having standing. Decreasing the standard of evidence increases $p(\bar{\theta})$, and $p(0.5) = 1$. Thus, for $\bar{\theta} < 1$, $\bar{\theta}$ depicts the extent of the environmental group's legal standing.

Timing. The timing of the game can be summarized as follows:

0. Society learns the possible investor types, q and the distribution of θ.
1. Legislators decide whether to grant limited discretion or not. When they grant discretion to the agency, they additionally choose a standard of evidence $\bar{\theta}$. When they do not grant discretion, they introduce uniform regulation.
2. The investor learns its type and applies for a permit. During the licensing procedure, the agency also learns the actual type. Information on the type is not verifiable.
3. When the agency does not have discretion, the uniform standard is implemented, and the game ends. When the agency has discretion, it can offer a side-contract to the investor, which specifies a payment to the agency in exchange for regulation preferred by the investor, provided that the agency decision is not overruled.
4. The agency announces a type S_i^a. Learning intended regulation, the environmental organization, if it has standing, decides whether to undertake research or not.
5. As research results, the group receives a signal s and quality information θ, which are both verifiable. If the environmental group does not undertake

research, or finds a signal $s = S_j$, or $\theta < \overline{\theta}$, or both, the agency's intended regulation is implemented.

6. When the environmental group takes action and presents the adequate signal, the court overrules the agency, if $\theta \geq \overline{\theta}$.

7. The regulated project will be executed (and a side-payment may be effected), if privately profitable under the implemented regulation.

3.3 AGENCY DISCRETION AND LEGAL STANDING

The environmental group. Consider first the group's decision whether or not to file suit, which presupposes that the agency announced S_h^a and the group did undertake research. As the group learns θ during research, $p(\overline{\theta}) \in \{0,1\}$ when it has to make this decision. It will take action if it received a signal $s = S_l$ as its research result, with higher accuracy than the prescribed minimal standard of evidence ($\theta \geq \overline{\theta}$). If at least one condition does not hold, the group will not sue. Consequently, the court, when brought in, will always rule in favor of the environmental organization. The group will never have to bear the legal costs C^c. However, it bears the risk of spending research costs C^r and obtaining either a signal useful in court, but with too low a quality, or a signal $s = S_h$ which, by itself, cannot be used to construct a case.

Consider now the environmental organization's incentive to undertake research. Recall that the group will always accept an announcement of S_l^a (meaning that the investor will be regulated under the stricter standard promulgated by the law) irrespective of its belief in regard to which type it actually confronts. Upon announcement of S_h^a, a court ruling against planned regulation will occur under one of two alternative constellations: either the agency did accept a bribe and the signal found by the group indicates the true type, or the agency did intend to regulate correctly and the group received a wrong signal. Thus, a signal not indicating the actual type may also be useful for the environmental group. It is this latter possibility that may provoke court errors.

Before research, the probability of finding a correct signal with sufficient quality is defined by

$$prob[(s = S_l, \theta \geq \overline{\theta}) | S = S_l] = p(\overline{\theta}) E(\theta | \theta \geq \overline{\theta})$$

$$= \int_{\underline{\theta}}^{1} f(\theta)d\theta \cdot \frac{\int_{\underline{\theta}}^{1} \theta f(\theta)d\theta}{\int_{\underline{\theta}}^{1} f(\theta)d\theta} = \int_{\underline{\theta}}^{1} \theta f(\theta)d\theta .$$

whereas the probability of finding a false signal of sufficiently high quality is

$$prob[(s = S_l, \theta \geq \overline{\theta}) | S = S_h] = p(\overline{\theta})[1 - E(\theta | \theta \geq \overline{\theta})]$$

$$= \int_{\underline{\theta}}^{1} f(\theta)d\theta \left(1 - \frac{\int_{\underline{\theta}}^{1} \theta f(\theta)d\theta}{\int_{\underline{\theta}}^{1} f(\theta)d\theta} \right) = \int_{\underline{\theta}}^{1} (1 - \theta) f(\theta)d\theta .$$

When observing S_h^a, the environmental group will update its belief that the investor is of the low type and, hence, that the agency intends wrong regulation according to Bayes' rule. Remember that the possible gain for the group of prevailing in court is given by ΔD. Hence, the condition for the environmental organization to undertake research is

$$\left(\frac{(1-q)b}{q+(1-q)b} p(\overline{\theta}) E(\theta | \theta \geq \overline{\theta}) \right.$$

$$\left. + \frac{q}{q+(1-q)b} p(\overline{\theta})(1 - E(\theta | \theta \geq \overline{\theta})) \right) \Delta D > C^r, \tag{3.7}$$

where the first bracketed term times ΔD depicts the expected gain from finding correct evidence that the announced type is the wrong one and the second bracketed term times ΔD depicts the expected gain of finding false evidence, suggesting a false announcement by the agency even while it was truthful.

The agency.   Consider now possible negotiations over a side-payment between the investor and the agency. When the bureaucrat detects that he has to regulate a low type, he may offer a side-contract to the investor, who, by assumption, can only accept or reject it. The investor will accept any contract for which

$$\Pi_0 - S_l^w - P \geq \Pi_0 - S_l^* .$$

Thus, the bureaucrat would ask for $P^B = S_l^* - S_l^w$. He has an incentive to do so, when

$$k[p(\overline{\theta})E(\theta|\theta \geq \overline{\theta})A(C^c) + (1 - p(\overline{\theta})E(\theta|\theta \geq \overline{\theta}))A(P^B)] \\ + (1-k)A(P^B) > 0. \tag{3.8}$$

The left-hand-side of (3.8) is the expected payoff from wrong regulation of the low type: the first term in brackets represents an overruling by the court (the group finding a signal indicating the actual type with sufficient quality), the second term depicts fruitless research, and the last term gives the payoff when the group does not undertake research. Re-arranging (3.8) gives

$$A(P^B) > \frac{-k\int_{\overline{\theta}}^{1} \theta f(\theta)d\theta \, A(C^c)}{1 - k\int_{\overline{\theta}}^{1} \theta f(\theta)d\theta} ,$$

which holds for $k = 0$, and for $k = 1$ and high $\overline{\theta}$. Even while the bureaucrat is not personally sanctioned for accepting the payment, legal costs serve as a sanction anticipated by an administrator taking his office's budget into account. Assume this effect deters the agency from accepting the payment for some lower $\overline{\theta} < 1$, given that $k = 1$.

Note that the legislature could reduce incentives to collude by choosing less differentiated environmental standards, thus reducing the possible surplus from collusion bargaining. However, when not granting legal standing and thus not relying on the environmental group's activities ($\overline{\theta} = 1$, or $k = 0$), the legislature would have to prescribe a uniform standard to deter the agency from collusion. Furthermore, when the legislature wants to rely on standing and the group's research activities, lack of differentiation would also reduce the group's incentive to undertake research. This can been seen from (3.7).

Enforceability of the side-contract. A side-contract covering a bribery payment cannot legally be enforced. Under the timing of the game presented in Section 3.2, transfers are paid after the agency issues the conditional project permit. When the agency is committed to the regulation that has been issued, it will never be rational for the investor to pay the agreed transfer sum in stage 8 of the game. Anticipating this, the agency may as well decide not to collude.

The usual assumption made in the literature is that of self-enforcement or 'quasi-enforceability' (Laffont and Tirole 1993, 478). Self-enforcement may result in a repeated game, where the investor and the agency have an ongoing relationship (Klein et al. 1978, Telser 1980). Indeed, facility decisions by investors are of a long-term nature. As facilities are in constant need of modernization or enlargement, operators will have to regularly request the corresponding permits to install new equipment. Agencies can then punish non-cooperative behavior of the investor (not to pay the agreed transfer) by also behaving non-cooperatively in future periods. This issue will be explored in detail in Chapter 4. In the present analysis, (quasi)-enforceability will be assumed.

Consider now a case which may emerge when the deterrence effect stemming from legal costs is very strong.

Overregulation and extortion. Legal costs to be borne by the agency will also influence the decision on to how to regulate a high-type investor: the agency may have an incentive to prescribe tighter environmental standards D_I^*, thereby avoiding a costly legal battle.

In reality, this case is less probable, because investors are also entitled to file suit against agencies' regulations. Consequently, a high-type investor may succeed in getting wrong regulation overturned by the court. The model presented here abstracts from this possibility to focus on the impact of standing for outside watchdog organizations. Such overregulation will then occur because

$$kp(\overline{\theta})[1 - E(\theta|\theta \geq \overline{\theta})]A(C^c) < 0. \tag{3.9}$$

A high-type investor, while not having the possibility, in the model, to sue the agency, may avert overregulation by also offering a payment. Because the threat of overregulation is credible, the agency can extort the high-type investor, that is, exchange correct regulation for a side-payment. Upon receipt of the additional transfer, the agency may prefer to regulate correctly and risk a subsequent overruling by the court. Assume a similar bargaining procedure as in the case of collusion with the low type.

Corollary 3.1. Under $\overline{\theta} < 1$ and the emerging incentives for overregulation, the extortion of investors can improve welfare.

Proof. The investor is ready to accept any side-contract in which

$$\Pi_0 - S_h^* - P \geq \Pi_0 - S_h^w .$$

Consequently, the parties will agree on a transfer level $P^{Be} = S_h^w - S_h^*$. Then, the agency will realize $A(P^{Be})$, when the environmental group's research activities are not successful, or the group does not undertake research. From reformulating and re-arranging (3.9), the administrator will not be ready to make the bargain, if

$$
\begin{aligned}
&k[\,p(\overline{\theta})(1 - E(\theta|\theta \geq \overline{\theta}))A(C^c) \\
&+ (1 - p(\overline{\theta})(1 - E(\theta|\theta \geq \overline{\theta}))A(P^{Be})] \qquad\qquad (3.9a) \\
&+ (1 - k)A(P^{Be}) < 0,
\end{aligned}
$$

which depicts a stricter condition than (3.9). Consequently, there will be P for which (3.9a) does not hold while (3.9) still does so. ∎

The positive effect on overregulation is maximized under the assumed bargaining procedure, in which the agency reaps the entire surplus. However, the effect will be substantial for every procedure under which the administrator receives at least a positive share.[6] Assume for now that (3.9a) does not hold under the applied bargaining procedure and, hence, the high-type investor is correctly regulated.[7]

Equilibrium analysis.   For given $\overline{\theta}$, equilibrium strategies $b^*(\overline{\theta})$ and $k^*(\overline{\theta})$ can be derived by operating with conditions (3.7) and (3.8). Depending on how $\overline{\theta}$ is chosen, specific equilibrium strategy combinations result, which can be classified according to the different impacts stemming from the legal

---

[6]Extortion within a setting of bargaining between the private parties will be addressed in Chapter 5.

[7]When agencies are not merely income maximizers, but also at least to some extent care for the quality of regulation (that is, are not completely indifferent to regulating correctly or wrongly), overregulation may not be a credible threat. This can been seen by a suitable adaptation of (3.9a) (let t and w indicate true and wrong regulation, substitute $A(P^{Be})$ by $A(t)$, $A(C^c)$ by $A(w,C^c)$ and 0 by $A(w)$, and let $A(t) > A(w) > A(w,C^c)$). Then, it is more difficult to motivate extortion.

system. First, the court may overturn wrong regulation by the agency; this is the *correction* function of the court. Second, the possibility of research and a subsequent trial may deter the agency from accepting a bribe for false regulation. Call this the *deterrent* function of the legal system. Third, the judge may wrongfully overturn correct high-type regulation, thus committing a *legal error*.

In the benchmark case without standing, $\overline{\theta} = 1$. Then, according to (3.7), the environmental group never has an incentive to undertake research: $k^* = 0$. The agency will never face the risk of bearing legal costs, and will thus always be ready to apply lenient regulation for a side-payment, according to (3.8): $b^* = 1$.

The explicit derivation of possible equilibrium constellations for $\overline{\theta} \in [0.5, 1)$ is relegated to the appendix. They can be summarized as follows:

- There is no correction and no deterrence in equilibrium ($b^* = 1$, $k^* = 0$). In this case, $\overline{\theta}$ is chosen such that the benchmark described above to still hold: the group will never investigate, and the agency will always accept the transfer. While third-party standing exists, it has no influence on the parties' decisions. Call standing to be non-substantive in this case.
- There is only correction and no deterrence ($b^* = 1$, $k^* = 1$). Here, $\overline{\theta}$ is chosen such that (3.7) holds for $b = 1$, and (3.8) holds for $k = 1$. When the environmental group files suit, the court will correct the regulation; however, due to the high standard of evidence, the risk for the agency of being overruled is too low to be deterred from collusion.
- There is collusion and deterrence ($b^* \in (0, 1)$, $k^* \in (\tilde{k}, 1)$). For the chosen standard of evidence $\overline{\theta}$ and for $b = 1$, (3.7) holds. When $\overline{\theta}$ is low enough for (3.8) not to hold for $k = 1$, the agency will not accept a bribe when the group always undertakes research. However, (3.7) may not hold for $b = 0$: When the agency always acts honestly, the environmental group will not investigate. Strategies are totally mixed.
- There is no correction and only deterrence ($b^* = 0$, $k^* = 1$). Here, (3.7) holds for $b = 0$, and (3.8) does not hold for $k = 1$. The group always investigates, and the agency never colludes. In this case, the judge will never overturn wrong regulation: The environmental organization, in undertaking research, only relies on possible court errors.

Note that there can be no $\overline{\theta} \in [0.5, 1)$ that give rise to the equilibrium strategy combination $b^* = 0$, $k^* = 0$. This can be readily ascertained from (3.7) and (3.8).

Expected welfare. Let W^e be the expected welfare for the legislature, when it prescribes the application of differentiated standards D_l^*, D_h^* and grants discretionary power to the agency:

$$
\begin{aligned}
W^e(\overline{\theta}) = & \, q[k^*(\overline{\theta})p(\overline{\theta})(1 - E(\theta|\theta \geq \overline{\theta}))(V_h^w - C^c) \\
& + (1 - k^*(\overline{\theta})p(\overline{\theta})[1 - E(\theta|\theta \geq \overline{\theta})])V_h^* - k^*(\overline{\theta})C^r] \\
& + (1 - q)[(1 - b^*(\overline{\theta}))V_l^* \\
& \quad + b^*(\overline{\theta})[k^*(\overline{\theta})p(\overline{\theta})E(\theta|\theta \geq \overline{\theta})(V_l^* - C^c) \\
& \quad + (1 - k^*(\overline{\theta})p(\overline{\theta})E(\theta|\theta \geq \overline{\theta}))V_l^w - k^*(\overline{\theta})C^r]].
\end{aligned}
\tag{3.10}
$$

In (3.10), the first line of the right-hand side gives the effect of legal errors on expected welfare: incorrect regulation prescribed by the court. The second line shows correct high-type regulation uncontested by the group and the impact of the research costs. The expression in the third line depicts the court's role as a deterrent, the fourth line depicts the correction function, and the first expression of the last line gives the effect of wrong regulation that is not contested in court. As the regulatory costs in equilibrium depend on the equilibrium strategies b^* and k^*, $W^e(\overline{\theta})$ is only piecewise differentiable, that is, for $\overline{\theta}$ generating the same equilibrium constellation. In the benchmark case where $\overline{\theta} = 1$ or under a non-substantive standing, $k^* = 0$, $b^* = 1$. Then, (3.10) gives

$$
W^e = qV_h^* + (1 - q)V_l^w .
\tag{3.11}
$$

As $W^e(\overline{\theta})$ is piecewise differentiable, the optimal standard of evidence can only be derived under numerical specifications. However, as was argued before, such an explicit derivation is not necessary for exploring whether the discretion-cum-standing solution can perform better at all in welfare terms.

3.4 THE CHOICE OF THE REGULATORY REGIME

The optimal uniform standard. Denote an optimal uniform standard by $\tilde{D}^*$. The legislature's problem is to maximize expected welfare

$$
\tilde{W}(\tilde{D}) = q[\Pi_0 + Cs - S_h(\tilde{D}) - \tilde{D}] + (1 - q)[\Pi_0 + Cs - S_l(\tilde{D}) - \tilde{D}] ,
$$

which yields the first-order-condition

$$qS_h'(\tilde{D}^*) + (1-q)S_l'(\tilde{D}^*) = -1 . \tag{3.12}$$

Clearly, for $q \in (0,1)$, $\tilde{D}^* \in (D_l^*, D_h^*)$. The first result can now be stated.

Proposition 3.1. If the legislators decide to grant agency discretion, they will always set a standard of evidence $\bar{\theta} < 1$ giving rise to a substantial standing.

Proof. Setting $\bar{\theta} = 1$ or granting non-substantive standing amounts, under the condition of a collusive agency, to a uniform regulation over the lenient standard D_h^*. Such a standard does not belong to the possible uniform standards maximizing expected welfare. ∎

For notational brevity, let $\hat{V}_h(\bar{\theta})$ be the expected welfare of regulating the high type under agency discretion, for a specific $\bar{\theta}$:

$$\begin{aligned}\hat{V}_h(\bar{\theta}) = &(1 - k^*(\bar{\theta})p(\bar{\theta})[1 - E(\theta|\theta \geq \bar{\theta})])V_h^* \\ &- k^*(\bar{\theta})p(\bar{\theta})[1 - E(\theta|\theta \geq \bar{\theta})](V_h^w - C^c) - k^*(\bar{\theta})C^r\end{aligned} \tag{3.13}$$

and denote $\tilde{V}_h^*$ and $\tilde{V}_l^*$ the welfare from regulation of the high and the low type under an optimal uniform standard $\tilde{D}^*$; thus

$$\tilde{W}^* = q\tilde{V}_h^* + (1-q)\tilde{V}_l^* , \tag{3.14}$$

Regime Comparison. In what follows, give attention to the equilibrium defined by

$$\bar{\theta}^\circ = \max[\bar{\theta}|b^* = 0],$$

which exists because of the assumptions made with respect to the regulatory costs. On account of deterrence, the low type will be adequately regulated. Welfare losses will result from high-type regulation, because the environmental group finds favorable evidence and sues the agency with positive probability. Hence, high-type regulation will be inefficient under both regulatory regimes. The question is then which regime generates a higher inefficiency in regulating the high type investors, and whether the possible relative efficiency gain, within high-type regulation, by changing the regime will be offset by an efficiency loss within low-type regulation.[8] Under $\overline{\theta}°$, expected welfare of the discretion-cum-standing regime is given by

$$W^e(\overline{\theta}°) = q\hat{V}_h(\overline{\theta}°) + (1-q)V_l^* \qquad (3.15)$$

Comparing (3.15) with (3.14) and solving for q yields the following result.

Proposition 3.2. Consider the standards of evidence $\overline{\theta}°$. When

$$q < \frac{V_l^* - \tilde{V}_l^*}{V_l^* - \tilde{V}_l^* + (\tilde{V}_h^* - \hat{V}_h(\overline{\theta}°))}, \qquad (3.16)$$

expected welfare from granting agency discretion and a substantial legal third-party standing will be higher than under a uniform standard.

The proportion of high-type investors q influences the relative performance of the regulatory regimes in two different ways. Reconsider condition (3.16):

- When high-type regulation is less efficient under agency discretion and $\overline{\theta}°$ than under a uniform standard ($\tilde{V}_h^* - \hat{V}_h(\overline{\theta}°) > 0$), introducing agency discretion and a substantial standing will improve welfare, when the fraction of high-type investors is below a threshold level given by (3.16). This depicts the influence of q on the frequency of court errors.
- When, on the contrary, $\tilde{V}_h^* - \hat{V}_h(\overline{\theta}°) \leq 0$, the welfare improvement resulting from introducing agency discretion and a substantive standing, according to (3.16), is not type-contingent. However, $\tilde{V}_h^*$, which denotes welfare from high-type regulation under a uniform standard, also depends on q. As can be seen by (3.12), the lower q, the closer the uniform standard $\tilde{D}^*$ will be to D_l^*, and the more inefficient regulation of the high type. A lower $\tilde{V}_h^*$, however, makes $\tilde{V}_h^* - \hat{V}_h(\overline{\theta}°) \leq 0$ more probable.

A comment may be in order with respect to the role of the regulatory costs. Clearly, as can be ascertained by (3.10), higher legal and research costs directly make the discretion-cum-standing solution less attractive. This

---

[8]To stress it again: It is not asserted that $\overline{\theta}°$ is the (globally) welfare-maximizing standard of evidence within the discretion-cum-standing regulatory regime. Therefore, the condition stated in the following proposition is sufficient, but may be stricter than necessary for the superiority of discretion–cum–standing regulation.

impact, however, plays no role within the comparison presented here. The relevant, indirect impact is that high regulatory costs may impede the emergence of an equilibrium which constitute the institutional solution's original attraction. In this case, the welfare comparison is trivial. Conversely, however, as long as equilibria exist where the agency is deterred from collusion without overregulation, q will exist for which the institutional solution is superior in welfare terms, irrespective of the specific level of regulatory costs.

3.5 THE COURT'S DECISION RULE

While the agency is granted discretion in decision-making, the court is committed by the legislature to use a simple decision-making rule in the form of a standard of evidence set by the legislators. The purpose of this section is to show that this commitment has value.

Consider the decision-making rule of a Bayesian court, which decides by weighing up expected costs and benefits. When being brought into the game, the court is presented a signal $s = S_l$ upon announcement of S_h^a. Learning the quality of the signal θ, the court updates beliefs that it confronts the high type. Consequently, the judge will reject intended regulation, if

$$\frac{q(1-\theta)}{q(1-\theta)+(1-q)b\theta}V_h^w + \frac{(1-q)b\theta}{q(1-\theta)+(1-q)b\theta}V_l^* >$$
$$\frac{q(1-\theta)}{q(1-\theta)+(1-q)b\theta}V_h^* + \frac{(1-q)b\theta}{q(1-\theta)+(1-q)b\theta}V_l^w.$$

Reformulating gives the standard of evidence $\tilde{\theta}$ endogenously set by the Bayesian court:

$$\tilde{\theta} = \frac{q(V_h^* - V_h^w)}{(1-q)b(V_l^* - V_l^w) + q(V_h^* - V_h^w)} = \beta(b), \qquad (3.17)$$

and $\beta'(b) < 0$, $\beta(0) = 1$. Note that the inverse function $b = \beta^{-1}(\tilde{\theta})$ monotonically decreases in a higher standard of evidence.

Proposition 3.3. The standard of evidence endogenously set by a Bayesian court according to (3.17) will implement a unique equilibrium. This equilibrium will not improve on the welfare level attainable under a standard of evidence exogenously set, and, in general, will perform worse.

(i)   Deterrence will never be complete in equilibrium.
(ii)   An equilibrium where deterrence is substantial, in the sense of $b^* < 1$, may not exist.

Proof.

(i)   Assume that the action of never accepting a bribe is an equilibrium strategy of the administrator ($b^* = 1$). Under rule (3.17), the court would then always dismiss a complaint ($\beta(0) = 1$). This, however, implies that the environmental group would never undertake research, according to (3.7), and the agency, according to (3.8), would always accept a bribe.

(ii)   Consider a standard of evidence $\tilde{\theta}_1 = \beta(1)$. Note that the equilibrium correspondence $b^*(\overline{\theta})$ derived in Section 3.3 is non-decreasing in a higher standard of evidence, and that $b = \beta^{-1}(\overline{\theta})$ monotonically decreases in a higher standard of evidence. These monotonicity properties imply uniqueness. When the agency, according to (3.8), is always ready to accept a bribe under a given standard $\tilde{\theta}_1$, the unique equilibrium implemented under decision rule (3.17) is characterized by $\tilde{\theta}^+ = \tilde{\theta}_1$, $b^*(\tilde{\theta}_1) = 1$ and $k^*(\tilde{\theta}_1) \in [0, 1]$.

When, however, the agency accepts a bribe under the standard $\tilde{\theta}_1$, the unique equilibrium consists of completely mixed strategies and is given by a standard of evidence $\tilde{\theta}^+ \leq \tilde{\theta}_1$ implicitly defined by $b^*(\tilde{\theta}^+) = \beta^{-1}(\tilde{\theta}^+)$, which is characterized by $b^*(\tilde{\theta}^+) \in (0, 1)$ and $k^*(\tilde{\theta}^+) \in (\overline{k}, 1)$. The equilibrium, in general, will perform worse, because (3.17) fails to take the welfare-improving deterrence effect into account. ∎

The weakness of the decision-making rule (3.17) is that it is efficient only *ex post* (after suit is filed), but not *ex ante*: it focuses only on the issue under dispute, and does not take into consideration the impact of the decision-making rule on the parties' equilibrium strategies. It is, however, these strategies which may give rise to inefficiencies and the initial grounds for the emergence of a legal dispute. A problem of credible commitment results, because the court, once confronted with a specific case, would like to use decision-making rule (3.17). The problem is solved by the institutional division between the legislature and the judiciary, whereby the former can commit the latter to apply a specific standard of evidence.[9]

As information disclosure models usually assume Bayesian behavior (see, for example Milgrom and Roberts 1986 or Froeb and Kobayashi 1996), this section contains a *caveat* with respect to the policy conclusions to be drawn from these models. This *caveat* applies when the decision-making institution under investigation is a court or another institution for conflict resolution, which becomes active only as a reaction to complaints concerning the decisions of other regulatory bodies.

3.6 MINIMIZING LEGAL COSTS

Return now to the model where the standard of evidence $\bar{\theta}$ is exogenously set by the legislature. In the legal discussion on liberalizing standing rights, it was sometimes argued that such reforms of administrative law would lead to an augmentation of filed suits and a subsequent increase in costs for running the legal system.

Remember from Chapter 2 that there are important objections to these concerns:

- First, there is a substantial difference between the number of filed suits and those actually going to trial. Incentives to bargain an out-of-court settlement will emerge precisely when legal costs are substantial. This will be the theme of the next chapters.
- Second, from the welfare perspective of the preceding sections, the objective of minimizing court costs is clearly of restricted value, as those costs are only one component of society's well-being.

The following analysis will not take into account these points, and will therefore accept the objective of minimizing legal disputes for the sake of the argument. To investigate this issue, it considers local variations of the standard of evidence $\bar{\theta}$.

Denote by ζ the *ex ante* probability of a legal dispute:

---

[9]Sobel (1985) presents a disclosure model in which, to select among multiple equilibria, it is the judge himself who commits to specific rules of evidence. Note, however, that the present problem is not one of selecting among multiple equilibria.

$$\zeta(\overline{\theta}) = qk^*(\overline{\theta})\int_{\overline{\theta}}^{1}(1-\theta)f(\theta)d\theta + (1-q)b^*(\overline{\theta})k^*(\overline{\theta})\int_{\overline{\theta}}^{1}\theta f(\theta)d\theta \quad (3.18)$$

Using (3.8) and denoting $K = A(P^B)/[A(P^B) - A(C^c)]$, equation (3.18) can be transformed into

$$\zeta(\overline{\theta}) = qK\left[\frac{\int_{\overline{\theta}}^{1}(1-\theta)f(\theta)d\theta}{\int_{\overline{\theta}}^{1}\theta f(\theta)d\theta} + \frac{C' - \int_{\overline{\theta}}^{1}(1-\theta)f(\theta)d\theta \; D_h^*}{\int_{\overline{\theta}}^{1}\theta f(\theta)d\theta \; \Delta D - C'}\right] \quad (3.18a)$$

(see equation 3.A1 in the appendix). The first term of the right-hand side of (3.18) is the probability of a legal error and the second one is the probability of the court correcting wrong regulation. $\zeta(\overline{\theta})$ is piecewise differentiable, that is, for $\overline{\theta}$ that give rise to the same equilibrium constellation. When standing is non-substantive, $\zeta(\overline{\theta})$ is trivially zero.

For constellations in which there is either correction or deterrence, lowering the standard of evidence indeed increases the probability of legal disputes. This can be seen immediately by setting $b^* = 1$ and $k^* = 1$, or $b^* = 0$ and $k^* = 1$, in (3.18) and differentiating $\zeta(\overline{\theta})$.

Focus now on totally mixed strategies, in which the court has both a correction and a deterrent function. The sign of the derivative of (3.18a) cannot be determined unequivocally without putting more structure on the model. Consider a variant of the model in which $\overline{\theta}$ is equally distributed; hence, $f(\overline{\theta}) = 2$. Then, (3.18a) transforms into

$$\zeta(\overline{\theta}) = qK\left[\frac{1-\overline{\theta}}{1+\overline{\theta}} + \frac{C' - (1-\overline{\theta})^2\Delta D}{(1-\overline{\theta}^2)\;\Delta D - C'}\right]$$
$$= qK\left[\frac{2\overline{\theta}C'}{(1+\overline{\theta})[(1-\overline{\theta}^2)\;\Delta D - C']}\right], \quad (3.18b)$$

the derivative of which is

$$\frac{d\zeta(\overline{\theta})}{d\overline{\theta}} = qK\left[\frac{2C'[(1-\overline{\theta}^2)\Delta D - C'] + 4\overline{\theta}^2(1-\overline{\theta})C'\Delta D}{[((1-\overline{\theta}^2)\Delta D - C')(1+\overline{\theta})]^2}\right] > 0.$$

To see the sign of the derivative, note that $(1-\bar{\theta}^2)\Delta D - C^r > 0$ for every equilibrium under this constellation. Hence, the following result can be stated.

Proposition 3.4. Assume $f(\bar{\theta}) = 2$. Consider a legal reform which strengthens third-party standing by lowering the standard of evidence required to prevail in court. When courts have both the role of *ex post* correction and *ex ante* prevention before and after the legal reform, a stronger third party standing unambiguously decreases the probability of a legal battle.

Thus, a stronger legal standing for environmental watchdogs does not generically lead to a higher caseload for courts. Even when any out-of-court dispute resolution is explicitly ruled out, the converse may be true, where a more restricted access to the legal system increases the number of filed suits.

In the model, legal costs can be avoided completely by abolishing standing for the environmental watchdog. Real-world legal reforms will probably be more incremental. Then, one has to doubt the wisdom of policy recommendations arguing for such standing restrictions in order to reduce the costs of the legal system. One has to do so, even when accepting the objective of a mere reduction in legal costs, which implies that other components of society's welfare are not considered.

3.7 COLLUSION WITH THE ENVIRONMENTAL GROUP

Up to now, it was ruled out that administrators may also collude with environmental organizations. By referring to their limited funds, it was said that they will be out-bidden by investors. This section will formalize the argument in a simplified version of the model where it is not possible to use the court system; hence, $\bar{\theta} = 1$.

For now, let us also introduce the following variations: Assume that the administrator does not observe the investor type. Introduce a parameter λ, drawn from a distribution on $(0, 1]$, which represents the limited ability for the environmental organization to collect funds, due, for example, to problems of collective action (a similar parameter is used by Laffont and Tirole 1991). The parameter λ is private information of the environmental group. Maximal funds which can be mobilized are given by $\lambda \Delta D$. It is useful for the following analysis to recall observation 3.2:

$$S_l^* - S_l^w < \Delta D < |S_h^* - S_h^w|$$

for $S(D)$ being strictly convex. Denote

$$\lambda^{cr} = \frac{S_l^* - S_l^w}{\Delta D}.$$

Two constellations may arise, dependent on whether the investor is of the low or the high type. Remember that the investor type and λ are now private information.

Low-type investor. Under correct regulation, the low type investor would be confronted with the more stringent environmental standard; therefore, it will be ready to bribe the agency up to the possible gain from incorrect regulation $S_l^* - S_l^w$. Note that b^* trivially equals one when legal standing is ruled out.

However, even while not having the opportunity to use the court system, the environmental group has another option to prevent lenient environmental regulation: it may also offer a payment in exchange for accurate regulation, up to $\lambda \Delta D$.

High-type investor. Under correct regulation, a high-type investor would be summoned to implement the lower environmental standard. The environmental group would be ready to offer a bribe up to $\lambda \Delta D$ in exchange for wrong regulation (implementation of the stricter environmental standard).

The high-type investor, however, may avert unfavorable regulation by offering a higher transfer. She will be ready to pay up to $S_h^w - S_h^*$ in exchange for correct regulation.

Consequently, bidding for preferred regulation results between the investor and the environmental group. Assume for illustration that the agency runs a second-price, sealed bid auction,[10] where each party submits a bid in ignorance of the other's party bid, and the winner pays the amount of the second-highest bid. Bids incur no costs for their submission; assume therefore that groups which surely lose the auction, i.e., with $\lambda < \lambda^{cr}$, will also submit bids.[11] It is a (weakly) dominant strategy to submit a bid equal to one's valuation (see for example Fudenberg and Tirole 1991, 10–11). Consequently, the low-type investor will bid $S_l^* - S_l^w$, the high-type investor will bid

---

[10]This second price sealed-bid auction yields the same expected price for the seller as an English auction, where parties drop out when bids reach their individual valuation (Vickrey 1961).

[11]They may hope that investors commit errors; e.g., by submitting a wrong bid, or by forgetting to submit the bid in the first place.

$S_h^w - S_h^*$, and the environmental group will bid $\lambda \Delta D$.[12] Assume that the agency decides in favor of the group when bids are equal (note that bids will never be equal when the investor is of the high type). The following proposition follows immediately from observation 3.2. and the definition of λ^{cr}.

Proposition 3.5. For technology $D(S)$ being strictly convex, collusion with the environmental organization will never decrease the efficiency of regulation.

(i) For $\lambda \geq \lambda^{cr}$, bidding for regulatory stringency will always result in efficient regulation.

(ii) For $\lambda < \lambda^{cr}$, the low investor type will buy lenient regulation at the auction (the environmental group is out-bidden). The high investor type will buy accurate regulation at the auction.

Under the established terminology (used with the reservations made above), bidding for incorrect regulation may be characterized as a bribery attempt, whereas bidding for correct regulation corresponds to the extortion context. For the agency, the option to collude with one party serves as a credible threat to extort the other party. The party to be extorted has a higher valuation of regulatory quality, and type-specific optimal regulation results.[13]

The second part of the proposition depicts the situation envisaged in the earlier parts, where it was argued that the environmental group is out–bidden due to limited funds. As the first part of the proposition makes clear, the argument is not to be interpreted in the sense that unlimited funds decrease efficiency. The possibility of the environmental group – under unlimited funds – to outbid low-type investors' bribes increases welfare, while high-

---

[12]Clearly, $\lambda \Delta D$ is not the group's actual valuation. It is nevertheless the relevant equilibrium bid, because it serves as a non–bankruptcy constraint. To see this, consider a group with $\lambda < \lambda^{cr}$ submitting an offer higher than $S_l^* - S_l^w$. It will win the auction when confronting the low investor type, but run bankrupt. When costs are involved with bankruptcy, the group will prefer to submit $\lambda \Delta D$, lose the auction and have zero payoff.

[13]Note that under discrete types, the second-price auction does not yield the maximal payoff for the agency. For instance, the agency can extract an additional rent from the high-type investor by stipulating that any investor offering more than $S_l^* - S_l^w$ has to pay a fixed price χ such that $S_h^w - S_h^* - \chi > prob[\lambda < \lambda^{cr}][S_h^w - S_h^* - E(\lambda | \lambda < \lambda^{cr}) \Delta D]$, where the right-hand side gives the expected payoff for the high-type investor who mimics the low type and submits $S_l^* - S_l^w$. As this payoff strictly increases in offers, the investor will do even worse by offering less than $S_l^* - S_l^w$. In consequence, to offer $S_h^w - S_h^*$ is still weakly dominant. See Fudenberg and Tirole (1991, 253, 288) for a similar argument. However, proposition 3.5 is not affected by this observation, as it holds for any auction where the parties bid their valuations in equilibrium.

type investors will always be able to outbid environmental groups offering bribes.

3.8 DISCUSSION AND CONCLUSIONS

3.8.1   Summary

This chapter presented a model where granting discretion to collusive agencies in environmental regulation can be supplemented with legal standing for environmental organizations, which empowers them to let the agency's decision-making be scrutinized by a court. Within the model, the extent of legal standing is given by the minimum quality of evidence required, which is a continuous parameter whose choice can be optimized by the legislature. The model allowed us to neatly analyze the interaction of the various impacts stemming from the legal system: the correction of wrong regulation, collusion deterrence and the possibility of legal errors. The deterrence effect lay at the core of the derived results.

First, it was shown that, for some type distributions, a discretion-cum-standing regime of type-specific optimal standards D_l^*, D_h^* is welfare-superior to direct regulation by the legislature *via* a uniform standard. Thus, the former solution, even while generating substantial regulatory costs, may have its economic merits.

Second, the superiority of granting agency discretion was shown to crucially hinge on a substantial standing for the environmental watchdog, which gives an economic rationale for the liberal standing doctrine applied in the United States.

The deterrent effect that legal standing has on the agency's incentive to collude provided some additional insights. When the legislature decides to grant discretion, the probability of 'meritless' suits, where plaintiffs exclusively rely on welfare-reducing court errors, will be positive in equilibrium: a welfare-maximizing legislature may be ready to trade court errors for the deterrence of collusion. Furthermore, restricting the courts' leeway in decision-making by committing them to simple decision-making rules will improve overall welfare, when deterrence from activities giving rise to trials is explicitly considered in the analysis. And, finally, it is because of the deterrence effect that the analysis casts doubts on the validity of the – seemingly reasonable – argument that extending standing will increase the courts' caseload. In contrast, it was shown that impeding access to the courts may increase the number of suits.

An additional result was derived which is of interest within a framework of collusive agencies: authorities open for transfers may use collusion with one party as a credible threat for the extortion of the other party. In such a setting and under a strictly convex technology, extortion was shown to possibly improve welfare.

3.8.2 Overregulation and the Allocation of Legal Costs

Under agency discretion, overregulation resulted either from legal errors or from the agency's incentive to issue overly strict regulation to avoid costly legal battles. The latter case was derived under the assumption of the British cost recovery rule, where the agency has to bear all legal costs if it loses the trial. Two lessons can be drawn from the analysis.

First, when administrators care about their budget, legal costs play the role of a fine.[14] Overly harsh fines (for bribery or for local bias) intended to avoid inefficiencies from collusion may thus generate inefficiencies from overregulation. Clearly, this adverse effect is countervailed to some extent when the investor can also sue against overly strict regulation; however, it can be concluded that punishment of agencies' misbehavior has to be fine-tuned.

Second, a conclusion can be drawn for the recovery of legal costs. As a departure from the general US principle that every party has to bear its own legal costs (attorney's and legal fees), the British rule was introduced under the citizen suit provisions of most environmental acts. The analysis depicts a possible adverse effect of this cost recovery rule, where agencies' budget considerations negatively affect the environmental allocation.

3.8.3 Information Rights

Recall that information rights are composed of the right to be given notice of intended regulation and of the right to access public records. Consider first a variant of the model in which giving notice of the intended project is not required. Then, affected parties can only file suit after (or during) realization of the project, when (part of) the environmental damage is observed. Even when assuming that gathering evidence does not consume time and that judicial review also occurs immediately, additional inefficiencies may result.

---

[14]See Lupia and McCubbins (1994) favoring such agency penalties, and Asimov (1994, 132) for a critique which, hence, does not address overregulation.

First, when the newly erected facility is closed down under a court error, sunk investment costs or an irreversible environmental harm will generate additional inefficiencies. Second, possible losses from sunk investment costs, under a court error, will reduce the investor's incentive to ask for a permit in the first place. Thus, giving public notice of intended projects also improves the investor's incentive to invest.

In reality, construction of the project is time-consuming. Affected parties may then file suit after observing the beginning of the construction works. They will have to get a temporary restraining order (T.R.O. – *einstweilige Verfügung*) from the court to stop construction, which, in turn, may also depend on the presented evidence. As the process of gathering evidence is also time-consuming, affected parties are then in a dilemma: they may either file suit on the basis of insufficient evidence and risk denial of a T.R.O., or spend time on gathering evidence and risk irrevocable environmental damage by the ongoing construction works. Under public notice, in contrast, they may use the time-consuming waiting period of the licensing procedure to gather evidence.

When investors observe the environmental group's activities and fear the loss of sunk costs because of the court overruling the regulation, they may have an incentive to slow down the construction works. This may reduce the inefficiencies from sunk costs and irreversible environmental harm; however, as the realization of a beneficial project is also postponed, this may additionally generate a welfare loss.

Consider next the role of access to the administrative records. Access may reduce the research costs the environmental group has to spend, which has direct positive welfare consequences. Furthermore, lower research costs will also increase the incentive of the environmental group to undertake research. In the mixed equilibrium, the agency has to lower the equilibrium probability (of accepting the bribe) to keep the environmental organization indifferent between undertaking research and not.

Access may also influence the quality of the research, that is, the distribution of θ. Evidence to be found within the agency's records may be better than those found outside the records (remember that the agency learns the investor type during the permitting process). This effect reduces the probability of legal errors and, hence, has also positive welfare implications.

3.8.4   Delay

This analysis did not consider a possible delay of the project execution by a time-consuming legal battle. The costs of delay may be depicted by discounting the social benefits V_i^* or V_i^w with a factor $\delta < 1$, when construction of the facility is delayed by a trial. This effect will clearly reduce welfare of the discretion-cum-standing regime. As the environment will remain in the state most preferred by the environmental group during this period of time, the group may also have an incentive to file suit when not undertaking research or after unsuccessful research. Even when such an incentive is ruled out because the legal costs the group ultimately has to bear are prohibitive, delay will increase the group's incentive to undertake research. Too see this, consider the following condition, which is a variant of (3.7). The group will undertake research, when

$$
D_h^* > \left[\frac{(1-q)b}{(1-q)b+q} p(\overline{\theta}) E(\theta | \theta \geq \overline{\theta}) + \frac{q}{(1-q)b+q} p(\overline{\theta})[1 - E(\theta | \theta \geq \overline{\theta})] \right] \delta D_l^*
$$

$$
+ \left[1 - \frac{(1-q)b}{(1-q)b+q} p(\overline{\theta}) E(\theta | \theta \geq \overline{\theta}) - \frac{q}{(1-q)b+q} p(\overline{\theta})[1 - E(\theta | \theta \geq \overline{\theta})] \right] D_h^*
$$

$$
+ C^r.
$$

The left-hand side depicts the costs of not undertaking research; the right-hand side expected costs of undertaking research. The first term on the right-hand side are expected environmental costs after successful research and a correct or incorrect overruling by the court, the second term depicts fruitless research. Setting $\delta = 1$ and reformulating this expression immediately gives (3.7).

The analysis presented in this chapter explicitly ruled out that the environmental group may enter the bargaining game between the investor and the agency. This assumption is now relaxed. When the project is not executed as long as the licensing procedure is ongoing, delay may result, because the group's interest in avoiding environmental damages generates incentives to drag on the bargaining procedure. This argument is often forwarded against the principle of more participatory rights of organized environmental interests. Subsequent chapters, *inter alia*, will examine this issue in more detail.

3.9 APPENDIX

In what follows, equilibrium strategies $b^*(\bar{\theta})$ and $k^*(\bar{\theta})$ under agency discretion are derived by operating with conditions (3.7) and (3.8), and parametrically decreasing the policy variable $\bar{\theta}$. Equilibrium strategy combinations are classified under labels A to D; within each classification, there is a unique equilibrium for a given $\bar{\theta}$. Figures 3.A1 and 3.A2 present the respective Nash correspondences. Note that in these figures, moving in eastern direction means to lower the standing barrier; hence, the abscissa denotes $(1-\bar{\theta})$.

A. No correction, no deterrence: $b^* = 1$ and $k^* = 0$. Equation (3.7) does not hold for $b=1$. The parameter $\bar{\theta}$ is high enough for the benchmark described above to still hold: the group will never investigate, and the agency will always accept the transfer. While standing formally exists, it has no influence on the parties' decisions. Standing is non-substantive.

Lower now $\bar{\theta}$ such that (3.7) holds as an equality, for $b=1$. Then, the environmental organization is indifferent as to whether or not to conduct investigations, and will thus be ready to randomize. One of two cases will apply:

Case I: $b^* = 1$ and $k^* \in [0, \bar{k}]$. Equation (3.8) will not hold for $k \in (\bar{k}, 1]$. When the research probability is too high, the agency will be deterred from a side-arrangement with the investor. Then, lowering $\bar{\theta}$ still further leads directly to the class of equilibria C where both parties randomize over their possible strategies (see below).

Case II: $b^* = 1$ and $k^* \in [0, 1]$. Equation (3.8) also holds for $k^* = 1$. Further lowering $\bar{\theta}$ leads to the following class of equilibria:

B. Only correction, no deterrence: $b^* = 1$, $k^* = 1$. Within equilibria B, (3.7) holds for $b=1$, and (3.8) holds for $k=1$. When the environmental group files suit, the court will correct the regulation; however, due to a high standard of evidence, the risk for the agency of being overruled is too low to deter it from collusion.

Lower now $\bar{\theta}$ to the point where, for $k^* = 1$, (3.8) holds as an equality. Then, the agency is indifferent as to whether or not to agree on bribery and will therefore be ready to randomize. One of two cases results:

Case IIa: $k^* = 1$, $b^* \in [0,1]$. Here, (3.7) holds for any b. The group will undertake research even when the probability of the agency accepting a side-payment approaches zero. Lowering $\overline{\theta}$ still further leads directly to equilibria D where the group undertakes research even if the agency does not collude.

Case IIb: $k^* = 1$, $b^* \in [\underline{b},1]$. Here, (3.7) does not hold for $b \in [0, \underline{b})$. For a probability of collusion that is too low, the environmental group does not have an incentive to undertake research. Lowering $\overline{\theta}$ leads to the following equilibria class:

C. Correction and deterrence: $k^* \in (\overline{\overline{k}},\overline{k})$, $b^* \in (0,1)$ *(case I) or* $k^* \in [\overline{\overline{k}},1)$, $b^* \in (0,\underline{b})$ *(case IIb).* For $b = 1$, (3.7) holds. When $\overline{\theta}$ is low enough for (3.8) not to hold for $k = 1$, the agency will not accept a bribe when the group

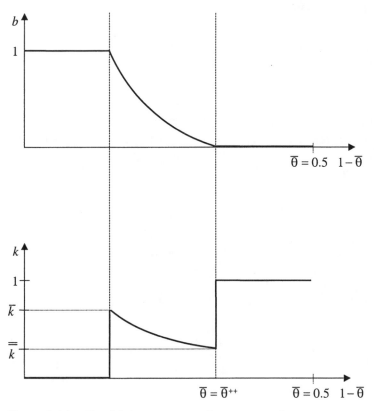

Figure 3.A1   Equilibrium correspondences – case I

always undertakes research. However, (3.7) may not hold for $b = 0$: When the agency always acts honestly, the environmental organization will not investigate. This constellation gives rise to an equilibrium in mixed strategies in which the parties randomize in choosing their actions. From (3.8), the equilibrium strategy of the group is given by

$$k^*(\overline{\theta}) = \frac{1}{p(\overline{\theta})E(\theta|\theta \geq \overline{\theta})} \frac{A(P^B)}{A(P^B) - A(C^c)}$$

$$= \frac{1}{p(\overline{\theta})E(\theta|\theta \geq \overline{\theta})} K, \tag{3.A1}$$

where $K \in (0,1)$ represents the propensity of the agency to accept the side-payment: A lower K means that the agency is less inclined to collude because of a low payment P^B or because of high legal costs. Solving (3.7) for b, the equilibrium strategy of the agency is

$$b^*(\overline{\theta}) = \frac{q}{1-q} \frac{C^r - p(\overline{\theta})(1 - E(\theta|\theta \geq \overline{\theta}))\Delta D}{p(\overline{\theta})E(\theta|\theta \geq \overline{\theta})\Delta D - C^r}, \tag{3.A2}$$

To double-check the sign of (3.A2), note that $C^r - p(\overline{\theta})(1 - E(\theta|\theta \geq \overline{\theta}))\Delta D > 0$, or the group will also investigate when the agency always regulates correctly (this will be the case under equilibria D). Furthermore, $\overline{\theta}$ is low enough for the group undertaking research when $b = 1$. Hence, from (3.7),

$$[(1-q)p(\overline{\theta})E(\theta|\theta \geq \overline{\theta}) + q\ p(\overline{\theta})(1 - E(\theta|\theta \geq \overline{\theta}))]\Delta D - C^r > 0.$$

These properties imply $p(\overline{\theta})E(\theta|\theta \geq \overline{\theta})\Delta D - C^r > 0$. Standing has two impacts here: the court will correct regulation ($k^* > 0$); anticipating this, the agency is deterred from collusion to a certain extent ($b^* < 1$). Deriving (3.A1) and (3.A2) with respect to $\overline{\theta}$ yields

$$\frac{db^*}{d\overline{\theta}} = \frac{q}{1-q} \cdot \frac{(1-\overline{\theta})f(\overline{\theta})\Delta D\left[\int_{\underline{\theta}}^{1}\theta f(\theta)d\theta\,\Delta D - C^r\right]}{\left[\int_{\underline{\theta}}^{1}\theta f(\theta)d\theta\,\Delta D - C^r\right]^2}$$

$$+ \frac{q}{1-q} \cdot \frac{\overline{\theta}f(\overline{\theta})\,\Delta D\left[C^r - \int_{\underline{\theta}}^{1}(1-\theta)f(\theta)d\theta\Delta D\right]}{\left[\int_{\underline{\theta}}^{1}\theta f(\theta)d\theta\,\Delta D - C^r\right]^2} > 0$$

and

$$\frac{dk^*}{d\overline{\theta}} = \frac{\overline{\theta}f(\overline{\theta})}{\left(\int_{\underline{\theta}}^{1}\theta f(\theta)d\theta\right)^2}K > 0.$$

Decreasing $\overline{\theta}$ decreases the equilibrium probabilities of undertaking research and of accepting the side-payment. Lowering standing barriers has a deterring effect on collusion. Then, the group can reduce its research activity in order to maintain the agency's indifference in regard to acceptance or non-acceptance of the side-payment. Conversely, a stronger standing for the environmental group increases the odds of prevailing in court. The agency is forced to reduce its probability of collusion in order to maintain the group's indifference towards conducting or not conducting an investigation.

Note that k^* never becomes zero for $b^* > 0$. This is so, because a decreasing $\overline{\theta}$ will eventually lead the group to always undertake research ($k^* = 1$) even when the agency does not collude.

Lower now $\overline{\theta}$ to the point for (3.7) to hold as an equality for $b^* = 0$, the group will still be ready to randomize. Equilibrium strategies are $b^* = 0$ and $k^* \in (\overline{\overline{k}}, 1]$, where $\overline{\overline{k}}$ is the equilibrium strategy of the group in the mixed equilibrium where $b^* = 0 + \varepsilon$, ε being 'very small'. Lowering $\overline{\theta}$ leads to the following equilibria:

D. No correction, only deterrence: $b^* = 0$, $k^* = 1$. (3.7) holds for $b = 0$, and
(3.8) does not hold for $k^* = 1$. The group always investigates, and the agency
never colludes. In this case, the judge will never overrule incorrect regulation:
The environmental organization, in undertaking research, relies only on
possible court errors.

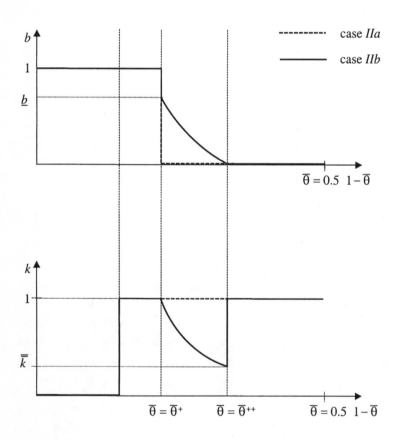

Figure 3.A2   Equilibrium correspondences – case II

4. Negotiations under Uncertain Court Outcomes: Asymmetrical Standing

4.1 INTRODUCTION

Chapter 2 presented a principal–agent analysis of regulatory capture, in which the investor and the administrator negotiated over the amount of the side-transfer. The investor was assumed not to have access to the judicial system. In contrast, the environmental group could challenge intended regulation in court, but was excluded from being a bargaining party. The analysis presented here and in Chapter 5 will relax these restrictions and address the parties' bargaining incentives under uncertain legal outcomes. This chapter will analyze the bargaining constellation characterized as typical of Germany. Therefore, first consider some evidence.

4.1.1   Environmental Bargaining in Germany

Important evidence on the importance of bargained agreements within administrative procedures of environmental law is given by the German literature on informal administrative action (*informales Verwaltungshandeln*), that is, administrators' actions beyond those formally prescribed by administrative law. Bilateral agreements of agencies with those they are supposed to regulate are described as forming a major part of these actions. They were intensely debated by legal scholars, starting with the paradigmatic contributions from Bohne (1981, 1984). According to the levels on which agencies exert discretionary power (see Chapter 2), agreements are usually divided into agreements on the regulatory level (*normabwendende Absprachen*) and those on the project-level (*normvollziehende Absprachen*) (Bohne 1981, 345; Kloepfer 1998, 294).[1]

---

[1] See for example the synopses by Scherer (1991), Ossenbühl (1987) for arrangements on the regulatory level, and Benz (1990), Bohne (1990), Breuer (1990), Bulling (1989), Dose (1989, 1997), Eberle (1984), Hennecke (1991), Kippes (1995), Schneider (1996) and Tomerius (1995) for arrangements on the project level. The list is by no means exhaustive; Kloepfer (1998,

Agreements on the regulatory level do not involve a single operator, but rather a whole industry.[2] Such agreements bear some similarities to the US-procedure of negotiated rulemaking, which will be discussed shortly in Chapter 5.

With respect to implementation at the project level, typical features of arrangements stressed by the literature are the following.

- They are the result of negotiations in which typical bargaining parties are the regulating agency and the investor or project operator (see, for example, Bohne 1981, 347; Eberle 1984, 440ff.; Kippes 1995, 60ff.; Tomerius 1995, 33–7).

- The aim of avoiding legal battles is regularly stressed as an important, although not exclusive,[3] objective of the agency when engaging in such a collaborative relationship (Eberle 1984, 442; Hennecke 1991, 269, 271, 272).[4]

- Negotiations take place within the licensing of new projects before the formal permit procedure starts (*Vorverhandlungen*), or within the regulation of existing facilities, upon implementation of tighter environmental policy (*Sanierungsabsprachen* or clean-up arrangements) (see Eberle 1984, Hennecke 1991, 271; Tomerius 1995, 37–8).

- Arrangements are typically informal; parties are not legally committed to the terms of the agreement (Bohne 1981, 347; Hennecke 1991, 270).[5] There are some possibilities for German agencies to enter contractual relations with private parties, *via* a so-called contract of public law (*öffentlich-rechtlicher Vertrag*, §§54ff. VwVfG))[6]. Clean-ups are

---

292–9) offers a concise summary from a legal viewpoint; and Peacock (1984, 133–54) an English synopsis.

[2] See Commission of the European Communities (1996), Leveque (1995), Segerson and Miceli (1998) for overviews. The latter contribution's theoretical analysis, however, only addresses agreements at the level of the firm, thus neglecting these crucial differences.

[3] Eberle (1984, 442), also stresses that the agency may overcome information deficits by cooperating with the investor. This was the assumption of Chapter 3.

[4] In turn, significant probabilities, for the agency, of ultimately losing costly lawsuits are usually derived by referring to the mere quantity of environmental norms, their vagueness and internal inconsistency (see for example Brohm 1986, 1987; Dose 1997, Benz 1992 and Kippes 1995 for a summary).

[5] Bulling (1989, 277, 280) differentiates into written 'agreements' and oral 'arrangements'. Under neither are parties formally committed.

[6] Such contracts are sometimes used to settle legal disputes. Agencies are entitled by administrative law (§55 VwVfG) to settle disputes both within legal procedure (*gerichtlicher Vergleich*) as well as out of the court (*außergerichtlicher Vergleich*). However, Kloepfer (1998, 287) comes to the conclusion that such contracts are 'rather the exception' in environmental policy implementation.

sometimes concluded by such a formal contract (Schapman 1997; Tomerius 1995). However, formal contracting is illegal within licensing procedures because of the danger of violating the participatory rights of third parties granted by the formal procedure (Kloepfer 1998, 287–8).

Because of this latter point, opinions diverge as to how to interpret informal licensing agreements from a legal viewpoint.[7] On the one hand, it is said that informality does not necessarily imply illegality, because of agencies' procedural discretion (§§10, 22 VwVfG; see Kloepfer 1998, 297). However, informal negotiations are often characterized as being in a legal 'gray zone' (Hennecke 1991, 269; Eberle 1984, 464). When taking place before the beginning of formal permit procedures, such negotiations may devaluate the participatory rights of third parties within the formal procedure: If the regulatory outcome is fixed beforehand, they would only be a sham (Eberle 1984, 439ff., 451ff.; Hennecke 1991, 273; Kloepfer 1998, 298; Tomerius 1995, 36, 122ff.). It is for this reason that an 'impartial negotiation style' of the agency is frequently required as a crucial precondition for the legality of informal bargaining (Bohne 1981, 351; Kloepfer 1998, 298).

The following analysis will examine these characteristic features of German environmental negotiations. Among these, the fact that bargaining typically occurs between project operators and regulating agencies is especially noteworthy, as it contrasts with the situation in the United States. In the most comprehensive empirical study on environmental negotiations (Bingham 1986), 78 percent of the investigated site-specific disputes (which, hence, would be subjected to a licensing procedure in Germany) involved environmental groups and/or local citizen groups.

Chapter 5 will argue that this difference in the typical bargaining constellation can be explained by the differing extent of associational standing. It will explore the efficiency implications of different standing doctrines on the bargaining constellation and the bargaining outcome. It will do so by comparing the stylized situation presented now, in which only the investor has standing, with a situation in which both private parties have standing. The former will be labeled 'asymmetrical standing', whereas the latter will be called 'symmetrical standing'.

To undertake this comparison, the theoretical analysis will again assume that the project under consideration generates environmental damage exclusively borne by persons who are not neighbors of the project. Under the

---

[7]See Benz (1990, 87ff.) and Kippes (1995, 67) for a classification of contributions.

German legal principle of protecting individual rights, those persons would not have standing, while they would do so under the more expansive US injury-in-fact standard. Externality victims, as before, are represented by the environmental group.

This chapter will present the general theoretical framework and will explore the case of asymmetrical standing. Besides stylizing the German situation, the case also allows for another interpretation. Even if an environmental group has standing, taking action is in reality costly. While some costs may be refunded after a successful case, environmental organizations will optimize the use of their given budget by fighting only against the most important projects. Therefore, the constellation may also depict a situation in which the damage, albeit substantial, is not important enough[8] to induce activities by environmental groups.

4.1.2   Agencies and the Courts

By assumption, the agency has wide discretion in implementing the law in a specific regulatory case. The underlying environmental act can be interpreted analogous to an incomplete contract: the legislature, when drafting the bill, did not consider the contingencies arising in the concrete regulatory case because of prohibitive transaction costs. Instead, two institutions are given power to deal with these contingencies. First, the legislature grants discretionary power to an implementing agency. Second, a court, when called in, may doubt the wisdom of the agency's decision and, subsequently, overrule it.

In reality, environmental law, while being vague, will rather not simply state that agencies can regulate as they wish. Instead, its quantity and internal inconsistency will often grant *de facto* wide agency discretion: These characteristics of environmental law make agencies believe that they are granted wide leeway in decision-making. Courts, however, may have a different opinion on the matter.

Being complementary to Chapter 3, this analysis will also incorporate a different flavor with respect to administrative and legal decision-making. The setting of Chapter 3, by taking the usual economic approach of modeling agencies as income maximizers,[9] relied on an essentially negative picture of administrators' motivations, asserting that, whenever possible and fruitful,

---

[8]In the US, such negotiations virtually 'happen all the time' in small-scale, local cases, as put it Larry Morgan, Deputy General Counsel, Florida Department of Environmental Protection.
[9]See the literature referred to in Chapter 2.

they will neglect their official duty to serve the general interest. In contrast, the role of the legal system appeared to be more positive, as it was the possibility of judicial review that deterred the agency from collusive behavior and improved welfare.

This combination of a negative picture of administrative decision-making and of a positive picture of the corresponding legal overruling has been challenged by several empirical contributions. Melnick (1992, 200) summarizes:[10]

> [M]ost of these studies show that judicial intervention has had an unfortunate effect on policymaking. Judicial review has subjected agencies to debilitating delay and uncertainty. Courts have heaped new tasks on agencies while decreasing their ability to perform any of them. They have forced agencies to substitute trivial pursuits for important ones. And they have discouraged administrators from taking responsibilities for their actions and for educating the public. ... Unsupported assertions about the malevolence of bureaucrats and the good will of judges do not constitute a convincing reply to these empirical studies.

Note for clarification that the analysis of Chapter 3 did not assume anything like the 'good will' of judges. Nor did it present an unambiguous positive role of the judiciary, as the emerging court errors, as such, had a welfare-decreasing effect. Also, the empirical studies referred to by Melnick, by analyzing concrete court rulings, do not address bargained outcomes emerging in the shadow of the law; that is, agreements reached just to avoid a legal battle. However, even while it is not intended here to discuss these studies in detail, it may be fruitful to incorporate their sense into the analysis, by emphasizing even more the possible inefficiencies of legal decision-making when compared with administrative decision-making.[11]

For this reason, the following model of a biased agency will allow, as a special case, for an unbiased, welfare-maximizing agency.[12] Decision-making by the court, however, will induce a stochastic legal error in favor of the party

---

[10]Beyond the contributions mentioned by Melnick (1992, 201, fn. 1), O'Leary's (1993) study presents a similar picture on the impact of federal courts' rulings on EPA's policy.

[11]In Germany, where opportunities to challenge administrative rules (*Verwaltungsverordnungen*) are limited, the impact of the courts on agencies' policies is restricted. The impact is more important under implementation at the project level. Asserted prolongation of licensing processes because of time-consuming legal battles led the German legislature to restrict participatory rights. See Chapter 2, 20.

[12]This case is in line with normative requirements as how agencies should act. Agencies have to 'weigh' competing objectives within licensing in Germany (this is the so-called *Abwägungsgebot*) as well as in the United States, under the permit program of section 404 of the Clean Water Act. See Chapter 2, 25–6. From an economic perspective, this requirement can be interpreted as efficiency norm.

which takes action against the agency. Therefore, even under a welfare-maximizing administrator, departures from efficiency are provoked by the court system.[13]

Specifically, the court ruling will be modeled as a lottery over the parties' pleadings, and parties, when they have standing and decide to sue, plead in accordance with their objectives. In line with the analysis of Chapter 3, one may argue that private parties will sometimes have the possibility to present misleading evidence, which, however, is convincing enough for the court to follow.

This court model presupposes that the judge rejects environmental regulation with positive probability. Such an assumption is not unrealistic in light of recent legal developments on property rights' regulation in the United States. Under the Fifth Amendment of the US Constitution, the taking of private property for public uses is prohibited without just compensation. This taking clause applies not only to physical takings, but also to regulation. Current proposals and recently enacted laws of the so-called New Property Rights Legislation tighten this standard by introducing the notion of a 'partial taking' (see Coursen 1996 for an overview). At the federal level, the Omnibus Property Rights Bill under debate in the Senate in 1995 mandated compensation for any regulation which affects the value of any portion of property by at least 33 percent. While this bill was ultimately rejected, similar legislation was passed in some states. For instance, the corresponding law in Florida grants a right for compensation when regulation puts an 'inordinate burden' on property owners. Then the loss of the 'fair market value' has to be compensated (ibid., 10246). When the agency cannot pay compensation due to tight budget constraints, this rule actually allows investors to push through lower regulation, when the court comes to the conclusion that the burden is 'inordinate'.

As the court sometimes decides in favor of a private party, the standing right of a private party may be interpreted as an attenuated, uncertain private property right. Under the technology assumptions made in Chapter 3, incentives to bargain over the amount on environmental spending S will be shown to emerge in such a setting of uncertain property rights. The

---

[13]In the present setting, when the agency is welfare-maximizing and completely informed, a complete abolishion of judicial review would restore efficiency. One may argue, however, that the court system has positive effects in other settings (like the one in Chapter 3), which are not explicitly modeled here. Such an approach is not uncommon in the literature. For instance, in analyses of three-tier hierarchies, hiring a supervisor is often set exogenously, because of asserted merits beyond supervision (see, for example, Tirole 1986, 188 or Schweizer 1992).

relationship to the Coasean analysis of private bargaining under secure private rights will be discussed in Chapter 5.

The negotiations will be modeled as a Rubinstein offer/counter-offer/bargaining game under complete (and perfect) information, in which the parties' opportunities to trigger a trial will be depicted as outside options (Rubinstein 1982, Sutton 1986). Information is still non-verifiable (or a stochastic court ruling would not make sense), but, in this chapter, observable for every bargaining party. Bargaining under private information will be addressed in Chapter six.

4.1.3   Literature

The effect of different standing doctrines within a bargaining context was discussed by Jensen at al. (1986), who express strong reservations about a more generous standing regime. They consider the case of a neighborhood externality, in which environmental damage from a facility is exclusively borne by the neighbor. Standing for the neighbor alone gives rise to a Coasean solution. Expanding standing means extending the right to sue the facility operator beyond this neighbor. Hence, as it is only the immediate neighbor who suffers damage, suits filed by other parties can only be frivolous, that is, in order to extract a settlement offer.[14] They argue that, if the number of potential plaintiffs is large, Coasean contracting between the neighbor and the facility owner may not happen in the first place due to high transactions costs.

Hence, the framework used here differs in several crucial respects from the one used by these authors:[15]

- First, by assuming that damage is borne by persons who are not neighbors of the project. These persons' stake is thus real.
- Second, the present analysis does not simply identify standing with secure rights to veto the project.
- Third, externality victims are represented by a collective actor, which lowers the transaction costs of bargaining.

---

[14]Incentives to bring frivolous lawsuits were investigated, for example, by Bebchuk (1988) and Katz (1990).

[15]Furthermore, their conclusion is doubtful in the first place, because they do not consider at all the credibility of the threat to sue. Given that the potential plaintiffs never have a substantial stake, probabilities to prevail in court are arguably not very high. Furthermore, litigation costs are substantial. Then, credibility of the threat may be doubted.

The approach used here comes close to Cheung (1988), who presents a Rubinstein game where only the plaintiff can use the outside option of going to court, after rejecting an offer. Spier (1992, 103–5) also assumes that only the plaintiff has the outside option, but assumes that the plaintiff also makes all offers. In this special setting, all feasible payoffs can be sustained as equilibria. A similar approach is also used by Mohr (1990), who presents a Rubinstein model of bargaining between the environmental agency and the firm to investigate the impact of different agency objectives on the bargaining outcome. In his model, both the agency and the firm can opt out by going to the court.

Furthermore, the court model used here is consistent with contributions modeling environmental disputes as contests, in which the probabilities of prevailing are endogenized by a contest function (see Baik and Shogren 1994 or Heyes 1997). However, contest models systematically disregard possibly emerging bargaining incentives.

To picture legal decision-making stochastically from an *ex ante* viewpoint is a usual approach within the vast literature on trial and settlement, whose earlier contributions also assume complete information (Landes 1971; Gould 1973; Posner 1973; Shavell 1982; see Cooter and Rubinfeld 1989, 1071ff., for an overview). These contributions, however, do not explicitly model the bargaining process, but only derive the set of possible bargaining solutions. This set is typically non-empty when actors are risk-neutral or risk-averse and litigation costs are positive. Porter (1988) transfers this approach to environmental regulation. He shows that under a strictly convex technology (as introduced in Chapter 3), bargaining incentives between private parties may emerge even when they are risk-neutral, legal costs are zero and compensation is ruled out. This result is shown in Section 4.3 to hold also for the case of bargaining involving a public party, that is, the regulating agency.

In contrast to these contributions, the setting applied here allows one to derive a unique bargaining outcome, which is a precondition for comparing the bargaining constellations under asymmetrical and symmetrical standing, as will be done in Chapter 5. However, the analysis shares a characteristic feature with the above contributions under complete information, that is, that no trial occurs in equilibrium. It is this property that has promoted the use of models in which parties are privately informed. A discussion of the corresponding literature will be relegated to Chapter 6.

The chapter proceeds as follows. The next section will introduce the model applied in this and the following chapters. Because of the investor's incentive to sue a non-negotiated permit, bargaining between the investor and the agency results. Section 4.3 derives the bargaining solution under this setting. By focussing on the role of the status quo payoffs during ongoing negotiations, it will compare the bargaining over the permit conditions for new projects and the bargaining over the regulation of existing facilities. Section 4.4 presents and discusses some variations of the basic model. Section 4.5 considers in more detail the issue of enforcing informal agreements. Section 4.6 gives a summary.

4.2 THE FRAMEWORK

The model presents a two-tier governance structure (an agency, a court). Private parties are the investor (or project operator) and the environmental organization. Potential bargaining parties (the agency, the investor and, in the next chapter, the environmental group) are risk-neutral and completely informed. Introducing risk aversion would not change the results as long as every party's degree of risk aversion is common knowledge. Relevant information is still non-verifiable, meaning the court cannot subpoena the parties to reveal it.

4.2.1 Notation

Different bargaining constellations will be analysed and compared within the framework presented now. This chapter will analyse the situation in which only the investor has the opportunity to file suit (asymmetrical standing), while Chapter 5 will address the situation in which both the investor and the environmental group can take legal action (symmetrical standing). Furthermore, this chapter will compare environmental bargaining over a planned project with negotiations over the regulation of an existing facility. Throughout the next three chapters, sub- and superscripts to the respective variables (payoffs, bargaining sets and bargaining frontiers) will be used to indicate which bargaining constellation is addressed. Specifically, the following notation will be used.

a indicates bargaining under *asymmetrical* standing

s indicates bargaining under *symmetrical* standing

n indicates bargaining over a *new* or planned project

e indicates bargaining over an *existing* facility

   c   denotes (expected) payoffs from going to *court*
   B   denotes payoffs under the solution of the *bargaining* game
   N   denotes payoffs under the *Nash* solution of the bargaining game

Under the model used here, the actual bargaining solution may differ from the Nash solution, for reasons that are spelled out below.

4.2.2   Technology and Actors

Technology. Assumptions on $D(S)$ correspond to those of Chapter 3. Chapter 3 depicted the realization of an indivisible project, which yielded consumer surplus $Cs > 0$. The variable S corresponded to spending on abatement technology. However, the framework allows also for a divisible project, where S denotes profit reductions because of a lower installed capacity.

    To see this, consider the usual microeconomic production framework. Assume the project produces a homogenous good x. The project operator is a price-taker.[16] Denote the exogenous price by q and variable production costs by $C(x)$. Production costs are strictly convex: $C'(x) > 0$, $C''(x) > 0$. The project profit is

$$\Pi(x) = qx - C(x),$$

which is strictly concave: $\Pi'(x) \gtrless 0$, $\Pi''(x) = -C''(x) < 0$. Optimal capacity of the project without regulation is given by profit-maximizing output x_0, where $q = C'(x_0)$. The profit level at output x_0 is denoted by Π_0.

    Environmental damage such as aesthetic harm may result from the mere magnitude of the project. Assume therefore that damages increase in capacity and $D(x)$ is convex: $D'(x) > 0$, $D''(x) \geq 0$. Assume also that abatement is not possible: Reducing environmental externalities means a reduction in capacity. Any reduction of x below x_0 reduces the firm's profit. Hence, the spending level on environmental protection is given by

$$S(x) = \Pi_0 - \Pi(x),$$

---

[16]One may assume significant entry barriers to rationalize $\Pi_0 > 0$ in such a competitive setting, under constant returns of scale.

which is strictly convex: $S''(x) = -\Pi''(x) > 0$. Denote the corresponding inverse function (the mapping from output into the spending level) by $x(S)$:

$$x(S) = S^{-1}(S),$$

where $x''(S) = 1/S''(x) > 0$. Using this inverse function, the mapping from the spending level into environmental damage is given by $D(S) = D[x(S)]$, and $D'(S) = D'[x(S)]x'(S)$. Now,

$$D''(S) = D''(x)(x'(S))^2 + D'(x)x''(S) > 0$$

implies that $D(S)$ is strictly convex, as was the assumption in Chapter 3.

For the analysis presented now, the role of the consumer surplus is minor; therefore, set $Cs = 0$ (which is, anyway, natural when the firm is a price-taker). Welfare is then given by $\Pi_0 - D(S) - S$. Assume $\Pi_0 - D(S^*) - S^* > 0$.

Furthermore, assume the investment to be eternal and non-depreciating; then Π_0 and D_0 are the present values of the respective periodical parameters:

$$\Pi_0 = \frac{1}{1-\delta}\pi_0, \quad D_0 = \frac{1}{1-\delta}d_0$$

where δ is the common discount factor.

In the present setting, neither monitoring nor enforcement costs are considered. This is not to say that these costs are negligible, nor that they may not induce incentives to negotiate because of potential cost savings[17]; rather, the exclusion of these costs makes it clear that they are not necessary to derive bargaining incentives under uncertain legal outcomes.

Actors. As in Chapter 3, because of the harmful effects on the environment, the project owner needs a permit from a regulating agency before operating the facility. The permit may be conditional: the agency has wide discretion in prescribing a specific spending level S on environmental protection.

Agency discretion can lead to an agency's abuse of its power. Therefore, a conditional permit can be taken to court by the investor or by the

---

[17]Amacher and Malik (1996, 1998) as well as Segerson and Miceli (1998) present bargaining models based on monitoring and enforcement costs. These contributions will be discussed in Section 4.3.2.

environmental group. The remainder of this chapter will explore the situation in which only the investor has standing. This means that the project, while generating environmental damage D, does not impair the (narrowly defined) individual rights of neighbors. Under the German principle of individual rights' protection, this damage would then not generate standing, while it would do so under the more generous US injury-in-fact test.

Consider, therefore, first the objectives of the investor and the agency. The objective of the investor is to maximize net profit

$$\Pi(S) = \Pi_0 - S;$$

thus, he will mostly prefer an unconditional permit. The agency is assumed to maximize

$$W(S) = \theta(\Pi_0 - S) - D(S),$$

where θ represents here an exogenous bias parameter. For $\theta < 1$ the agency is biased against the investor (is 'environmentalist'); for $\theta > 1$, it is biased against the externality victims (is 'industry-friendly').

In the following chapters, the focus will often be on a welfare-maximizing agency ($\theta = 1$); this is why the agency payoff is also given by W. However, W stands for welfare only if $\theta = 1$.

Note that S also stands for the stringency of environmental regulation. The administrator will prefer regulation over

$$S^A = \arg\max_S W(S).$$

Denote the corresponding agency payoff level by W^A and $W_0 = \theta\Pi_0 - D_0$. Implicitly restrict the support of θ by making the following assumptions.

- $W^A > 0$. The administrator will never reject the permit application.
- $S^A \in (0, \Pi_0)$. When being regulated according to S^A, the investor will build the project.

Within these restrictions, the following analysis applies for any θ, when not otherwise indicated. As in Chapter 3, stars indicate efficient solutions; hence, Π^* is the investor's payoff under efficient spending. The condition for an interior agency payoff maximum W^A is $D'(S^A) = -\theta$, which implies, for a strictly convex $D(.)$, $S^A > S^*$ for $\theta < 1$, and vice versa. Note that, for $\theta = 1$, $S^A = S^*$. Also, denote

$$W_0 = \frac{1}{1-\delta} w_0 .$$

4.2.3 The Trial Subgame

The court model. The trial will be modeled as a lottery over the parties' pleadings: the parties plead in line with their objectives, and the court decides immediately in favor of one of the parties with some positive probability. Some comments concerning a more general model of the court will be made when discussing the result; specifically, it will be shown that the model also holds when the investor can get the court only to lower the required spending level.

Parties can sue without cost. Introducing litigation costs does not change the qualitative results of bargaining, but may restrict bargaining incentives. The impact of positive court costs will be considered in Section 4.3.3.

The subgame after failed bargaining. In the situation in which an environmental group does not have standing, a trial results when the agency, after unsuccessful bargaining, issues a specific conditional permit against which the investor decides to sue. Note the sequence of moves: the agency always moves first by issuing a non-negotiated permit; then, the investor decides whether to file suit or not. This sequencing gives rise to the question as to whether the investor's threat to sue the non-negotiated permit is credible, and how the agency will react strategically in response to this threat.

The investor, when fighting the agency's regulation, pleads for an unconditional permit (in line with its objective), while the agency, when sued, will defend the conditional permit it issued. Consider first the choice of the agency as to which spending level to prescribe for a non-negotiated permit. For a specific spending level S, the expected outcome from a trial is given by the following expressions:

$$\Pi^{ca} = \Pi_0 - (1 - p_I)S \tag{4.1}$$

for the investor and

$$W^{ca} = p_I(\theta\Pi_0 - D_0) + (1 - p_I)[\theta(\Pi_0 - S) - D(S)] \tag{4.2}$$

for the agency, where the superscript c stands for court, a stands for asymmetrical standing, p_I denotes the probability that the court rules in favor of the investor, and $p_I \in (0,1)$ for the court outcome being uncertain. Hence,

$$S^A = \arg\max_S [p_I(\theta\Pi_0 - D_0) + (1 - p_I)(\theta(\Pi_0 - S) - D(S))]$$

and the agency, when it seeks to issue a permit after a breakdown of negotiations, sets $S = S^A$.[18]

When litigation costs are zero, the investor has an incentive to fight any permit issued without negotiations, as $S^A > (1 - p_I)S^A$. It is this feature that yields bargaining incentives between the investor and the agency.[19]

In the bargaining game, the possibility of using the legal system is modeled as an outside option for the parties, meaning that, at a specific stage of the bargaining game specified below, one party has the opportunity to quit the negotiations and trigger a trial. Specifically,

- the investor may terminate the negotiations. In this case, the agency will issue a permit over S^A, and the investor will sue this permit, as $(1 - p_I)S^A < S^A$.
- The agency's outside option is to quit the bargaining table and issue the permit S^A, against which the investor will take action.

4.2.4   The Bargaining Model

The bargaining process will be modeled as a strategic offer/counter-offer bargaining game (Rubinstein 1982, Sutton 1986), in which parties may take

---

[18]This formulation assumes common beliefs of the agency and the investor with respect to the expected court outcome. When agents have differing access to information, these beliefs may differ (indeed, the Harsanyi doctrine says that differing prior beliefs have to be explained by differing access to information; see Aumann 1987). Empirical evidence stress the relevance of 'optimistic overconfidence' (Kahneman and Tversky 1995, 46–50). Denote by p_A the agency's subjective probability of prevailing in court. When at least one party is overly optimistic, $p_I + p_A > 1$, and bargaining incentives may not exist. Within complete-information analyses, this is the standard explanation of why trials may result in equilibrium (see the referenced literature on trial and settlement, or Cooter and Ulen 1988, 486–7).

[19]The investor will not necessarily file suit for positive litigation costs and some S^A. This issue will be addressed in Section 4.3.3.

their outside option after they rejected an offer.[20] For the general description, call these parties one and two:

- Party one starts the negotiations in period $t = 0$ with an offer of a specific spending level S. The adversary (party two) may accept or reject this offer. If it accepts, the game ends with the payoffs (Π^{Ba}, W^{Ba}). If it rejects, it may quit by taking its outside option. In this case, the trial subgame, as described above, is played, and the game ends immediately with the payoffs (Π^{ca}, W^{ca}). However, party two may also submit a counter-offer. Preparation of this counter-offer needs time, meaning that
- Party two submits a counter-offer in period $t = 1$. Acceptance by party one investor terminates the game. A rejection again opens up two opportunities: party one may take its outside option, in which case the trial subgame is played, or decides to submit a second offer in period $t = 2$.
- The game is repeated until one party accepts an offer or takes its outside option.

Denote the period's length by Λ. Thus, the common discount factor of both parties is $\delta^\Lambda \in (0, 1)$. When not indicated otherwise, $\Lambda = 1$. Hence, bargaining is costly, because the payoffs associated with a delayed agreement must be discounted. Any party realizing a specific payoff in period t has to be offered at least the discounted value of this payoff by its adversary in order to accept an agreement one period earlier, in $t-1$.

Call the payoffs the parties realize during each negotiation round the periodic status quo payoffs. For instance, in the case of a planned project, the periodic status quo payoff pair for the investor and the agency is $(0,0)$ whereas in negotiations of the regulation of an existing facility it is (π_0, w_0).

The bargaining solution. Explicit solutions of the strategic game are relegated to the appendix. In the following sections, the axiomatic characterization of the bargaining solution will be used. This characterization

---

[20]Thus, parties have always a chance to submit a counter-offer before their adversary quits the negotiations and goes to the court. Shaked (1994, 422) argues that such a model should be used to depict bazaar-like bargaining where 'it is commonplace for the seller to shout after the leaving customer and make a last price offer'. In contrast, models where parties can opt out immediately after their own offer was rejected should be used when analyzing negotiations in 'Hi Tech' markets, in which communication occurs via telephones or computers (ibid.). Clearly, environmental bargaining comes closer to the former than to the latter. When parties can opt out immediately after their own offer was rejected, a multiplicity of equilibria may result (see also Osborne and Rubinstein 1990, 58–63 and Spier 1992). The inefficiency result stated in Lemma 4.1 (i) below, however, would not be affected by using such an alternative bargaining protocol.

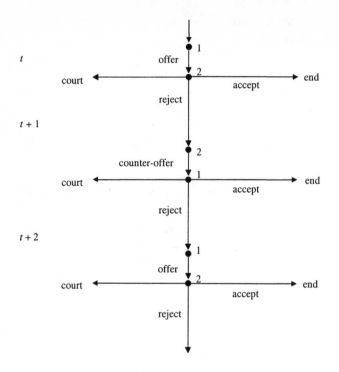

Figure 4.1   Offer/counter-offer bargaining

applies when $\Lambda \rightarrow 0$, the time period elapsing between offer and counter-offer being 'very small'. The solution is based on two well-known results from bargaining theory:

- The solution of a strategic model of offer/counter-offer bargaining without outside options converges, for a common discount factor δ^Λ and for $\Lambda \rightarrow 0$, to the symmetric Nash solution[21] (Nash 1950) of the game (Sutton 1986, Binmore et al. 1986, 182–3).
- The *outside option principle*: Outside options affect the solution of the bargaining game only when a party's threat to take the outside option is credible in a given subgame. In this case, the other party has to agree on a bargaining solution which guarantees the value of the outside option to the threatening party. If the threat is not credible, the outside option does not

---

[21]When discount factors differ, the solution can be characterized, for $\Lambda \rightarrow 0$, by an asymmetric Nash solution. See Osborne and Rubinstein (1990), 84–6.

affect the bargaining solution.[22] (Sutton 1986, Binmore et al. 1986, 185–6, Binmore et al. 1989). Hence, the impact of the outside options can be analytically separated, as will be done in the following analysis. A formal proof of this property is given in the appendix.

Notice that the parties exert two threats, within bargaining and when triggering a trial:

- The investor can threaten to sue against a non-negotiated permit. This threat will always be credible, as long as litigation costs are not too high (see Section 4.3.3). It will be shown that bargaining incentives result. Second, the investor can threaten to take its outside option by quitting the negotiations (upon which the agency will issue a non-negotiated permit). This threat, in turn, may or may not be credible.
- The agency can threaten to issue a permit requiring a specific spending level, should negotiations fail. When litigation costs are not too high, the threat to issue regulation S^A is always credible. Second, when bargaining incentives exist, it can threaten to take its outside option in the bargaining game. This threat may or may not be credible.

Compensation. In the Coasean analysis of private environmental negotiations under well-defined, secure property rights, the possibility of compensation payments is crucial for the existence and efficiency of a bargaining solution. In the present analysis under an uncertain legal outcome, compensation will be revealed as non-crucial for the existence of a solution. The Coasean case of secure property rights will emerge, in Chapter 5, as a benchmark case in which the court always decides in favor of one private party.

The possibilities of compensation payments may be limited in reality. First, the payment of compensation may not lie within regulatory discretion; then, it is legally prohibited for agencies to pay compensation in the form of a cost-sharing of protective activities. Even if there are no legal obstacles, such arrangements will be limited by the tight budget restrictions of governmental agencies. This same 'fallacy-of-bankruptcy' argument applies to

---

[22]The outside option principle underlines the difference between the status quo, whose present value is realized when the parties agree to not agree, and an outside option. The introduction of outside options should not be modeled by shifting the status quo point, when they offer a second opportunity to the parties besides a possible 'agreement to disagree'. This is so, because the status quo also influences the negotiations insofar as (periodic) status quo payoffs are realized as long as negotiations are ongoing. See Binmore et al. (1986) for a discussion.

compensation payments from citizens' groups or environmental organizations. However, it does not apply to compensation payments from investors, as they could, in principle, be financed out of the project's profit. To reflect this argument, the following analysis will assume that compensation opportunities are asymmetric in the sense that only the operator of the project under dispute can pay compensation, as long as the remaining profit is positive.

4.3   THE ROLE OF THE STATUS QUO

The following analysis will compare bargaining within the licensing of new projects and within the regulation of existing facilities. Negotiations will happen under different status quo payoffs. Intuition suggests that the agency is in a better bargaining position in the former case. As the project is not executed as long as the permit procedure (and corresponding negotiations) is ongoing, 'the enterprise is dependent upon a positive decision of the agency' (Jarass 1990, 261).

For now, the bargaining solution is assumed to be laid down by an enforceable contractual agreement. Section 4.5 will focus on the issue of informality.

4.3.1   Licensing New Projects

Consider now the constellation between an investor and an agency within a licensing procedure for a planned facility. As the project is not executed as long as the permit procedure is ongoing, the status quo payoff pair is $(0,0)$.

When bargaining incentives exist, the investor and the regulating agency will bargain over a specific spending level S, which corresponds to a specific level of technical abatement. As any spending level S induces a specific payoff for each party, any possible candidate for a bargaining equilibrium can be characterized by a specific pair (Π, W). The solution of the bargaining game will be denoted by (Π_n^{Ba}, W_n^{Ba}), where a stands for asymmetric standing and n stands for *new* project. The spending level in bargaining equilibrium is $S_n^{Ba} = \Pi_0 - \Pi_n^{Ba}$.

Denote the set of feasible bargaining equilibria by Φ_a. For $W^A > 0$ and $\Pi(S^A) > 0$, this set is non-empty. Denote the mapping from a given payoff of the investor (associated with a specific spending level) into the maximal negotiated payoff of the agency by

$$\varphi_a(\Pi) = \theta(\Pi) - D(\Pi_0 - \Pi).$$

Graphically, φ_a is the locus of all pairs $(\Pi(S), W(S))$; hence, this bargaining frontier contains the set of all cost-efficient spending levels, where $D = D(S)$. Under strict convexity of $D(S)$ and the payoff functions specified in Section 4.2, $\varphi'_a(\Pi^A) = 0$, $\varphi'_a(\Pi) < 0$ for $\Pi \in (\Pi^A, \Pi_0]$, and $\varphi''_a(\Pi) < 0$. A graphical presentation of $\varphi_a(.)$ and Φ_a is pictured in Figure 4.2.

Define by $\varphi^I_a(.)$ the function giving the maximal payoff for the investor for a given (bargained) agency payoff. Specifically, $\varphi^I_a(.)$ incorporates the inverse function for the segment of $\varphi_a(.)$ on domain $[\Pi^A, \Pi_0]$. Consider now the possibility that $W_0 > 0$. For any $W \in [0, W_0]$, $\varphi^I_a(W) = \Pi_0$. Any welfare level strictly lower than W_0 may also be realized by zero environmental spending: in the negotiations, the investor cannot gain more than Π_0. Clearly, these points are not cost-efficient.[23]

Furthermore, for all given agency payoffs $W < W^A$, any $\Pi < \varphi^I_a(W)$ is Pareto-dominated. It may be concluded that any bargaining solution must be such that $\Pi^{Ba} \in [\Pi^A, \Pi_0]$.

Consider now the axiomatic characterization of the bargaining solution, holding for $\Lambda \to 0$. Denote Nash's solution of the game by (Π^N_n, W^N_n), where N stands for Nash and p for project; thus, (Π^N_n, W^N_n) maximizes the Nash-product[24] ΠW subject to $(\Pi, W) \in \Phi_a$. The main result can be stated by

Lemma 4.1. For a common discount factor δ^Λ and for $\Lambda \to 0$,

(i)   When bargaining incentives exist, bargaining between the investor and a welfare-maximizing agency will result in an immediate agreement on $S^{Ba}_n < S^A$.

(ii) Bargaining incentives between the investor and the agency exist for any $p_I \in (0, 1)$.

(iii) The unique solution of the bargaining game is characterized as follows:

---

[23]This formulation of $\varphi_a(.)$ and $\varphi^I_a(.)$ avoids technical ambiguities in deriving the possible bargaining solution (Π_0, W_0). See the appendix for details.

[24]The general formulation of the Nash-product is the product of the gains in von Neumann-Morgenstern utilities over the respective status quo outcome (see, for example, Osborne and Rubinstein (1990, chap. 2). As it is abstracted from attitudes towards risk, and the status quo outcome is just (0, 0), the formulation is simpler.

- When $\Pi^{ca} > \Pi_n^{Na}$ and $W^{ca} \leq W_n^{Na}$,

  the investor's outside option is a credible threat. The bargaining solution is $(\Pi_n^{Ba}, W_n^{Ba}) = (\Pi^{ca}, \varphi_a(\Pi^{ca}))$.

- When $\Pi^{ca} \leq \Pi_n^{Na}$ and $W^{ca} \leq W_n^{Na}$,

  no outside option is credible, and the Nash solution is the solution of the game: $(\Pi_n^{Ba}, W_n^{Ba}) = (\Pi_n^{Na}, W_n^{Na})$.

- When $\Pi^{ca} \leq \Pi_n^{Na}$ and $W^{ca} > W_n^{Na}$,

  the agency's threat with its outside option is credible, and the solution is $(\Pi_n^{Ba}, W_n^{Ba}) = (\varphi_a^I(W^{ca}), W^{ca})$.

Proof. See the appendix. ■

Figure 4.2 gives an illustration of this result for $\theta = 1$; hence, it pictures the case of a welfare-maximizing agency. In the figure, the parameter p_I is chosen such that the investor's threat to take her outside option is credible, and the bargaining solution is given by $(\Pi_n^{Ba}, W_n^{Ba}) = (\Pi^{ca}, \varphi_a(\Pi^{ca}))$. As the Nash solution has to be on the downward-sloping segment of $\varphi_a(.)$, an inefficiently low spending level also results when the Nash solution is valid, that is, when both threats to opt out are not credible ($\Pi_n^{Na} \in (\Pi^*, \Pi_0]$).

Thus, legislators cannot avoid negotiations when regulating agencies have to be given discretion because of regulatory complexity, and when discretionary decisions by the agency may be scrutinized by the courts in favor of investors. Under the formulation of the court used here, bargaining incentives may result even in the absence of legal costs or risk aversion. Furthermore, even when the agency is welfare-maximizing, the bargaining will always result in too low a spending level on protective activities. Thus, the analysis yields an explanation from a viewpoint of bargaining theory for the implementation deficits of German environmental policy.[25] However, welfare under the bargained outcome will not be worse, and possibly better than expected welfare from trial. In this sense, informal negotiations improve efficiency when compared with an agency than only relies on the court system to implement environmental law.[26]

When $p_I \in \{0, 1\}$, public or, respectively, private property rights relating to the environment are sure. If $p_I = 0$, bargaining degenerates into the

---

[25]Path-breaking for the German discussion on implementation deficits was Mayntz et al. (1978). See also Lahl (1993) for a recent discussion.

[26]This corresponds to the assessment often made in the German literature (see, for example, Benz 1990, 91ff.).

investor's immediate acceptance of a permit prescribing an spending level S^A.

Given the assumption that the court decides with positive probability against the agency, the result that equilibrium spending is inefficiently low for $\theta = 1$ may not seem too surprising. Indeed, the investor's outside option, which is its reservation value, requires too low a spending level. However, the result's emphasis is that the inefficiency stems from bargaining. In the negotiations, the agency will not always simply guarantee the outside option payoff to the investor. The inefficiency result does not depend on the credibility of the investor's threat to trigger a trial *during* negotiations: the Nash solution also implements too low a spending level.[27]

The intuition behind this result is that the agency is interested not only in reducing environmental damage through environmental spending, but also in realization of the investor's profit, which is as well part of society's well-being. The agency will take a 'soft' stance even in negotiations where no outside option is a credible threat. Consequently, the simple picture of the court as a lottery over the parties' pleadings could be replaced be a more general model. As long as $\Pi_0 - S^A < \Pi^{ca}$, the investor will sue against the permit, and the resulting negotiations will lead to a lower spending level than S^A.[28]

When the agency is only interested in efficiency ($\theta = 1$) and can pay compensation, it could restore efficient regulation by financing the difference between the negotiated and the efficient spending level. While such cost sharing of protective activities indeed sometimes takes place in German environmental policy,[29] despite the proclamation of the polluter-pays-principle, the general viability of such a solution is restricted under tight public budgets. Furthermore, as state revenues are usually generated by distortionary taxes, financing environmental subsidies would also imply a welfare loss *via* a rising excess burden.

This analysis allows some insights concerning the bargaining power of a specific party. When, for example, the investor credibly threatens with its outside option, the agency will have to 'pay it off' by guaranteeing it the

---

[27]Mohr (1990, 612), while assuming a welfare-maximizing agency, implausibly models the negotiations as a simple linear division problem over the 'pie' Π_0. As the limit of the Rubinstein game for $\Lambda \to 0$, he therefore gets $S_n^{Na} = 0.5\,\Pi_0$, which may also imply too high a spending level. Consequently, he only states that the bargaining outcome will be inefficient.

[28]Specifically, one may assume that the investor can only get the court to lower the spending level, but not to rule in favor of an unconditional permit. Also, the court may decide with positive probability on a spending level higher than S^A.

[29] Funke (1990, 216–17) presents a German clean-up case where 40 percent of environmental investments were financed by the Federal *Umweltbundesamt*.

value of the outside option as a bargained outcome. Consequently, the agency will reap all gains from trade (in Figure 4.2, this is the difference $W_n^{Ba} - W^{ca}$), and, hence, has 'all the bargaining power'. The present analysis derives bargaining power endogenously from a specific value of the parameter p_I (which implies specific values of the parties' outside options) and the subsequent credibility of the related threats to opt out. It does not allocate all the bargaining power to a party by simply assuming a specific bargaining protocol (under which the powerful party is assumed to submit all offers). Furthermore, having all bargaining power in this sense does not lead the agency to push through a higher spending level, when compared with a situation where it does not have all the bargaining power. This seemingly paradoxical result can be explained readily with the help of Figure 4.2. Note that the outside option values depend on the parameter p_I. The credibility of the investor's threat to opt out (which implies that the agency has all the bargaining power) presupposes a 'high' p_I. Such a high probability of prevailing in court, however, implies a lower equilibrium spending level in the first place, when compared with the situation in which no party's threat is credible, or the agency's threat is credible.

For the case of an indivisible project yielding a positive consumer surplus Cs, the following result can additionally be stated.

Corollary 4.1. Define a consumer surplus level $Cs_{\min}$. For any $Cs > Cs_{\min}$, the agency's outside option is a credible threat for any $p_I \in (0,1)$. Therefore, the bargaining outcome is always $(\Pi_n^{Ba}, W_n^{Ba}) = (\varphi_a^I(W^{ca}), W^{ca})$.

Proof. See the appendix. ∎

Again, this result can be explained by using Figure 4.2. Introducing (or parametrically increasing) Cs means shifting $\varphi_a(.)$ upwards. For a high enough Cs, the Nash solution will be a corner solution, in which $(\Pi_n^{Na}, W_n^{Na}) = (\Pi_0, W_0)$. As $W^{ca} > W_0$ for any $p_I \in (0,1)$, the agency's outside option is then always credible. The intuition behind this result is straightforward: the higher the 'social benefit' of the project, the more lenient the agency will act as a bargaining adversary of the investor, as long as its outside option is not credible. When $Cs > Cs_{\min}$, the agency's threat is always credible, and the investor will have all the bargaining power for any $p_I \in (0,1)$.

4.3.2   Regulation of Existing Facilities

A considerable part of environmental regulation focuses on facilities that already exist and are in operation. This aspect is especially important when environmental policy, as was the general trend in the last decades, introduces ever more numerous and more stringent norms, producing constant pressure on regulating agencies to ensure the compliance of existing plants with the new requirements.

This bargaining constellation can be analyzed in the setting presented in the preceding section. The solution to the corresponding bargaining game will be denoted by (Π_e^{Ba}, W_e^{Ba}), where e stands for existing facility.

Assume without loss of generality that, before the new legislation, there were no prescribed environmental standards at all, the damage produced by the facility thus being D_0. Then, the status-quo point of the negotiations over the implementation of a new environmental act is (Π_0, W_0). This means that, as long as the negotiations are ongoing, the facility will yield a periodic payoff π_0 for the investor and w_0 for the agency, where $\pi_0 = (1-\delta)\Pi_0$ and $w_0 = (1-\delta)W_0$. Hence, the parties' periodic status-quo payoffs during a

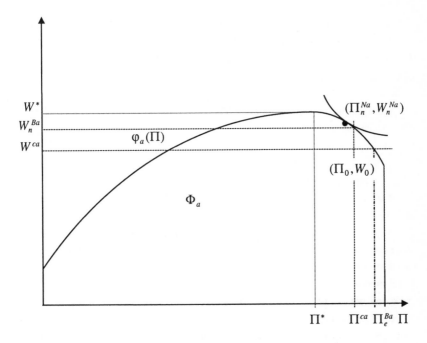

Figure 4.2 Negotiations between the investor and the agency

negotiation round are given by the pair (π_0, w_0). The bargaining protocol of the strategic game may also be depicted by Figure 4.1.

In this bargaining constellation, two effects influence the equilibrium payoffs within the strategic game. The first one is, like in the preceding analysis, the effect of discounting. However, in the case considered now, there is a second effect: to reach an earlier agreement, the adversary also has to offer the value of the periodical status-quo payoff the party realizes in period t. When bargaining over the regulation of a new project, these periodic payoffs are (trivially) zero, as the project is executed only after termination of the permit procedure and the corresponding negotiations.

The solution of the strategic game is again presented in the appendix. Consider now the axiomatic characterization of the game.

Lemma 4.2. For $\Lambda \rightarrow 0$, the solution of the bargaining game within the regulation of an existing facility is $(\Pi_e^{Ba}, W_e^{Ba}) = (\varphi_a^I(W^{ca}), W^{ca})$ for $p_I \in (0, 1)$.

Proof. See appendix 1. ∎

To explain this result, consider first the Nash solution to the game. It is given by payoffs which maximize $(\Pi - \Pi_0)(W - W_0)$ subject to $(\Pi, W) \in \Phi_a$. But any technically efficient point in Φ_a except (Π_0, W_0) yields a $\Pi^{na} < \Pi_0$. Thus, the Nash solution is given by (Π_0, W_0). The intuition is that any positive level of environmental spending would reduce the company's payoff, when compared to the status quo. Therefore, the company would reject any offer from the agency implying a positive spending level. The negotiations would drag on forever, the company realizing the periodic status quo payoff in every period. The only offer the company will accept is just the discounted sum of these periodic payoffs, which is, of course, the status quo outcome. The result is that there are no incentives to actually bargain without outside options.

As, however, $W^{ca} > W_0$ for $p_I \in (0, 1)$, the agency's threat to quit the negotiations and issue regulation on S^A is always credible. Remember that the company has an incentive to take action against such a prescription, which is anticipated by the agency. Thus, the Nash solution will never be relevant in the game with outside options. The threat of the investor to opt out will never be credible, as $\Pi^{ca} < \Pi_0$. Under complete information, the incentive to drag on the negotiations does not lead to actual delays in agreement; instead, the company gains bargaining power. When compared with the value of its own outside option, the company gains $\Pi_e^{Ba} - \Pi^{ca}$, whereas the agency only gets its reservation payoff, that is, the value of its outside option.

4.3.3 Comparing Clean-Up Arrangements and Agreements over New Projects

When licensing a new project, the investor does not have an incentive to drag out the negotiations. Thus, intuition suggests that, other things being equal, a clean-up arrangement should grant more favorable conditions for the project operator than a negotiated permit for a new facility (Jarass 1990). However, this intuition holds only for a specific parameter range. Consider the case where $\Lambda \to 0$:

Proposition 4.1. Define

$$\tilde{p}_I = \frac{\theta S_n^{Na} + D(S_n^{Na}) + \theta S^A + D^A}{\theta S^A + D^A - D_0},$$

where S_n^{Na} is the spending level associated with the Nash solution in negotiating a permit for a new project.

(i)   For $p_I \in [\tilde{p}_I, 1)$, the clean-up arrangement will imply a lower spending level than negotiating the permit for a new project.

(ii)   For $p_I \in (0, \tilde{p}_I)$, both bargaining situations yield the same outcome. The project operator does not have additional bargaining power in clean-up negotiations.

Proof. From the definition of $\tilde{p}_I$,

$$W_n^{Na} = \tilde{p}_I(\theta \Pi_0 - D_0) + (1 - \tilde{p}_I)[\theta(\Pi_0 - S^A) - D^A],$$

where W_n^{Na} is the agency's Nash payoff when bargaining over the new project. For $p_I \geq \tilde{p}_I$, the agency's outside option is not a credible threat in negotiations over the new project. Hence, the investor possesses additional bargaining power in clean-up negotiations, as $\max [\Pi_n^{Na}, \Pi^{ca}] < \Pi_e^{Ba}$; Π_n^{Na} being the investor's Nash solution payoff in negotiations over the planned project. For $p_I < \tilde{p}_I$, the agency's outside option is a credible threat in both bargaining constellations, and the outcomes will not differ for given p_I. ∎

The example in Figure 4.2 depicts part (i) of proposition 4.1 for $\theta = 1$. Here, in bargaining over the permit for a new project, the outside option of the investor is a credible threat, and the solution is $(\Pi_n^{Ba}, W_n^{Ba}) = (\Pi^{ca}, \varphi_a(\Pi^{ca}))$. The bargaining power of the company within clean-up negotiations leads, p_l being given, to a lower environmental spending level, by the amount $\Pi_e^{Ba} - \Pi^{ca}$.

The proposition allows us to differentiate the possible reasons as to why existing facilities may be regulated less strictly than planned projects. In reality, differences in the applied regulatory stringency are often defended in terms of investment security. A German keyword often used in this respect is *Vertrauensschutz*, meaning that investors should have the legal right to prevent project-specific regulation from being changed after investment costs have been sunk (Maurer 1988). When judges adhere to this conception, a setting of 'legal grandfathering' may apply, where the probability of winning in court may be higher for a company taking action against the regulation of its old facilities when compared with a company trying to get standards lowered for its new facility.

However, the analysis makes clear that such court-induced grandfathering is not crucial for deriving differing bargaining outcomes for the two constellations; instead, these may also have pure bargaining-inherent reasons. But this result holds only to a limited extent. Part (ii) of the proposition shows that the bargaining outcome will be identical under both constellations for a specific parameter range. For this range, assuming legal grandfathering is crucial in order to derive the more lenient regulation of existing facilities.

For the case of an indivisible project with positive consumer surplus, the following result is immediate from Corollary 4.1 and Proposition 4.1.

Corollary 4.2. For any consumer surplus $Cs > Cs_{min}$, both bargaining constellations yield the same outcome for $p_l \in (0, 1)$.

In this case, $\tilde{p}_l = 1$. Thus, an investor bargaining over the conditions of its permit does not have less bargaining power, if the new facility under dispute will generate high enough 'social benefits'. In this case, one has to rely on legal grandfathering to explain the differences in negotiated outcomes.

4.4 DISCUSSION

In this paragraph, some extensions and possible modifications to the model presented so far will be discussed. Assume for now that agencies are welfare-maximizing; hence, $\theta = 1$.

4.4.1 The Role of Green Agencies

In the present analysis, a welfare-maximizing agency $(\theta = 1)$ is not a sufficient condition for welfare-efficiency. Amacher and Malik (1996) derive a similar result in a bargaining model without outside options where an agency and a facility operator trade a more lenient emissions level against lower enforcement costs implied by a specific technology choice. They conclude that an 'ideal' regulator should be biased against the investor to a specific degree, which they depict by $\theta < 1$.

Their result can readily be restated within the context of the present analysis. Consider the case of bargaining over the permit for a new project,

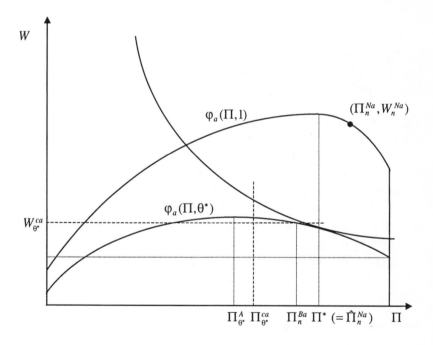

Figure 4.3 Efficiency and biased agency

and compare a welfare maximizing agency ($\theta = 1$) with an agency which is biased against the investor to a specific degree ($\theta < 1$). As $\varphi'(\Pi^*, \theta < 1) < 0$, there will be an θ^* for which S^* can be implemented by the Nash solution (Π_n^{Na}, W_n^{Na}) on $\varphi_a(\Pi, \theta^*)$; that is, $\hat{\Pi}_n^{Na} = \Pi^*$ (see figure 4.3).

While Amacher and Malik's result makes clear that biased decision-making is not necessarily welfare-decreasing, the efficiency result does not hold in the presence of an uncertain legal outcome. In court, the biased agency will plead for a spending level $S^A > S^*$ leading to an investor payoff $\Pi^A < \Pi^*$. When the outside option of the agency is a credible threat, $\Pi_n^{Ba} = \varphi_a^I(W^{ca}, \theta^*) < \Pi^*$: the spending level will be inefficiently high. This situation is depicted in Figure 4.3. When the investor is credible in threatening with legal action, $\Pi_n^{Ba} = \Pi^{ca} > \Pi^*$, and the spending level will be inefficiently low.

In the case of clean-up negotiations, the agency's outside option is always a credible threat. Then, efficiency may result for a specific combination of $\theta^*, \hat{p}_I$, for which

$$\Pi_e^{Ba} = \varphi_a^I[\theta^* \Pi_0 - (1 - \hat{p}_I)(\theta S - D(S)) - \hat{p}_I D_0] = \Pi^*.$$

In both bargaining constellations, efficiency induced by a biased agency is a special case and does not hold generally. However, the bias parameter θ represents the agency's preferences and, hence, cannot be fine-tuned like a policy variable.

4.4.2 Litigation Costs

Positive litigation costs, by affecting the expected value of trial, influence the credibility of the parties' threats to opt out during bargaining, as well as the incentive of the investor to sue a non-negotiated permit. This latter impact may restrict incentives to bargain in the first place. Instead, the agency may have an incentive to issue a non-negotiated permit prescribing an inefficient low spending level, against which the investor does not take action.

Assume the British allocation rule for legal costs, where the loser pays all legal costs.[30] This is the usual allocation rule in Germany. Denote total legal costs by C_t. Expected payoffs from trial are then

---

[30]The analysis can also be formulated for the US rule, where every party bears its own legal costs. Results do not differ qualitatively. The impact of the British and the American recovery rules on settlement incentives between private parties was investigated by several contributions. Shavell (1982) shows that, when subjective probabilities to prevail may diverge due to excessive optimism, settlement rates decline under the British rule. This result can be reproduced in the

$$\Pi^{ca} = \Pi_0 - (1 - p_I)(S^A + C_t) \tag{4.3}$$

for the investor and

$$W^{ca} = \Pi_0 - (1 - p_I)[S_A + D(S_A)] - p_I D_0 - C_t \tag{4.4}$$

for the agency. A merely welfare-maximizing agency[31] does not care who actually bears legal costs. Consider now the investor's incentive to sue a non-negotiated permit. Denoting the spending level in a non-negotiated permit by S_A, it will take action, if

$$S_A > (1 - p_I)(S_A + C_t)$$

or

$$C_t < \frac{p_I}{1 - p_I} S_A . \tag{4.5}$$

When legal costs are not too high, (4.5) holds for $S_A = S^*$: the investor will sue against a permit prescribing the efficient spending level. Then, for any positive level of legal costs, (4.5) will hold as an equality for a specific spending level $S_A^+ < S^*$, implying that the investor is indifferent as to whether or not to sue when confronted with a conditional permit over S_A^+. Assume that the investor does not sue when being indifferent. Denote the payoff pair associated with S_A^+ by (Π^+, W^+); clearly, $(\Pi^+, W^+) \in \varphi_a$. The agency may prefer to issue such an inefficient permit over S_A^+ in order to avoid the even higher costs of a legal battle (remember that, when legal costs are zero, the agency never has an incentive to deviate from S^*, because the investor will sue any conditional permit implying a positive spending level, as long as $p_I > 0$). The agency will do so, if

$$\Pi_0 - (S_A^+ + D(S_A^+)) > \Pi_0 - (1 - p_I)[S^* + D(S^*)] - p_I D_0 - C_t. \tag{4.6}$$

---

present setting. Bebchuk (1984) get a similar result in a model of asymmetric information, where the uninformed party makes a take-it-or-leave-it offer. However, when it is the informed party who submits the last offer and the probability of winning is common knowledge, Reinganum and Wilde (1986) show that the disadvantage of the British rule vanishes.

[31] 'Merely' means that the agency does not have specific distributive goals and is not biased.

When (4.6) holds for a S_A^+, a threat by the agency to issue efficient regulation over S^*, should negotiations fail, would not be credible. Let $\hat{C}_t$, $\check{C}_t$ be critical levels of legal costs, where $\hat{C}_t$ is given by

$$\hat{C}_t = \frac{p_I}{1-p_I} S^*$$

and $\check{C}_t$ defines a S_A^{++} by

$$\check{C}_t = \frac{p_I}{1-p_I} S^{++}$$

such that

$$\Pi_0 - (S_A^{++} + D(S_A^{++})) = \Pi_0 - (1-p_I)[S^* + D(S^*)] - p_I D_0 - \check{C}_t.$$

Proposition 4.2. Consider a welfare-maximizing agency.

(i)   For $C_t \geq \hat{C}_t$, no bargaining incentives exist. The agency issues a non-negotiated permit over the efficient spending level S^*. The investor does not have an incentive to sue against this non-negotiated permit.

(ii)   For $\hat{C}_t > C_t \geq \check{C}_t$, no bargaining incentives exist. The agency issues a non-negotiated permit over an inefficiently low spending level S_A^+. The investor does not have an incentive to sue against this non-negotiated permit, but would sue any permit prescribing a spending level $S_A > S_A^+$.

(iii)   For $C_t < \check{C}_t$, bargaining incentives exist. The agency issues a negotiated permit over an inefficient low spending level S^{Ba}. The investor has an incentive to sue against any non-negotiated permit the agency might be willing to issue.

Proof. (i) follows from (4.5) and the definition of $\hat{C}_t$. To prove (ii) and (iii), notice that the lower the legal costs, the more interesting it is for the investor to sue against a non-negotiated permit, according to (4.5). Consequently, the lower the legal costs, the more the agency has to give in (with respect to the prescribed spending level) to make the investor indifferent between suing against and accepting a non-negotiated permit. This decreases the agency's payoff from giving-in (the left-hand-side of (4.6)), while the expected welfare from trial over the optimal permit increases for lower court costs (this is the right-hand side of (4.6)). Consequently, for $C_t < \check{C}_t$, (4.6) does not hold for any S_A^+ which would induce the investor not to sue. Hence, the agency, when not negotiating, will stick to a permit over S^*, which will be taken to court by the investor. The analysis of Section 4.3.2 applies accordingly. When $\hat{C}_t > C_t \geq \check{C}_t$, (4.6) holds, and the agency issues a permit over S_A^+, which the investor accepts. Because of (4.6), a threat by the agency to issue an efficient permit over S^* would not be credible. Bargaining incentives do not exist, because $(\Pi^+, W^+) \in \varphi_a$. ∎

Note that the solution under $\hat{C}_t > C_t \geq \check{C}_t$, even while bargaining is not involved, also implements an inefficiently low spending level.

For the following analyses, assume again that litigation costs are zero.

4.4.3 Commitment and Offset Duties

This section discusses strategic opportunities for a welfare-maximizing agency to improve the inefficient bargaining outcome when the investor's threat to take its outside option is credible. Thus, these opportunities exist only during negotiations over the permit for a new project.

Commitment
Should negotiations break down because one of the parties triggers a court dispute, it is optimal for the agency to issue a permit with an associated spending level $S^* = \arg\min[S + D(S)]$, and to defend this level in court. A threat to issue a permit over an $S^t > S^*$ would not be credible without commitment (Mohr 1990, 614). Assume, as before, that p_I is parametrical. Then, a commitment is attractive, because the investor's expected value of a trial decreases for $S^t > S^*$:

$$\Pi_0 - (1 - p_I)S^t < \Pi_0 - (1 - p_I)S^*.$$

Assume that the investor's threat to trigger a trial is credible without commitment. Then, the agency would have to 'pay it off' by guaranteeing the value of its outside option within a bargained agreement. Consequently, as a commitment reduces the investor's outside option value, the welfare inefficiency of the bargaining outcome could be reduced, possibly up to the Nash solution.

However, the investor will retain its incentive to sue against any non-negotiated permit, because $(1 - p_I)S^t < S^t$. Consequently, the agency cannot prevent environmental bargaining from happening in the first place. Efficiency cannot be restored by commitment.[32]

In the US literature on *Environmental* or *Alternative Dispute Resolution*, public announcements by agencies are discussed as possible commitment devices (Bacow and Wheeler 1984, 39). During a dispute over a project permit, the agency could publicly announce that it will at least require technical safeguards associated with a spending level S^t. The agency would stick to this announcement in court because of fear of losing reputation when deviating from this announced pleading strategy, provided that it values this reputation loss more than the corresponding efficiency loss.

To apply such a public announcement as a strategic commitment when bargaining, a specific perception of the environmental dispute by the general public is necessary. On the one hand, the public has to disapprove any deviation by the agency from the announced S^A. On the other hand, however, it has to approve the bargained agreement on a lower S^{Ba}. Thus, the general public not only has to perceive the process of policy implementation (and corresponding subsequent disputes) as a bargaining game, but, moreover, it also has to *accept* these disputes as a bargaining game in which the agency has to act strategically.

For the United States, these conditions may be fulfilled at least partially. This could be inferred from the prominence of *environmental* or *alternative dispute resolution* techniques, which were also formally recognized by federal legislature. Hence, such an acceptance by the general public may seem more improbable in a situation in which negotiations occur informally, externally and prior to formal licensing procedures. In Germany, regulating agencies engaging in negotiations with investors contradict the official norm of agencies being the omnipotent executors of the public interest. This is why, in the German debate on Informal Administrative Action, such agency activities were criticized by some authors as reflecting a merchandizing spirit of the public administration (*Händlermentalität*), which clandestinely collaborate with industry (*Kungelei*) (see Hennecke 1991, 269). If public opinion follows such a perception, it would also mean a reputation loss for the agency to first

---

[32]This contradicts Mohr (1990), who comes to the conclusion that commitment within bargaining may restore efficiency. This results from his implausible modeling of the Rubinstein game without outside options. See the appendix for details.

announce the taking of a tough stance, should negotiations fail, and to agree then on a more lenient (bargained) agreement. It may be concluded that German agencies cannot apply a public announcement as a means of strategic commitment in informal negotiations.

Conservation offset duties

Consider now the situation in which the agency is entitled not only to prescribe a specific spending level for environmental protection, but, additionally, may ask for compensation of the remaining environmental damage. Such possibilities exist both for German and US agencies in conservation law.

In Germany, conservation law prescribes the offsetting of major interference with nature and landscape. Specifically, the Federal Conservation Act prescribes that

- Avoidable interference must be prohibited (§8, 2 BNatSchG). The avoidability criterion – under the usual interpretation – is met when the project is optimized with respect to the objective of nature conservation

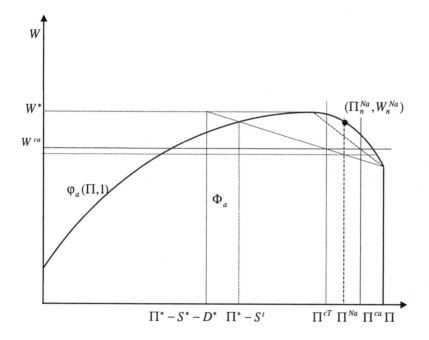

Figure 4.4 Commitment and offset duties

(Kloepfer 1998, 723).

- Non-avoidable interference has to be offset on-site or off-site (§8, 2, 9 BNatSchG). This means, in principle, physical measures by the investor, leading to a compensation in kind (for example, planting trees, or restoring a wetland). However, the *Länder* Conservation Acts (with the exception of Bavaria) also allow for compensation payments, in the form of conservation offset duties (*Naturschutzrechtliche Ausgleichszahlungen*; see Kloepfer 1998, 724).

Thus, a welfare-maximizing agency would prescribe the avoidance of the interference up to S^*, and may ask for additional offset duties. Note, however, that the law is less clear than it might appear from §8 BNatSchG as to what extent the agency is bound to ask for a total compensation. This is so because of the general weighting requirement of §1 BNatSchG: the agency has to weight the objective of nature conservation against competing objectives, hence, against the interests of the investor. In consequence, the agency has leeway in fixing the amount to be paid by the investor.

A similar provision exists in the United States in regulation focusing on the protection and restoration of wetlands. For projects interfering with wetlands, developers have to obtain a section-404 permit. The guidelines formulated by the Army Corps of Engineers and EPA also provide a sequencing mechanism for avoidance and mitigation/compensation (see Beck 1994, 800):

- Potential impacts of the project have to be avoided to the maximum extent practicable;
- Remaining unavoidable impacts have to mitigated/compensated.

Compensation of the remaining damage will usually occur in kind and on-site. However, recent experiments also allow for off-site compensation in cash, whereby investors have to acquire credits from a wetland mitigation banking system.[33] Payments by developers are consolidated for specific projects concerned with the restoration of degraded wetlands[34] (see Silverstein 1994, Gardner 1996).

---

[33]In Germany, revenue from offset duties is also tied up for conservation purposes (Kloepfer 1998, 725). The present analysis, which focuses on the strategic value of offset duties within informal negotiations, does not consider effects on welfare emerging from the expenditure side.

[34]One advantage of such schemes is that mitigation possibly occurs before the development activity takes place. Therefore, the time lag until a mitigation project will generate the same ecological value may be avoided. Furthermore, the consolidation effect of having one large

To adapt the theoretical analysis to this institutional setting, assume that the agency is legally entitled to ask, as part of a permit, for a monetary transfer D^* in addition to the optimal spending level S^*. To ensure comparability with the situation in which the agency does not have this opportunity, assume an identical p_I under both situations. Asking for a transfer D^* reduces the investor's outside option value, while it does not reduce expected welfare from trial. Denote the investor's outside option value by

$$\Pi^{cT} = \Pi_0 - (1 - p_I)(S^* + D^*).$$

For a welfare-maximizing agency, asking for an additional transfer beyond S^* would not affect its payoff – the transfer would be mere redistribution. The following proposition can be stated without formal proof.

Proposition 4.3. The legal prescription, for a welfare-maximizing agency, to ask for total compensation of the remaining environmental damage D^* beyond the welfare-efficient spending level S^* (*conservation offset duty*) will constitute a credible threat. When, for a given p_I, the investor's threat to opt out is credible in the game without offset duty, the welfare inefficiency of the bargaining outcome can be reduced, possibly up to the welfare level of the Nash solution.

An agency with no interest in distribution will be interested in additional compensation only for strategic reasons, because the problem of making ist commitments credible does not arise. Again, the agency cannot prevent the bargaining from happening in the first place, because the investor still has an incentive to sue against every non-negotiated permit.

Figure 4.4 depicts this result. Note that in the Nash bargaining equilibrium, no additional transfer is paid. Conservation offset duties are only used as a strategic device. While this may not seem realistic, it results from the assumptions of mere welfare maximization and wide discretion with respect to offset duties. However, the result is not unrealistic even from an empirical perspective. As part of the German debate on implementation deficits, some authors indeed complain about the poor implementation of this offset rule, even when stipulated in the permit. Instead, the agency tolerates such a permit violation (Lübbe-Wolf 1993, 219; Lahl et al. 1992, 582). The

---

mitigation wetland instead of multiple small ones is said to be more cost-efficient and ecologically more beneficial (Gardner 1996, 10075, 10077).

issue that agencies are sometimes ready to tolerate permit violations will be
addressed in Section 4.5.

4.4.4   Cost-Efficiency and Differentiated Norms

So far, it was assumed that the (welfare-maximizing) agency has wide
discretion, implying that, should negotiations fail, it will issue welfare-
efficient regulation. In reality, implementing agencies may be formally
required to apply a set of technical standards (fixed, for example, by a higher-
level bureaucracy in an executive ordinance) which are not even cost-efficient
because of excessive uniformity. When marginal abatement costs are facility-
specific (and the project consists of several facilities), the agency may then be
ready to circumvent formal, uniform regulation and informally agree with the
operator to apply more differentiated standards leading to lower compliance
costs for the operator and to higher welfare.

This situation can be depicted readily with the help of Figure 4.5. A set of
technical standards that are cost-inefficient will lead to a payoff pair
$(\Pi^s, W^s) \in \Phi_a$, but $(\Pi^s, W^s) \notin \varphi_a$. Differentiating standards in informal

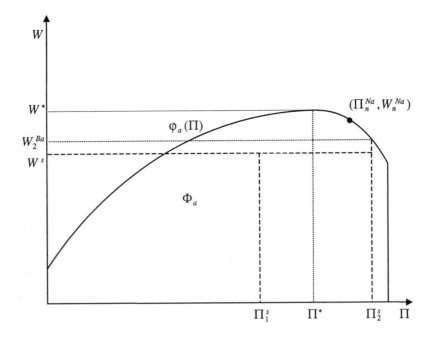

Figure 4.5 Cost-inefficient standards and negotiations

bargaining will move payoffs in a north-eastern direction towards φ_a, implying lower compliance costs and, possibly, lower environmental damage. Given that the investor will take action against any non-negotiated permit, , the administrator, after failed bargaining, will prefer to adhere to the formal requirements and issue a permit leading to payoffs (Π^s, W^s) (any other permit would be illegal, and the administrator prefers to let illegal activities not be detected by the courts)[35]. Note that, depending on the values of (Π^s, W^s), the agency's threat to opt out may never be credible. Clearly, a welfare-maximizing agency will not be interested in enforcing inefficient technical standards when it can agree on a negotiated solution (Π_n^{Ba}, W_n^{Ba}) which is also welfare-inefficient $(W_n^{Ba} < W^*)$, but at least cost-efficient $((\Pi_n^{Ba}, W_n^{Ba}) \in \varphi_a)$ and, as such, more efficient than the set of excessively uniform technical standards ($W_n^{Ba} > W^s$).

In Figure 4.5, (Π_1^s, W^s) is chosen such that no outside option constitutes a credible threat: the parties will agree on the Nash solution. In contrast, (Π_2^s, W^s) is chosen such that the investor's threat to opt out is credible ($\Pi_2^s > \Pi_n^{Na}$). Remember from the preceding part that in this case, the agency has all the bargaining power; consequently, the investor's spending on environmental protection is the same under the bargained agreement and under the set of technical norms. Cost savings are exclusively used for the reduction of environmental damage: in Figure 4.5, this is the difference $W_2^{Ba} - W^s$. In this sense, the bargained outcome leads to over-compliance; however, from a welfare perspective, the spending level is still inefficiently low in equilibrium.[36]

---

[35]This is why this analysis does not adequately depict EPA's project XL. Here, the agency is formally entitled to negotiate; consequently, a threat to implement inefficient regulation will never be credible. The setting presented in Section 4.3.1 may fit better. See Chapter 2, 18–19, for a short summary on project XL.

[36]This contradicts Segerson and Miceli (1998, 117), who derive the possibility of a first-best outcome when the welfare-maximizing regulator has all the bargaining power. In their analysis, bargaining power is allocated exogenously, via the assumption of a specific bargaining procedure (they assume that either the investor or the regulator makes a take-it-or-leave-it offer). In the present setting, their result of a possible first-best outcome may be restated by assuming a set of technical standards leading to a payoff pair (Π^*, W^s) and exogenously assuming an agency having all the bargaining power. However, when bargaining power is derived endogenously, via the credibility of the outside options in the bargaining game, such an approach would not make sense: the investor's threat to opt out will never be credible for (Π^*, W^s); consequently, the regulator will never have all the bargaining power in this case.

4.4.5   Bargaining Transitional Periods

Restrict now the welfare-maximizing agency's leeway further by assuming that the agency has to implement ultimately the set of technical standards laid down in the administrative ordinance. However, the agency may still have leeway by granting project-specific transitional periods for adaptation to the standards. Such temporary exemptions from implementation are especially relevant when regulating existing facilities.[37] It is here that long transitional periods are defended on the ground that companies have to be protected from too rapid an implementation of new regulatory norms because of investment security. This grandfathering by transitional exemptions can be readily analyzed in the framework presented here.

Consider a situation in which the set of environmental standards is fixed in an administrative ordinance, such that the agency does not have discretion about the level of environmental quality to be implemented under the law. Assume for presentational reasons that this set of standards is efficient and, hence, leads to a payoff pair (Π^*, W^*). The agency has leeway in granting a transitional period for adaptation to the standard. The potential legal dispute concerns the length of this period: while the agency would prefer to grant no temporary exemption at all,[38] companies may have a chance to convince courts to grant such an exemption. Thus, denoting the length of a transitional period by l, assume that there is an $l > 0$ for which $p_l > 0$.

The correspondence between the parties' maximal payoffs associated with a specific l is given by φ_l; thus, $W(l) = \varphi_l[\Pi(l), l]$. Denote discounting in continuous time, to obtain a continuous φ_l:

$$S^* = \int_0^\infty s^* e^{-rt} dt , \quad D^* = \int_0^\infty d^* e^{-rt} dt , \quad D_0 = \int_0^\infty d_0 e^{-rt} dt ,$$

where r is the parties' common discount rate. The respective payoffs of the parties are

---

[37]In Germany, clean-up agreements regularly stipulate periods for adaptation to new requirements. See Funke (1990) for examples.

[38]The analysis does not consider the firm's adaptation costs. When adaptation cost are positive and decreasing in the period granted for adaptation, granting temporary exemptions may be rational from a welfare viewpoint.

$$\Pi(l) = \Pi_0 - \int_l^\infty s^* e^{-rt} dt \tag{4.7}$$

and

$$W(l) = \Pi_0 - \int_0^l d_0 e^{-rt} dt - \int_l^\infty (d^* + s^*) e^{-rt} dt \tag{4.8}$$

A 'very long' transition period amounts to (almost) no environmental spending: $\lim_{l \to \infty} \Pi(l) = \Pi_0$ and $\lim_{l \to \infty} W(l) = W_0$, whereas $\Pi(0) = \Pi^*$ and $W(0) = W^*$.

Deriving (4.7) and (4.8) gives

$$\frac{d}{dl} \Pi(l) = s^* e^{-rl} \tag{4.9}$$

and

$$\frac{d}{dl} W(l) = (d^* + s^* - d_0) e^{-rl}. \tag{4.10}$$

Solving (4.9) and (4.10) for e^{-rl} and substituting gives the slope of φ_l:

$$\frac{dW(l)}{d\Pi(l)} = \frac{(d^* + s^* - d_0)}{s^*} < 0.$$

Thus, φ_l is linear and decreasing on the interval $[\Pi^*, \Pi_0)$. As φ_l is not strictly concave on $[\Pi^*, \Pi_0)$, either risk-aversion or legal costs have to be introduced for strictly positive gains from bargaining and, hence, non-degenerated bargaining. Then, the analysis presented so far can be applied accordingly.

4.5 INFORMALITY AND SELF-ENFORCEMENT

Up to now, enforceability of the bargaining outcome (Π^{Ba}, W^{Ba}) was assumed. When signing a formal contract over the set and level of protective activities associated with a negotiated spending level S^{Ba}, the investor waives its right to sue against these stipulations. This section focuses on the situation where the signing of formal contracts is not possible. Assume again the possibility of agency bias.

Quasi-enforceability better reflects the German situation in which environmental bargaining occurs informally in a legal 'gray zone'. While it is possible, in principle, to set up contractual agreements between private and public parties in the form of so-called contracts of public law (*öffentlich-rechtliche Verträge*), such contracts are problematic when used in conjunction with formal permit procedures (Kloepfer 1998, 287–8). It would be illegal to sign a contract before termination of the formal permit procedure and the related public hearings. The rationale behind this rule is protection of the interests of affected third parties: an agency committing to a contractual agreement before the public hearing would have to neglect positions and objections made during the hearing. As is obvious from the literature, this possible illegality does not prevent a regulating agency from entering agreements with project operators. Instead, agreements are informal. This part shows that specific administrative instruments used by German agencies in the case of informal administrative action have also the function of coping with the problem of enforcing informal agreements.

Note that the term 'enforcement', as it is used here, only refers to the bargaining solution, but not to the environmental regulation itself. As will become clear shortly, the investor may even have an incentive to sue against a permit whose conditions were (informally) negotiated. Distinct from this incentive, the investor has in any case an incentive to cheat by not complying with the requirements, irrespective of whether or not they are the result of bargaining. By assuming that a (possibly negotiated) permit can be monitored and enforced without cost, this issue is not considered in the present setting.

Self-enforcing agreements rely on repeated interactions between the parties. Parties will not deviate from an informal agreement when the other party can threaten to break off a cooperative relationship and when the long-term losses from such a break-off are higher than the short-term gains from defection (Klein et al. 1978 and Telser 1980). This argument will be reiterated in the next paragraph. It will then be shown that specific instruments developed by German administrative practice ensure or improve the self-enforcement properties of repeated interaction. Instruments to be discussed are, again, the possibility of asking for additional compensation beyond S^A; furthermore, the practice of grading permits for big projects

(*Teilgenehmigungen*) and the practice of tolerating of permit violations (*Duldung*) will be addressed.

4.5.1   The Problem

Reconsider bargaining over the issuance of a permit for a new facility or over regulation of an existing one, when it is not possible to conclude a formal contract. Assume that the agency writes the negotiated outcome into the formal permit, that is, issues a permit prescribing the bargained spending level S^{Ba}. This means that in court, the agency will no longer be able to plead for S^A, but can only defend its permit over S^{Ba}. Once deadlines for legal challenges are passed, the investor has to comply with the negotiated spending level. However, the investor still has an incentive to fight the (negotiated) permit for any (possibly small) chance $\breve{p}_I \in (0, p_I]$ that the court rules in its favor,[39] because

$$\Pi_0 - S^{Ba} < \Pi_0 - (1 - \breve{p}_I)S^{Ba} \text{ for any } \breve{p}_I > 0.$$

It is one of the main objective of agencies, within informal administrative action, to reach 'court-proofness' (*Rechtssicherheit*) of a permit. Courts may be more inclined to rule in favor of cooperative agencies.[40] The difference $p_I - \breve{p}_I$ may depict the gain in 'court-proofness' induced by bargaining.

Consequently, environmental negotiations may be depicted as a two-stage game:

- In stage one, the agency decides whether or not to bargain. Note that the investor will always be ready to bargain, even when having an incentive to fight the outcome in court *ex post*.
  When bargaining occurs, the permit will prescribe S^{Ba}; when not, the agency will issue a permit over S^A.
- In stage two, the investor decides whether to sue against the permit or not.

Figure 4.6 depicts this two-stage game in extensive form, where (Π^c, W^c) denotes the parties' payoffs when the investor sues against the negotiated permit:

---

[39]This will not hold for any S^{Ba}, when litigation costs are positive. See the analysis under 4.3.2.
[40]They could take into consideration the German *cooperation principle*, prescribing that regulators should have a cooperative relationship with those subjected to regulation (Kloepfer (1998, 185ff.).

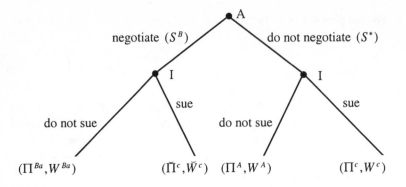

Figure 4.6 Implementation of an informal agreement

$$\check{\Pi}^c = \Pi_0 - (1 - \check{p}_I)S^{Ba},$$
$$\check{W}^c = \check{p}_I(\theta\Pi_0 - D_0) + (1 - \check{p}_I)[\theta(\Pi_0 - S^{Ba}) - D(S^{Ba})].$$

The game has a unique equilibrium whose outcome depends on the difference $\check{p}_I - p_I$:

- when $W^c > \check{W}^c$, the agency does not bargain and the investor sues against the permit over S^A,
- when $W^c \leq \check{W}^c$, the agency bargains, and the investor sues against the permit over S^{Ba}.

Under both constellations, the investor has an incentive to sue against any negotiated permit. In the first constellation, this deters the agency from bargaining in the first place. The second constellation results from a large difference $\check{p}_I - p_I$: agencies may then use bargaining to signal their willingness to cooperate to the judge.

4.5.2   Negotiations and Long-Term Cooperation

Typically, investment decisions by investors are of a long-term nature. As facilities are modernized or enlarged, operators will regularly have to request for the corresponding permits for new equipment. The model will depict the case of licensing the installation of new equipment.

Assume that the investment decision is not limited in time; thus, the investor's planning horizon for the investment is infinite (remember that the project was assumed to be an eternal, non-depreciating asset). Assume for ease of presentation that all investments are identical. Denote by Π_i^B the present value of net profits of the investment in period $i = 0, 1, 2,...,\infty$, when the investor accepts the associated bargained spending level S_i^B. Note that the subscript now indicates a time index, whereas the index in the superscript denoting different bargaining constellations is omitted. Note furthermore that periods elapsing between investments will be arguably much longer than periods elapsing between offers in the bargaining game. In a slight abuse of notation, the length of periods between investments will be normalized to one.

In the following analysis, separate licensing bargaining will occur for every such investment. In principle, these bargaining constellations may be connected. Specifically, when later investments technically depend upon the realization of earlier investments, a delayed bargaining agreement with respect to an earlier project will also delay realization of later projects. In such a setting, agreement is reached immediately over every project, as was shown by Muthoo (1995).[41] However, when projects are not interconnected and contracts are binding, repeated play of the Rubinstein equilibrium for every project will be the unique (stationary) equilibrium (ibid., 597). To focus on the role of a refusal to bargain as a punishment strategy, the present analysis will consider the latter case. Thus, the game consists of an infinite repetition of the two-stage game depicted in Figure 4.6.[42]

Assume that the agency acts cooperatively and bargains with the investor in a given period. The investor may now defect and sue against the negotiated permit, yielding payoffs Π_i^c. The agency may punish a defecting operator by acting non-cooperatively in future periods, that is, by rejecting negotiations over subsequent investments and just issuing a permit over S_j^A, $j > i$. In this case, the investor may realize its expected payoff from going to court, Π_j^c. Assume that net profits occur at the end of each period.

Consider the toughest punishment strategy the parties may apply, which prescribes that, while starting cooperatively, do never cooperate again after the first defection is observed. This 'grim strategy' means that the agency will never agree to bargain again after the investor's first defection, that is, after the investor sues against a negotiated permit for the first time. For any project

---

$j = i+1,...,\infty$, the agency will refuse to bargain. Conversely, the investor will sue against every permit after a defection by the agency, that is, after the agency refuses to bargain. The usual result is that the investor will cooperate unless being too impatient, that is, being too interested in short-term gains:

Lemma 4.3. The cooperative equilibrium can be sustained by the grim strategy profile, if

$$\delta \geq \frac{(\tilde{\Pi}_i^c - \Pi_i^B) - (\Pi_j^B - \Pi_j^c)}{(\tilde{\Pi}_i^c - \Pi_i^B)}. \tag{4.11}$$

Proof. Consider first subgames starting with a cooperative move by one party (that is, the agency bargains, or the investor does not sue):

- The agency can never gain by deviating from the grim strategy, by refusing to bargain in the next period. When the investor also plays the grim strategy, it will contest any permit after this defection by the agency. Because of the sequential nature of the one-shot game, a rejection of bargaining by the agency can be immediately punished by the investor, by contesting the permit over S^A in court, and by contesting any permit afterwards. This will clearly reduce welfare.
- Consider now the investor's incentive to deviate from cooperation by contesting a negotiated permit. It will not sue, if

$$\delta\Pi_i^B + \frac{\delta}{1-\delta}\Pi_j^B \geq \delta\tilde{\Pi}_i^c + \frac{\delta}{1-\delta}\Pi_j^c. \tag{4.12}$$

Reformulating (4.12) gives (4.11).

Consider now subgames starting after one party acted non-cooperatively (that is, the agency rejects negotiations, or the investor contests a negotiated permit):

- When the adversary adheres to the grim strategy and starts punishment, it is better to also adhere to the grim strategy (which prescribes eternal non-cooperation after the first defection by any party).
- Conversely, if the deviating party adheres to the grim strategy again afterwards, it will always refuse cooperation. Thus, it is rational for the other party to adhere to the grim strategy by starting punishment and to

also reject cooperation. Again, the grim strategy is the best reply in any such subgame, given that the other party adheres to this strategy. ∎

Inspection of condition (4.11) in lemma 4.3 reveals an additional role of conservation offset duties for a welfare-maximizing agency: when the investor can credibly threaten to take its outside option, $\Pi_i^B = \Pi_i^c$. Substituting into (4.12) shows that cooperation will break down for $\delta < 1$. Monetary transfers may then induce cooperation for some discount factors because they reduce the value of the investor's outside option according to the reasoning presented under proposition 4.3.

When the investor's threat is not credible in the first place, the strategic requirement of a monetary transfer will reduce the critical discount factor for which the investor is willing to cooperate.

Proposition 4.4. Consider the welfare-maximizing agency ($\theta = 1$).

(i)   When a threat by the investor to take its outside option is credible when bargaining the permit over an investment, a self-enforcing agreement may only be implemented when the agency is entitled to ask for additional compensation.

(ii) The strategic requirement of additional compensation may induce cooperation when the investor's outside option is not credible, but (4.6) does not hold.

The proposition states that a welfare-maximizing agency entitled to ask for additional compensation will not only be in a stronger bargaining position, but, by ensuring self-enforcement of an informal agreement, may induce bargaining incentives in the first place.

Note that proposition 4.4 does not allude to a specific equilibrium strategy profile. The point is that even the toughest punishment strategy an agency may have, in form of the grim strategy, will not induce cooperation when the investor only gets its reservation payoff in future bargaining. Then, as it does not lose anything by being punished even under the grim strategy, the less it will do under milder subgame-perfect punishment strategies.

Consider again the general framework in which agencies may be biased. An objection usually made with respect to the grim strategy is that, while subgame-perfect, it may not be 'Pareto-perfect'[43] – the point being that the

---

[43]For the following reasoning and the concept of Pareto-perfection, see Farrell and Maskin (1989), v. Damme (1989), and Fudenberg and Tirole (1991, 179–82) for a summary.

agency, by rejecting bargaining in every future period after an initial defection by the investor, foregoes potential welfare gains. Thus, in a sense, the punisher also punishes himself. The question is then whether the grim strategy constitutes too tough a punishment for being really plausible. Why should the agency not treat the investor's defection as an accident, under a 'let bygones be bygones'-philosophy and, instead of eternal punishment, use a strategy which concentrates on the restoration of cooperation?

In the present setting, this objection holds only to a limited extent.

Corollary 4.3. When the agency's threat to trigger a court decision is credible in bargaining over the investment projects, the grim strategy is Pareto-perfect for the agency.

Proof. Denote the agency's outside option value when bargaining over an investment by W_j^c, whereas W_j^B denotes the agency's bargained outcome. Under a credible outside option, $W_j^B = W_j^c$. Thus, the agency does not lose when refusing to bargain. ■

4.5.3   Graded Permits

Consider now a situation in which (4.12) does not hold. The result of the preceding paragraph suggests that bargaining incentives then break down even in a setting of repeated interactions.

However, the agency has an additional parameter in decision-making when the execution of the project under consideration is technically complex enough to grade the permit. This means that the project is split into technically different partial projects, which are constructed sequentially. Every partial project gets its own permit before execution. In Germany, this practice of dividing the permit for a large project (*Teilgenehmigungen*) is a major element within the so-called graded administrative procedures (*gestufte Verwaltungsverfahren*, see Schmidt-Aßmann 1978). As Kloepfer (1998, 247–8) notes, such graded procedures are 'the rule' when licensing large technical projects. The use of such a mechanism by agencies is allowed, under procedural discretion, even when explicit rules are absent (Kloepfer 1998, 247).

In the analysis previously presented, the investor's net payoffs occur at the end of each period. Assume that graded permits stretch the investor's net profit over period i. In reality, only the (environmental) investments will be stretched over period *i*, as gross profit only occurs after realization of the entire investment. Because the model focuses on the difference between the investor's cost savings of contesting a negotiated or a non-negotiated permit, it is not crucial when the payoff of gross profit occurs. This modeling favors the investor; therefore, no loss of generality is implied.

Thus, assume the total net profit to be additively separable on identical partial projects. Denote the number of partial projects chosen, that is, the number of permits issued by the agency during execution of the entire investment project, by *m*. Thus, total periods' length being 1, the length of a period in which a partial project is realized is $1/m$.

Proposition 4.5. When the investor's outside option is not credible, the agency, for a given δ, can always induce cooperation by the investor when the technical complexity of the project allows for a large enough number *m* of permits for partial projects.

Proof. Under graded permits, condition (4.12), which give the investor's incentive to cooperate, transforms into

$$\delta^{\left(\frac{1}{m}\right)}\frac{\Pi_i^B}{m} + \sum_{t=2}^{m}\delta^{\left(\frac{t}{m}\right)}\frac{\Pi_i^B}{m} + \frac{\delta}{1-\delta}\Pi_j^B \geq \delta^{\left(\frac{1}{m}\right)}\frac{\tilde{\Pi}_i^c}{m} + \sum_{t=2}^{m}\delta^{\left(\frac{t}{m}\right)}\frac{\Pi_i^c}{m} + \frac{\delta}{1-\delta}\Pi_j^c ,$$

and

$$\lim_{m\to\infty}\left(\frac{\tilde{\Pi}_i^c}{m}\right) = 0 . \blacksquare$$

Thus, by introducing a sequence of partial permits, the agency can reduce the investor's incentive to contest a negotiated permit *ex post*, as the possible gain from defection only concerns the stipulated safeguards of the partial permit.

The legal literature perceives the advantage of graded procedures in reducing the complexity of the regulatory problem by introducing the possibility of decision-making in parts (Schmidt-Aßmann 1978, 569–71). However, the analysis presented makes clear that graded permits may also have a strategic importance within informal environmental negotiations. This point is all the more important as informal negotiations do also emerge when regulatory issues are complex. Thus, informal negotiations and graded permits are analytically interconnected.

4.5.4 Tolerating Permit Violations

The agency may also induce cooperative behavior by the investor under the German concept of toleration (*Duldung*). This expression was coined by German legal scholars to describe the fact that agencies, as part of their informal decision-making, are often ready to tolerate a (temporary) violation of environmental law and the subsequent permits (Hermes and Wieland 1988, 5–6; Randelzhofer and Willke 1981, 58; Hennecke 1991, 271). The usual explanations forwarded in the literature are tight budget constraints under substantive enforcement costs.

It was debated by German legal scholars whether agencies, after a specific period of time, should be legally committed to the tolerated status quo, that is, whether courts should not declare as void a permit which the agency did not enforce (Randelzhofer and Willke 1981, 58). This question also appears to be important for using toleration as a self-enforcement mechanism, where the agency issues a formal permit over S^A, but informally agrees to tolerate a lower spending level S^B.

Note that investors who intend to take action against the regulation usually must consider legal deadlines for filing suit. After the deadline, the investor no longer has standing. It seems reasonable to assume that the time period before the deadline is shorter than the time period before the agency would be committed to the tolerated spending level S^B. After issuance of the permit, one thus has three time periods, in which (1) no party is committed, in which (2) only the investor is committed and in which (3) both parties are committed to S^B. For reasons that will become clear in a moment, call this second period of time the 'commitment gap'. The following proposition also considers, as a special case, the situation in which the commitment gap does not exist, that is, in which the second time period is zero.

Proposition 4.6. Self-enforcement of an informal agreement may be assured by the agency's issuing a permit over S^A after successful negotiations, and agreeing to tolerate a spending level S^B.

(i)   *No commitment gap.* The agreement is self-enforcing even in the static setting in which the investor will never ask for another permit.

(ii) *Positive commitment gap.* Self-enforcement can only be assured within a setting of repeated negotiations because the investor needs to have access to punishment strategies.

Proof.
When both parties are committed, they have both trivially lost the opportunity to defect *ex post.* Consider first the incentive of a non-committed investor to sue against a negotiated permit. As a commitment of the agency includes a commitment by the investor, only the following case is relevant.

- *Agency is not committed.* In this case, the agency, when sued, keeps the possibility of defending a permit over S^A. As $S^B \leq (1 - p_I)S^A$, the investor has no incentive to sue after successful negotiations.

Consider now the incentive of the agency to stick to S^B.

- *Investor is not committed.* Enforcing the formal permit would lead the investor to sue, which is not in the interest of the agency.
- *Investor is committed.* In this case, when the agency is not yet committed (positive commitment gap), the administrator can enforce S^A without triggering a trial. The agency has an incentive to defect. ∎

In consequence, 'bridging a positive commitment gap' requires a repeated setting and the related possibility of punishment, analogous to the analysis presented above where the negotiated spending level was stipulated in the formal permit. In contrast to this analysis, however, it is now the investor who needs a punishment strategy because it is the agency which has an incentive to defect during the commitment gap. Consequently, for an effective punishment, the credibility of the investor's outside option is irrelevant in this case, while the agency's outside option becomes relevant. To see this, assume that the agency's threat to opt out is credible during the negotiations over the follow-up projects, and assume that the agency defects, that is, insists on S^A even while having agreed before to tolerate S^B. Punishment by the investor, by refusing to bargain over the follow-up projects, would not reduce (expected) welfare. Consequently, the informal agreement over S^B cannot enforced by a toleration in such a case.

Here, the agency tolerates the implementation by the operator of lower technical standards and the corresponding lower spending level. However, the concept of toleration also applies, and is empirically observed, when the agency informally grants temporary exemptions from compliance with environmental laws. By informally agreeing to postpone the fulfillment of the requirements in the formal permit, the agency can effectively forestall any legal action by the investor against this permit. Within the licensing of new projects, such tolerations can be empirically observed for nature conservation issues (Lahl et al. 1992, 582): while the formal permit prescribes a specific set of measures for protecting nature, the agency tolerates a postponement of these measures.

The approach presented here makes it clear that explaining such an observed difference between the formal requirements of the permit and the actual compliance of facility operators does not need to rely on the existence of positive enforcement costs, together with tight enforcement budgets. Instead, this difference may be the result of an informally bargained agreement, where bargaining incentives exist because it is impossible to issue a court-proof conditional permit. Informal negotiations and the concept of toleration (*Duldung*) are connected via the issue of how to implement an informal agreement.

4.6 SUMMARY

This chapter presented an analysis of the emerging bargaining incentives in policy implementation under a setting of legal uncertainty. It investigated the bargaining constellations under asymmetrical standing, where only investors or project operators can contest permit requirements in court. This constellation was argued to be the typical one in Germany. The most important results of this chapter can be summarized as follows.

- Bargaining may result between the agency and the investor when the investor has a positive chance to have the agency's regulation overturned by the court. The negotiated permit will implement an inefficiently low spending level even under a welfare-maximizing agency. Agency bias in the sense of a 'green agency' will generally not restore the efficiency of the regulation.
- Although intuition would dictate otherwise, bargaining over the regulation of an existing project does not always favor the investor, when compared with bargaining over the permit conditions for a planned project.
- An entitlement for agencies to demand the compensation of environmental damage beyond efficient spending on protective activities may have

strategic value in bargaining and, hence, may reduce the inefficiency of the bargaining agreement. However, it cannot restore efficiency when a welfare-maximizing agency has to bargain with project operators because of legal uncertainty.

- Specific instruments developed within German informal administrative action, namely, the practice of grading permits for big projects and tolerating permit violations, have the function of ensuring the self-enforcement of informal agreements within long-term cooperative relationships.

The following chapter will extend the presented framework by introducing legal standing for an environmental group.

4.7 APPENDIX

Proof of Lemma 4.1

The proof assumes that it is the investor who submits the first offer. It can be restated for the case in which the agency submits the first offer. For $\Lambda \to 0$, the same bargaining outcome results.

Bargaining without credible outside options
Existence and inefficiency. The proof exploits the stationarity property of the bargaining game in the tradition of Shaked and Sutton (1984).[44] As the game is repeated infinitely, every subgame respectively starting in an odd even period is identical for the players, apart from rescaling. Consider Figure 4A.1. Denote by Π^{sup} the supremum payoff the investor may realize in an equilibrium of a subgame in which it is its turn to submit an offer (this is period $t = T$ in Figure 4A.1). In the preceding period, it is up to the agency to submit an offer. The investor will accept an offer equal to $\delta\Pi^{sup}$, which is the present value of its supremum possible payoff in $t = T - 1$, when $\delta\Pi^{sup} \geq \Pi^c$. In this case, its threat to opt out is not credible, and the agency may realize at least $\varphi(\delta\Pi^{sup})$ [45]. To strike a bargain in the preceding period ($t = T - 2$), the

---

[44]See also Sutton (1986) and Binmore et al. (1986).

[45]This is the difference to the analysis presented by Mohr (1990, 608), who assumes a welfare-maximizing agency, but models the bargaining between the agency and the investor as a linear division problem of the pie Π_0. Thus, $\varphi(\Pi) = \Pi_0 - \Pi$. This is clearly not plausible for a welfare-maximizing agency.

investor would have to offer $\max[W_0, \delta\varphi(\delta\Pi^{sup})]$. The agency's threat to opt out is not credible, when $\delta\varphi(\delta\Pi^{sup}) \geq W^c$, which implies that the investor can realize at most $\varphi'(\delta\varphi(\delta\Pi^{sup}))$ in period $t = T - 2$. From the definition of φ', $\varphi'(\delta\varphi(\delta\Pi^{sup})) = \Pi_0$ if $\delta\varphi(\delta\Pi^{sup}) < W_0$. As the subgame starting in $t = T - 2$ has the same structure as the one starting in $t = T$, it must hold that $\Pi^{sup} = \varphi'(\delta\varphi(\delta\Pi^{sup}))$.

By exchanging the words infimum/supremum, more/less, respectively at least/at most, the argument can now be repeated for the infimum payoff Π^{inf} the investor can realize in equilibrium in a subgame starting in an even period; thus, $\Pi^{inf} = \varphi'(\delta\varphi(\delta\Pi^{inf}))$.

Π^{inf} and Π^{sup} are fixpoints of $\varphi'(\delta\varphi(\delta.))$. Denote such a fixpoint by Π^+ and corresponding welfare by W^+. As $\varphi'(\delta\varphi(\delta.))$ is a continuous mapping from the compact interval $[\Pi^A, \Pi_0]$ into itself; Brouwer's fixpoint theorem applies: (At least) one fixpoint exists on $[\Pi^A, \Pi_0]$. Furthermore, it is evident from $\varphi'(\delta\varphi(\delta.))$ that Π^A cannot be a fixpoint. This proves (i) and (ii) of lemma 4.1 for the game when the parties' threats to opt out are not credible: a bargaining solution exists, and any bargaining solution will yield a lower spending level than S^A.

Period	offer made by	inv. receives at most /at least	agency receives at least/ at most
$t = T - 2$	investor	$\varphi'\delta\varphi(\delta\Pi^{sup/inf})$ $\varphi'(\delta\varphi(\Pi^c))$ $\varphi'(W^c)$	$\delta\varphi(\delta\Pi^{sup/inf})$ $\delta\varphi(\Pi^c)$ W^c
$t = T - 1$	agency	$\delta\Pi^{sup/inf}$ Π^c	$\varphi(\delta\Pi^{sup/inf})$ $\varphi(\Pi^c)$
$t = T$	investor	$\Pi^{sup/inf}$	

Figure 4A.1   Subgame payoffs and discounting: new project

Uniqueness. Uniqueness implies $\Pi^{inf} = \Pi^{sup}$. A formulation will be used that leads, for $\Lambda \to 0$, directly to the Nash solution of the bargaining game. For $[\Pi^A, \Pi_0]$, $\varphi(.)$ is decreasing in Π; furthermore, as $D(S)$ is strictly convex by assumption, $\varphi(.)$ is strictly concave. The proof needs only concavity.

It follows from the definition of (Π^*, W^*) that $W^+ = \max[\delta\varphi(\delta\Pi^+), W_0]$. Consider two cases:

(1)   For $\delta\varphi(\delta\Pi^+) > W_0$, a fixpoint may also be defined by (Π^c, W^c), where trivially $W^+ = \varphi(\Pi^+)$. Thus, it can also be written as a fixpoint condition that

$$\frac{\varphi(\Pi^+) - \varphi(\delta\Pi^+)}{(1-\delta)\Pi^+} = \frac{\delta\varphi(\delta\Pi^+) - \varphi(\delta\Pi^+)}{(1-\delta)\Pi^+} \qquad (4A.1)$$

Geometrically, the left-hand side of (4A.1) is the difference quotient $\Delta\varphi/\Delta\Pi^+$. Rearranging the right-hand side yields

$$\frac{\varphi(\Pi^+) - \varphi(\delta\Pi^+)}{(1-\delta)\Pi^+} = -\frac{\varphi(\delta\Pi^+)}{\Pi^+} \qquad (4A.1a)$$

Differentiating the right-hand side with respect to Π yields

$$\left[-\frac{\varphi(\delta\Pi)}{\Pi}\right]'_{\Pi} \equiv \frac{\varphi(\delta\Pi) - \varphi'(\delta\Pi)\delta\Pi}{\Pi^2} \qquad (4A.2)$$

This expression is positive, if $\varphi(\delta\Pi) - \varphi'(\delta\Pi)\delta\Pi > 0$. Expanding gives

$$\varphi'(\delta\Pi)\Pi < \varphi(\delta\Pi) + \varphi'(\delta\Pi)(\Pi - \delta\Pi) \qquad (4A.3)$$

It is known that $\varphi(.)$ being concave implies that

$$\varphi(\Pi) \leq \varphi(\delta\Pi) + \varphi'(\delta\Pi)(\Pi - \delta\Pi)$$

(compare Chiang 1984, 345). As $\varphi'(.) < 0$ for $\Pi > \Pi^*$, $\varphi'(\delta\Pi)\Pi < \varphi(\Pi)$. Condition (4A.3) is fulfilled under concavity of $\varphi(.)$ The derivative (4A.2) is positive, and the right-hand side of (4A.1) is monotonically increasing in Π. It is immediate that the difference quotient is non-increasing in Π for $\varphi(.)$ being concave. This property, taken together with the monotonicity property of the right-hand side in (4A.2) implies that, when (4A.2) holds, it does so for a unique Π^+.

(2)   When $\delta\varphi(\delta\Pi^+) \leq W_0$, a corner solution applies, where $\varphi'(\delta\varphi(\delta\Pi^+)) = \Pi_0$, and $(\Pi^+, W^+) = (\Pi_0, W_0)$. When the corner solution applies, it is also unique. As $\delta\varphi(\delta\Pi^+) < \varphi(\Pi^+)$, the above properties of the expressions in (A.2) imply:

$$\frac{\varphi(\Pi) - \varphi(\delta\Pi)}{(1-\delta)\Pi} > -\frac{\varphi(\delta\Pi)}{\Pi} \qquad\qquad \text{for all } \Pi < \Pi_0 .$$

This unique bargaining equilibrium can be implemented by the following (stationary) strategies of the parties:[46] The investor offers $W^+ = \varphi(\Pi^+)$ in every even period and accepts in every odd period any offer of at least $\delta\Pi^+$. The agency offers $\delta\Pi^+$ in every odd period and accepts, in any even period, any offer of at least $W^+ = \varphi(\Pi^+)$. It results that the investor will offer, in $t = 0$, $\varphi'(\delta\varphi(\Pi^c) + (1-\delta)W_0) < \Pi_0$; this offer will immediately be accepted by the agency.

Convergence to the Nash solution. The symmetric Nash solution is

$$(\Pi^N, W^N) = \underset{S}{\text{argmax}}\,[\Pi W] \text{ s.t.}$$

(i) $W = \varphi(\Pi)$,   (ii) $\Pi \leq \Pi_0$.

Solving for the first-order conditions gives

$$\varphi'(\Pi^N) = -\frac{\varphi(\Pi^N) - y}{\Pi^N}, \qquad\qquad (4A.4)$$

$$y \geq 0, \qquad \Pi_0 - \Pi^N \geq 0, \qquad y(\Pi_0 - \Pi^N) = 0, \qquad (4A.5)$$

where y is the Lagrange multiplier of constraint (ii) and (Π^N, W^N), $W^N = \varphi(\Pi^N)$ denotes the Nash solution.

Consider the condition $\delta\varphi(\delta\Pi^+) > W_0$ for an interior solution $\Pi^+ < \Pi^*$ in the strategic game. For $\Lambda \to 0$, this turns into $\varphi(\Pi^+) > W_0$, or $\Pi^+ < \Pi_0$, which corresponds to the second expression of (4A.5). Then, constraint (ii) is not binding, and y=0. An interior solution results: by using L'Hôpital's rule, the limit of (4A.1) for $\Lambda \to 0$ yields (4A.4) for $y = 0$. For $\varphi(\Pi^+) \leq W_0$, constraint (ii) is binding. The corner solution results: $y \geq 0$, and $(\Pi^N, W^N) = (\Pi_0, W_0)$. Thus, $(\Pi^+, W^+) = (\Pi^N, W^N)$ for $\Lambda \to 0$.

---

[46]Osborne and Rubinstein (1990), 43–8, show uniqueness of the equilibrium for more generic assumptions over the parties' preferences.

Credibility of the outside options

Reconsider Figure 4A.1. The investor has the opportunity to quit the bargaining table in any odd period. The threat to take this option is credible, if $\Pi^c > \delta\Pi^+$. In this case, the agency has to offer the value of the outside option in order to keep the investor from quitting the bargaining table. By assumption, the investor would accept any offer which equals the value of its outside option; it prefers an out-of-court settlement, whenever possible. The reasoning presented above may now be repeated; it results that the investor will submit an offer $\delta\varphi(\Pi^c)$ in $t = 0$, which the agency will accept immediately.

The agency has the opportunity to take the outside option in every even period. In Figure 4A.1, this is period $T - 2$. The agency's outside option is a credible threat, when $W^c > \delta\varphi(\delta W^+)$. In this case, a similar reasoning yields that the investor has to submit a corresponding offer, thus realizing $\varphi^I(W^c)$.

The limit of these outcomes for $\Delta \to 0$ yield the corresponding expressions in part (iii) of lemma 4.1.

Consider part (i): When an outside option is a credible threat, an inefficiently low spending level is immediate from the values of the outside options for $p_I \in (0, 1)$.

To see the bargaining incentives under outside options, note that (Π^c, W^c) is a convex combination of (Π^*, W^*) and (Π_0, W_0). However, φ is strictly concave on $[\Pi^*, \Pi_0]$, implying that (Π^c, W^c) must lay below φ for $p_I \in (0, 1)$. ∎

Proof of corollary 4.1

Note that Cs is an additive parameter within the function $W = \varphi(\Pi)$. Differentiating the right-hand side of (4A.2a) with respect to Cs thus gives

$$\left[-\frac{\varphi(\delta\Pi)}{\Pi} \right]'_{Cs} = -\frac{1}{\Pi} .$$

Increasing Cs exogenously will decrease the right-hand side of (4A.2a), Π being given. As the difference quotient does not change by a variation of Cs, Π^+ has to increase. For a high enough Cs, the corner solution will result. However, $W^c > W_0$ for $p_I < 1$: the agency's threat of the opting out is then always credible, while the investor's threat will never be credible. Therefore, $(\Pi^{Ba}, W^{Ba}) = (\varphi^I(W^c), W^c)$ for all $p_I \in (0, 1)$. ∎

Proof of lemma 4.2

The periodic status-quo payoffs π_0 and w_0 are integrated into Figure 4A.2.

Consider first the situation without outside options. Then, Shaked and Sutton's technique yields

$$\Pi^+ = \varphi^I(\delta\varphi(\delta\Pi^+ + \pi_0) + w_0) \qquad (4A.6)$$

or

$$\Pi^+ = \varphi^I(\delta\varphi(\delta\Pi^+ + (1-\delta)\Pi_0) + (1-\delta)W_0) \qquad (4A.7)$$

It is evident that $\Pi^+ = \Pi_0$ solves (4A.7). To check uniqueness, consider an offer $W^n > W_0$ by the project operator (the company), implying $\Pi^n < \Pi_0$. Hence,

$$\varphi^I(\delta\varphi(\delta\Pi^n + (1-\delta)\Pi_0) + (1-\delta)W_0) < \Pi_0 \,,$$

meaning that the project operator (the company) would never submit such an offer. Thus, $(\Pi^+, W^+) = (\Pi_0, W_0)$ uniquely solves (4A.7).

period	offer made by	company receives at most/at least	agency receives at least/ at most
$t = T-2$	company	$\varphi^I(\delta\varphi(\delta\Pi^{\text{sup/inf}} + \pi_0) + w_0)$ $\varphi^I(\delta\varphi(\Pi^c) + w_0)$ $\varphi(W^c)$	$\delta\varphi(\delta\Pi^{\text{sup/inf}} + \pi_0) + w_0$ $\delta\varphi(\Pi^c) + w_0$ W^c
$t = T-1$	agency	$\delta\Pi^{\text{sup/inf}} + \pi_0$ Π^c	$\varphi(\delta\Pi^{\text{sup/inf}} + \pi_0)$ $\varphi(\Pi^c)$
$t = T$	company	$\Pi^{\text{sup/inf}}$	

Figure 4A.2   Subgame payoffs and discounting: existing project

As $W^c > W_0$, the agency's threat of taking the outside option is always credible, whereas this is never so for the company ($\varphi^I(\delta\varphi(\Pi^c) + (1-\delta)W_0) < \Pi_0$). Therefore, the bargaining outcome is $(\Pi^B, W^B) = (\varphi^I(W^c), W^c)$ for $p_I \in (0,1)$. ∎

5. Negotiations under Uncertain Court Outcomes: Symmetrical Standing

5.1 INTRODUCTION

This chapter uses the framework presented in Chapter 4 to consider the situation in which, within project licensing, both the investor and the environmental organization have standing against a non-negotiated permit. It is argued that this corresponds more to the US situation. To see this, consider first some evidence concerning environmental negotiations in the United States.

Environmental Bargaining in the United States. Several general empirical studies point to the importance of bargained outcomes in legal disputes, thus confirming the widespread wisdom that 'most cases settle':[1]

- Kritzner (1986) found that out of 1649 civil cases analyzed in five federal judicial districts and seven state courts, only 7 percent went to trial; an additional 15 percent was adjudicated by arbitration or dismissal.
- Furthermore, parties may go to the courts to test how strong their case is, and settle after a first ruling has clarified their expectations. Kritzner (1986) found that 9 percent of all analyzed cases settle after a ruling on a significant motion. Schuck and Elliott (1990, 213–15) got a similar result. Their study on remanded cases is especially interesting in the present context because it considered administrative law cases. In 40 percent of all analyzed cases, no further proceedings occurred after remand. Whereas agencies reaffirmed their decision in 20–25 percent of cases only, major changes occurred in 40 percent of the remanded cases. Out of these 40 percent, approximately another 40 percent led to 'much more favorable results' for the challenging party. While they do not explicitly explore

---

[1] Galanter and Cahill (1994) give a comprehensive discussion on this issue.

how these changes are actually made, it seems reasonable to assume that negotiation-oriented processes played a role.

These studies do not explicitly focus on cases involving environmental law. Within environmental policy implementation, bargaining occurs at three different levels (Caldart and Ashford 1999):

- On the level of agency rulemaking: this is the so-called *Negotiated Rulemaking*. After initial proposals on how to broaden the notice-and-comment approach by EPA with a more consensus and negotiation-oriented procedure, including not only representatives from the industries to be regulated, but also third parties representing environmental or consumer interests (Harter 1982; Susskind and McMahon 1985), the process gained momentum in the late eighties. The US Congress acknowledged this process of agency decision-making by passing, in 1990, the Negotiated Rulemaking Act. Negotiated Rulemaking is now a still innovative, but accepted procedure. Participation of third parties in the negotiations is regularly stressed as an important component (see Pritzker and Dalton 1995, for a comprehensive description of the process, and Dalton 1993 for an overview).
- On the level of project approval and licensing, as is shown by the vast literature on *environmental dispute resolution*.[2] This literature focuses on how to improve the chances of successful negotiations, for example, through the intervention of a mediator. The most comprehensive compilation of cases only covers mediated disputes (Bingham 1986). Bingham's study presents 161 cases from 1974–84, out of which 115 are site-specific. It seems reasonable to assume that only the most important disputes get mediated (mediation is sophisticated and costly[3]); thus, this number probably represents only a lower bound of all negotiated cases.

    Furthermore, under the 'Program XL', the federal EPA now tries to implement more flexible regulation by more negotiation-inclined procedures within licensing processes (Caldart and Ashford 1999, 182–86).

---

[2]See, as a selection, Amy (1990), Bacow and Wheeler (1984), Bingham (1986), Crowfoot and Wollondeck (1990), Elliott (1996) O'Hare et al. (1983), Susskind and Cruikshank (1987), Susskind and Field (1996).

[3]The charge of a professional mediation entity for a typical mediation case may range from $50,000 to $300,000 (interview with Gail Bingham, RESOLVE).

Federal legislators in the United States accept policy implementation at this level to be a bargaining process. This can be concluded from the passing, in 1990, of the *Alternative Dispute Resolution Act* which allows and encourages agencies to use specific instruments to facilitate negotiations (for example, mediation). This formal recognition contrasts with the German situation.

- On the compliance level with environmental regulations, bargaining occurs as settlement negotiations in enforcement cases, possibly after citizen suits (see Habicht II and Hunt et al. 1999). The issue at stake here is the amount to be paid as a penalty, and the potential alternative uses of the penalty. Instead of just paying the penalty to the treasury, a negotiated agreement may stipulate payment for environmentally beneficial projects or, as the EPA calls it, supplemental environmental projects (SEPs; see Lawrence 1996). Here, environmental organizations play an important role by filing citizen suits (ibid., 10180).

The present analysis, which focuses on negotiations at the project level, will address the difference with respect to negotiated rulemaking at the end of the chapter. Also, negotiations within enforcement cases will not be analyzed. Some enforcement aspects, however, will be addressed, because Section 5.7 will argue that the private enforcement *via* citizen suits may also have a substantial impact on permit conditions.

The widespread participation, in negotiations at the project level, of parties representing environmental interests contrasts with the German situation. Remember from Chapter 4 the result of Bingham's study: 78 percent of the investigated site-specific disputes (which, hence, would be subjected to a licensing procedure in Germany) involved environmental groups and/or local citizen groups.[4]

The current analysis will focus on the differing extent of associational standing to give an explanation for this difference in the typical bargaining constellation. It argues that environmental organizations gain bargaining power through legal standing,[5] implying that an environmental group which is granted standing enters the bargaining game.

---

[4]See Bingham (1986, 44–5). The number is 35% for environmental groups alone. Note that even a local citizen, while injured-in-fact, may not be injured in his individual rights. As Bingham's study only considers disputes important enough to get mediated, it may overrate the importance of environmental groups' participation: due to their limited budgets, they will not participate in every small-scale environmental bargaining process.

[5]As Babich (1995, 10141) puts it alluding to citizen suits, standing rights are the 'teeth of public participation' (see also Bacow and Wheeler 1984, 176; Treiber 1990, 277–8). The role of standing to gain bargaining power is also stressed by environmental organizations'

The chapter proceeds as follows. The next section introduces associational standing into the framework presented in Section 4.2. Section 5.3 characterizes the solution of bargaining over the permit conditions for a new project. Section 5.4 compares the constellation of asymmetrical and symmetrical standing, and describes the differences to the Coasean analysis of private bargaining under secure property rights. Sections 5.5 and 5.6 present two variations of the model. First, a situation will be analyzed in which the environmental group, by filing suit, can only delay realization of the project. Section 5.6 relaxes the assumption that trial occurs instantaneously. Bargaining can then proceed until the date of trial, which amounts to an analysis of a finite version of the bargaining game. Section 5.7 presents two empirical cases to illustrate the theoretical analysis. Section 5.8 explores the role of litigation costs. The impact of associational standing on informal agreements will be analyzed in Section 5.9. Section 5.10 considers the investor's incentive to commit at the pre-bargaining stage to a specific technology in order to extort additional rents. Section 5.11 investigates the impact of associational standing within negotiated rulemaking. Section 5.12 summarizes and comments on possible political implications of the analysis.

5.2 THE FRAMEWORK

The analysis presented now only addresses bargaining over a new project; therefore, the subscript n will be omitted. Assume the agreement is still stipulated by a binding contract. Any party signing the contract waives its right to sue against the stipulated permit conditions. As before, litigation is costless. Assume that the agency is welfare-maximizing ($\theta = 1$). Remember that in this case, the agency's payoff W also depicts welfare.

Legal standing, besides offering the formal right to sue against an agency permit, is assumed to be substantial, in the sense the court will indeed decide in favor of the organization with a possibly small, but positive probability. Assume that the environmental organization is not legally entitled to ask for

---

representatives. According to Peter Lehner (NRDC), frequent litigation during the seventies and eighties raised awareness within industry and regulatory agencies that the NRDC is a powerful adversary; as a response to this learning process, these parties are now more inclined to enter negotiations with NRDC. A similar relationship can also be detected by comparing the main strategies of NRDC's regional offices: offices found more recently have to be more litigious, because they still have to prove that they have to be taken seriously.

compensation for environmental damage. The organization will then plead for a rejection of the economic activity.[6] Denote by

p_E the probability that the court decides in favor of the environmental organization.

The organization has an incentive to sue against any permit negotiated without its participation. To see this, denote the environmental damage associated with this permit by D^B. Then, for any $p_E > 0$,

$$-(1 - p_E)D^B > -D^B \qquad (5.1)$$

Therefore, the other parties will accept the environmental organization as a bargaining party, when it has standing.[7]

Consider now the bargaining situation in which the environmental organization participates. As soon as one of the private bargaining parties decides to quit the bargaining table, bargaining breaks down. This is so, because the investor, as well as the environmental organization, also has an incentive to sue against a permit negotiated without its participation:

$$(1 - p_I)S^B < S^B, \qquad (5.2)$$

for any $p_I > 0$, where S^B denotes the investor's spending level under a permit negotiated without its participation. Thus, when the environmental group has standing, bargaining either occurs with the participation of both private parties or does not happen at all.

When bargaining breaks down, the agency issues a non-negotiated permit over S^{nn}. The question is whether at least one private party has an incentive to sue this non-negotiated permit. After failed bargaining, no party waives its

---

[6] Such a far-reaching second-guessing by the court may seem rather improbable within the licensing of a new project. The analysis also holds when the group can convince the court only to raise the spending level. In reality, even a mere remand by the court would favor persons affected by environmental externalities. Since the decision-making process of the agency is time-consuming, a remand means that the construction of the project is delayed. For this period of time, the environment remains in the state most preferred by the affected citizen. Section 5.5 presents an alternative court model where associational standing only empowers the group to delay the date of trial.

[7] Analogously to the investor's incentive to contest a non-negotiated permit, condition (5.1) may also hold for positive litigation costs and some D^B.

right to sue. Thus, when one party sues the permit, the other private party will plead in court as well, in order to defend its stake. Denote by

p_I the probability of the investor being granted an unconditional permit,
p_A the probability of the agency obtaining confirmation of the permit S^{nn},

and $p_E + p_I + p_A = 1$. The permit will be contested, if at least one of the following conditions holds

$$p_I\Pi_0 + p_A(\Pi_0 - S^{nn}) > \Pi_0 - S^{nn}, \tag{5.3}$$
$$-[p_ID_0 + p_AD(S^{nn})] > -D(S^{nn}), \tag{5.4}$$

in which case the expected welfare from trial is

$$(p_A + p_I)\Pi - p_A(D(S^{nn}) + S^{nn}) - p_ID_0.$$

Again, it can be concluded that it is optimal to set $S^{nn} = S^*$ when negotiations break down. This is trivially so when the permit will not be challenged. When at least one of the conditions (5.3) and (5.4) holds, it comes to trial, and

$$S^* = \arg\min_{S^{nn}}[(p_A + p_I)\Pi_0 - p_A[D(S^{nn}) + S^{nn}] - p_ID_0].$$

Denoting the negative payoff for the citizen group by $-D^{cs}$, the values of the trial for the respective parties are then given by:

$$\Pi^{cs} = p_I\Pi_0 + p_A(\Pi_0 - S^*), \tag{5.5}$$
$$-D^{cs} = -(p_ID_0 + p_AD^*), \tag{5.6}$$
$$W^{cs} = (p_A + p_I)\Pi_0 - p_A(D^* + S^*) - p_ID_0, \tag{5.7}$$

where s stands for symmetrical standing. It is assumed that the probability of the investor's winning in court does not change. Furthermore, it captures the following assumption.

Assumption 5.1. Expected welfare from trial is reduced by the introduction of standing for externality victims: $W^{cs} < W^{ca}$.

Plausibly, the expected payoff for the investor is also reduced: $\Pi^{cs} < \Pi^{ca}$.[8]

Note the difference between having an incentive to sue and pleading in court to present one's stake. When the latter is not possible without filing suit, parties will take legal action in response to other parties' going to the court, even while, according to (5.3) and (5.4), they may not have an incentive to do so independently of the other party's activities.

Again, parties exert two threats: first, they may threaten to opt out during negotiations, in which case the agency issues a permit over S^*. Second, they may decide whether to contest this permit or not.

In the following analysis, it is the investor and the environmental group which are actually bargaining, whereas the agency takes a passive role. The agency is better of by accepting any negotiated agreement when compared with its option to risk a trial. This can be seen by restating the incentives to negotiate in terms of the associated costs. Incentives to negotiate exist between the private parties, if there is a pair S_m, D_m , for which

$$S_m \le p_A S^* + p_E \Pi_0,$$
$$D_m \le p_A D^* + p_I D_0.$$

These two inequations add up to

$$S_m + D_m \le p_A(S^* + D^*) + p_I D_0 + p_E \Pi_0,$$

whose right-hand side depicts the agency's costs of refusing the private bargaining solution, issuing a permit over S^* and thus triggering a legal dispute. Hence, when the first two inequations hold (which has to be the case for every bargained outcome between the private parties) the last inequation also holds, and the agency will accept the negotiated agreement.

This formulation allows for an immediate comparison with an analysis of private environmental bargaining under secure property rights and complete information (Coase 1960), and secure rights and incomplete information, in the spirit of Farrell (1987). The Coasean analysis will emerge as a benchmark of the model presented here. Farrell's analysis will be addressed in Chapter 6.

Because of (5.3) and (5.4), the values of the parties' outside options in the subsequent bargaining game are no longer given automatically by the

---

[8]Probabilities could also be redistributed between p_I and p_E without affecting the results; however, the introduction of standing for the environmental group may then improve expected welfare from trial, which may appear to trivialize the result.

respective expected values of the court outcome. Denote the values of the respective party's outside option by $(\Pi^{out}, -D^{out})$. Then,

$$(\Pi^{out}, -D^{out}) = \begin{cases} (\Pi^*, -D^*) & \text{iff } \Pi^{cs} \leq \Pi^* \text{ and } -D^{cs} \leq -D^*, \\ (\Pi^{cs}, -D^{cs}) & \text{else.} \end{cases} \tag{5.8}$$

The structure of the bargaining game can be summarized as follows:

- The agency is asked to undertake a regulatory activity, either by the submission of a permit application by an investor, or by the passing of a new environmental law which has to be implemented.
- Because of (5.1) and (5.2), the agency will initiate private negotiations over the conditions to be stipulated in the permit, that is, the corresponding spending level. Analogously to Section 4.2, the bargaining game between the investor and the environmental group (the agency being passive) is modeled as a strategic game of offer/counter-offer bargaining, in which each party may take its outside option after rejection of an offer from the adversary.
- Parties opt out by quitting the bargaining table. Then, the agency will immediately issue a permit over S^*, against which each private party may sue when it has an incentive to do so. If a party has an incentive to sue, the agency and the other private party will also defend their respective stake in court. Again, the court will also decide immediately.
- When agreeing on a negotiated permit, each private party waives its right to sue.

5.3 THE BARGAINING OUTCOME: A COMPARISON WITH COASE

The solution of this strategic game is presented in the appendix. Here, the axiomatic characterization of the game will again be used, which holds for a common discount factor δ^Λ and $\Lambda \to 0$.

To characterize the bargaining solution, consider first the bargaining frontier of the game. Denote by $\varphi_s(\Pi)$ the maximal (negotiated) payoff level of the environmental group for a given payoff level of the investor $\Pi \in (0, \Pi_0)$. Again, the subscript s stands for symmetrical standing. Introduce now the assumption regarding compensation possibilities presented in Section 4.2. In addition to spending on protective activities, the investor can pay a compensation financed out of profit, while the environmental organization cannot due to a tight budget. Denote a specific negotiated level of compensation by $C \geq 0$. The parties' payoff for given S and C is $\Pi_0 - S - C$ for the investor, and $-D(S) + C$ for the environmental group. From the definition of $\varphi_s(.)$,

$$\varphi_s(\Pi) = \max_{S,C}[-D(S) + C], \tag{5.9}$$

s.t. $S + C = \Pi_0 - \Pi$ and $C \geq 0$.

First-order conditions of (5.9) are

$$-D'(S) - y = 0,$$

$$1 - y \leq 0, \ C \geq 0, \text{ and } C(1-y) = 0,$$

where y is the Lagrangean multiplier. For $C = 0$, $D'(S) \geq -1$, implying that $S \leq S^*$. For $C \geq 0$, $D'(S) = -1$, implying $S = S^*$. Thus,

$$\varphi_s(\Pi) = \begin{cases} -D(S) & \text{for } \Pi_0 - \Pi < S^*, \\ -D(S^*) + C & \text{for } \Pi_0 - \Pi \geq S^*. \end{cases} \tag{5.10}$$

The graph of $\varphi_s(.)$ is depicted in Figure 5.1. Denote the transfer level which compensates completely the environmental damage $D(S^*)$ by C_{min}, and the corresponding profit by $\Pi_{min} = \Pi_0 - S^* - C_{min}$.

When bargaining a new project, the status-quo point is $(0, 0)$. Thus, the project is not executed as long as the negotiations are ongoing. Denote the equilibrium outcome of the bargaining game between the investor and the citizen group by (Π^{Bs}, Q^{Bs}), where, according to (5.10), either $Q^{Bs} = -D^{Bs}$ or $Q^{Bs} = -D^* + C^{Bs}$.

Lemma 5.1. For a common discount factor δ^Λ and $\Lambda \to 0$, the unique solution of the bargaining game between the investor and the environmental group, when negotiating over the conditions for a new project, is characterized as follows.

(i)   Bargaining incentives exist for $p_I, p_A, p_E > 0$.

(ii) The unique solution of the bargaining game is given by as follows.

- When $\Pi^{out} \leq 0.5\,\Pi_{min}$,

  the outside options of both parties do not constitute credible threats. The bargaining outcome is

  $(\Pi^{Bs}, Q^{Bs}) = (0.5\,\Pi_{min}, 0.5\,\Pi_{min})$.

- When $\Pi^{out} > 0.5\,\Pi_{min}$,

  the investor's threat to quit the bargaining table is credible. The solution results from (5.8) and (5.9):

  $(\Pi^{Bs}, Q^{Bs}) = (\Pi^*, -D^*)$, if $\Pi^{cs} \leq \Pi^*$ and $-D^{cs} \leq -D^*$,

  $(\Pi^{Bs}, Q^{Bs}) = (\Pi^{cs}, \varphi_s(\Pi^{cs}))$ else, where

  $$\varphi_s(\Pi^{cs}) = \begin{cases} -D(\Pi_0 - \Pi^{cs}) \text{ for } \Pi^{cs} > \Pi^*, \\ -D(S^*) + C^{Bs} \text{ for } \Pi^{cs} \leq \Pi^*. \end{cases}$$

Proof. See the appendix. ∎

The reasoning behind lemma 5.1 can be given with the help of Figure 5.1.

Credibility of the outside option and bargaining power. The threat of the environmental group to opt out during negotiations (thus triggering the issuance of a permit over S^* and a possible trial) will never be credible. Its expected outcome of taking the outside option is negative, whereas its status quo payoff is zero.

Figure 5.1 depicts the difference between the credibility of the threat to opt out and the decision to contest the permit over S^*. In the figure, the investor's threat to opt out is credible; however, when a permit over S^* is issued, it will be the environmental group which files suit, according to (5.4).

Consider the case in which $(\Pi^{Bs}, Q^{Bs}) = (\Pi^{cs}, \varphi_s(\Pi^{cs}))$, and $\varphi_s(\Pi^{cs}) < 0$. When compared to the status-quo payoff, the environmental organization is worse off in a bargained agreement. This explains why the group may have an incentive to drag out the negotiations. Given complete information, this incentive turns into bargaining power: whereas the investor just gets its reservation payoff Π^{cs}, the environmental group reaps the gains from trade $\varphi_s(\Pi^{cs}) - D^{cs}$.

Property rights and Coasean bargaining. The Nash solution results when no party's threat to quit the negotiations is credible. In this case, the parties share the profit remaining after spending S^* for environmental protection and complete compensation for the damage D^*. In Figure 5.1, the Nash solution is denoted by $(\Pi^{Ns}, Q^{Ns}) = (0.5\,\Pi_{min}, 0.5\,\Pi_{min})$.

This solution also results for the case of Coasean bargaining under secure property rights. To see this, note that all expected court outcomes (5.5) to (5.7) turn zero for $p_E = 1$, implying a secure property right for the environmental group. Coasean bargaining corresponds to the bargaining game in which the outside options' values coincide with the status quo

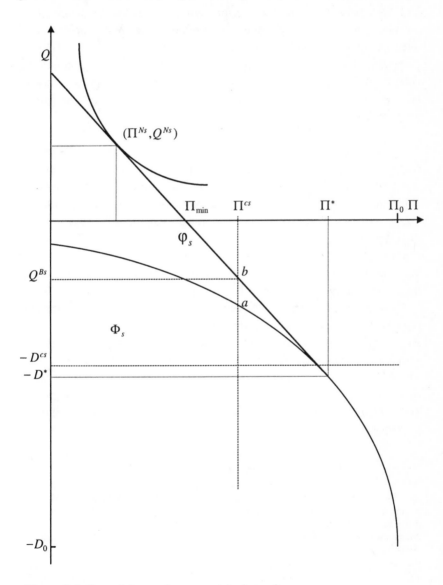

Figure 5.1 Bargaining under symmetrical standing

values.

Therefore, the Coasean analysis is a special case of the more general setting presented here. Specifically, it can be concluded that secure property rights are not a prerequisite either for the existence or for the efficiency of a bargaining solution. The Nash solution resulting under secure property rights will also emerge for 'almost secure' property rights, as long as the investor's outside option does not constitute a credible threat. When the investor's threat is credible, an efficient solution will result as long as $\Pi^{cs} \leq \Pi^*$ (this restriction is due to the assumption that the environmental group cannot compensate[9]). In this sense, complete or 'well-defined' property rights are not necessary for bargaining incentives and an efficient bargaining outcome.[10]

Insecure Property Rights, Compensation and Existence. The possibility of compensation payments is necessary for bargaining incentives to emerge under secure-rights bargaining à la Coase. Under insecure rights, however, compensation is not necessary for the existence of a bargaining solution. When compensation payments are ruled out, (5.10) always gives $\varphi_s(\Pi) = -D(\Pi_0 - \Pi)$. Then, the investor's outside option will always be credible. As long as $(\Pi^{cs}, -D^{cs}) \in \Phi_s$ (where Φ_s is suitably redefined for the no-compensation case),[11] the parties will agree on an outcome as given by the second part of (ii) in lemma 5.1.

Furthermore, in the case in which compensation is possible, insecure rights may generate bargaining incentives, while these do not exist under secure rights. To see this, consider the case of a project generating a substantial consumer surplus, and assume that $Cs + \Pi_0 - D^* - S^* > 0$, while $\Pi_0 - D^* - S^* \leq 0$. An incentive to negotiate will not exist under a secure right ($p_E = 1$), while they may exist under insecure rights (as long as $(\Pi^{cs}, -D^{cs}) \in \Phi_s$). This can been seen by suitably adapting the reasoning to prove part (i) of lemma 5.1.

---

[9]When the group can also pay compensation, it will be ready to co-finance protective activities up to the efficient level in the case where the negotiated payment from the investor $\Pi_0 - \Pi^{cs}$ implies too low a spending level. Then, the outcome of bargaining between the private parties will always be efficient.

[10]Within an informal analysis, a similar result is stated by Usher (1998). See also Lehmann (1996, 1997).

[11]It was assumed that the damage cannot completely be avoided in the case of positive profit. Then, bargaining incentives may not exist for some $(\Pi^{cs}, -D^{cs})$. This can been seen by reconsidering the proof of lemma 5.1, part (i), for the no-compensation case.

Insecure Rights, Compensation and Efficiency. Obviously, compensation is crucial for the efficiency of the bargaining solution when the investor's threat to opt out is not credible. When its threat is credible, compensation is crucial, as long as a non-negotiated permit by the agency would be challenged in court by at least one of the private parties. However, in the case in which $\Pi^{cs} \leq \Pi^*$ and $-D^{cs} \leq -D^*$, the investor threatens not to trigger a trial, but, by allowing negotiations to fail, the issuance of a permit S^* by the agency, against which no party has an incentive to sue. It results that the parties, in (degenerate) negotiations, would also agree on a spending level S^* (under complete information, the agency may anticipate this outcome and simply issue an efficient permit over S^*, which the private parties accept). The standing rights of the private parties against the agency's decision cancel each other out. When standing is symmetrical, the agency may gain leeway in implementing a permit according to its own objectives.

The analysis also yields an argument as to why environmental organizations may be ready to accept compensation when bargaining over a new project. Consider the case where $\Pi^{out} > 0.5 \Pi_{min}$, $\Pi^{cs} < \Pi^*$ and $-D^{cs} > -D^*$. The investor's threat to trigger a trial is credible, and the bargaining outcome, following (5.10), contains a positive compensation payment. As the investor is guaranteed only its reservation value (the expected profit from triggering a trial Π^{cs}), it is the environmental group which reaps all efficiency gains from compensation. In Figure 5.1, these efficiency gains are depicted by the distance a–b.

5.4 COMPARING ASYMMETRICAL AND SYMMETRICAL STANDING

Comparing lemmas 4.1 and 5.1. yields the following result.

Proposition 5.1. The introduction of legal standing for affected third parties leads, in private bargaining over the permit conditions for a new facility, to an efficient outcome or to an efficiency improvement when compared to the bargained outcome under asymmetrical standing.

Proof. Bargaining under asymmetrical standing resulted in an efficiently low spending level. In the symmetrical standing situation, as long as $\Pi^{cs} \leq \Pi^*$, bargaining will be efficient; the parties either agree on the efficient permit

S^*, or on the efficient spending level S^*, plus an additional compensation payment.

When $\Pi^{cs} > \Pi^*$, the investor's threat to trigger a trial is credible, and it results from (5.10) that the investor and the environmental group will agree on an inefficiently low spending level. To see the efficiency improvement, consider the following situations under asymmetrical standing:

- The investor's threat is also credible under asymmetrical standing. For a given p_I, the expected value of going to court is smaller, for the investor, under symmetrical than under asymmetrical standing: $\Pi^{cs} < \Pi^{ca}$. This implies a higher negotiated spending level.
- The investor's threat is not credible under asymmetrical standing. In this case, either the Nash solution applies, or the agency's threat is credible, implying either

$$\Pi^{ca} < \Pi^{Na}, \text{ or}$$
$$\Pi^{ca} < \varphi_a^I(W^{ca}).$$

As $\Pi^{cs} < \Pi^{ca}$, the negotiated spending level under symmetrical standing will again be higher. ■

The result is that a standing to sue for affected third parties of environmental regulation will improve efficiency in a setting of complete information. This is so, even while the expected welfare from trial is reduced. [12]

The possibility of compensation payments under symmetrical standing is crucial for proposition 5.1 to hold unambiguously. When compensation is ruled out, an efficiency improvement will result, as long as $\Pi^{cs} > \Pi^*$ in the symmetrical standing situation. When $\Pi^{cs} \leq \Pi^*$ and $-D^{cs} \leq -D^*$, the parties' options to use the court system neutralize each other. They would agree on the efficient permit over S^*. However, when $\Pi^{cs} < \Pi^*$ and $-D^{cs} > -D^*$, the spending level may overshoot in the sense that the investor and the environmental group may agree on too high a spending level, and the

---

[12]The result may appear to depend crucially on the reduction of the investor's value of its outside option by the introduction of legal standing for the environmental group: $\Pi^{cs} < \Pi^{ca}$. However, this is only the case when the investor's threat to opt out is credible under both bargaining constellations: Consider the case in which both parties' outside options do not constitute credible threats under asymmetrical standing, and the Nash solution applies. This implies $\Pi^{ca} < \Pi^{Na}$. An efficiency improvement will result under symmetrical standing for $\Pi^{cs} < \Pi^{Na}$. This condition, however, may also imply $\Pi^{cs} > \Pi^{ca}$.

inefficiency associated within this spending level may be even higher than the inefficiency resulting from too low a spending level under asymmetrical standing.

This possibility of overshooting is not very plausible from a theoretical perspective, because it presumes that the environmental group foregoes all efficiency gains from compensation.

5.5 A VARIANT: STANDING AND DELAY

Consider now the following variant of the court model, in which the environmental organization, when having standing, cannot ultimately prevent realization of the stipulated permit conditions. The only thing it can do is to delay the date of trial for T periods. Delayed trial dates are partly caused by the court's high caseload, which is beyond the group's influence. However, the environmental group may use legal procedures for tactical maneuvers (for example, to file motions) to further delay the court's ultimate decision and, hence, implementation of the project.

When the group does not participate in the negotiations, the agency and the investor still agree on a negotiated permit yielding (Π^{Ba}, W^{Ba}). Denote the group's payoff under the bargaining equilibrium by $-D^{Ba}$. Note that, as neither the agency nor the investor has an incentive for delay when licensing a new project, both will strive for a rapid legal decision even when negotiations between them fail. Thus, it is still reasonable to assume that a trial would be concluded more quickly (or, in the model, immediately) under asymmetrical standing. Hence, this court model depicts the concern often raised within the German discussion that associational standing may lead to the further delay of court decisions.

When contesting the permit, the group's payoff is given by $-\delta^T D^{Ba}$. The group has an incentive to sue against any permit negotiated without its participation and the non-negotiated permit in terms of the efficient spending level.

Consider now the bargaining between the private parties. When one of the parties opts out, the agency issues an efficient permit, which can be contested by the private parties. Payoffs from trial are

$$\Pi^{cs} = \delta^T \Pi^{ca},$$
$$-D^{cs} = \delta^T (-D^{ca})$$

where $-D^{ca} = -[p_I D^* + (1 - p_I)D_0]$. Deriving these expressions for T and solving the equation yields

$$\frac{dD^{cs}}{d\Pi^{cs}} = \frac{D^{ca}}{\Pi^{ca}}.$$

Hence, for any T, $(\Pi^{cs}, -D^{cs})$ is a convex combination of $(\Pi^{ca}, -D^{ca})$ and $(0, 0)$, and $(\Pi^{ca}, -D^{ca})$ is a convex combination of $(\Pi^*, -D^*)$ and $(\Pi_0, -D_0)$. Consequently, bargaining incentives exist for $T > 0$, and the analysis of 5.4 applies accordingly.

5.6 BARGAINING AND EXOGENOUS TRIAL DATE

Reconsider now the model in which the environmental group, in court, can effect a rejection of the project with probability p_E. Even when the group cannot strategically delay the trial, substantial time may elapse between the moment of filing suit and the judge's ruling because of the high caseload. Then, bargaining may continue after a party has filed suit.

This point can be investigated within a bargaining game with an exogenously fixed date of trial at period T. Consequently, as long as the preparation and submission of an offer requires time, parties can only submit a finite numbers of offers and counter-offers. The bargaining outcome will crucially depend on which party submits an offer in the last period before trial, which, in turn, depends on T being odd or even and on which party submits the first offer in the game. As the last offer that can be submitted before a trial effectively amounts to a take-it-or-leave-it offer, the party submitting this offer will have all the bargaining power.

Spier (1992, 95–103) uses a bargaining model with an exogenous date of trial in a liability dispute in which the defendant has to pay an indemnity to the plaintiff with certainty, when it comes to trial. In this case, the plaintiff wants to settle as early, and the defendant as late as possible. A delayed settlement may even result under complete information, when no bargaining costs are incurred beyond discounting (Spier 1992, 97). [13] It may be suspected that a similar result applies in the present setting because it was argued that

---

[13]A similar result is derived by McKenna and Sadanand (1995), where external arbitration occurs at time T.

the environmental group may want to delay execution of the project, while the investor wants to start construction as early as possible.

Omit, for brevity, the superscript s in this section. Consider the case where $-D^c > -D^*$, $\Pi^c < \Pi^*$ and the investor's threat to opt out is credible. When it opts out, it is the environmental organization which will file suit against the efficient permit. Assume that the trial was erroneously triggered by a mistake of one of the bargaining parties. It is the environmental group which submits the first offer in the subsequent game with T bargaining periods. The trial will take place in period T, immediately after a rejection of the last offer. When T is even, the investor can submit a take-it-or-leave-it offer at T. Under the assumption of $-D^c > -D^*$, this implies an efficient spending level and a positive level of compensation. According to (5.10), payoffs are then defined by $\Pi = \Pi^* - C$ and $Q = -D^* + C$, or

$$Q = -D^* + \Pi^* - \Pi. \tag{5.11}$$

The investor will submit an offer such that $-D^* + C^B = -D^c$, which yields a payoff of $\Pi^* - C^B$ for the investor. To settle in an earlier period t, the investor will at least require a payoff $\delta^{(T-t)}(\Pi^* - C^B)$, meaning that, when it receives such a payoff, it will be indifferent as to whether to settle at t or to wait until trial.

When submitting such an offer, the environmental group, from (5.11), will realize a payoff of

$$-D^* + \Pi^* - [\delta^{(T-t)}(\Pi^* + C^B)]. \tag{5.12}$$

The group will submit this offer and hence, agree to settle earlier, when

$$-D^* + (1 - \delta^{(T-t)})\Pi^* + \delta^{(T-t)}C^B > \delta^{(T-t)}(-D^* + C^B)$$
$$\Rightarrow \Pi^* > D^*,$$

where the left-hand side is a reformulation of (5.12) and the right-hand side gives the discounted value of waiting until trial: $\delta^{(T-t)}(-D^* + C^B) = \delta^{(T-t)}(-D^c)$. When $\Pi^* = D^*$, the group will also be indifferent as to whether to settle now or to wait until trial. It is only in this case that Spier's result applies.

The argument can be reiterated for T being odd, implying that it is the group which will make a take-it-or-leave-it offer in the last period.

Consequently, for $\Pi^* = D^*$, the bargaining outcome $(\Pi^* - C^B, -D^* + C^B)$ can be sustained as an equilibrium in any $t \in [1, T]$. Spier's analysis only holds when, aside from inefficiencies that are inherent to the trial, there is no surplus to share from the issue under dispute. Indeed, her model features a zero-sum dispute, by assuming that, under a court ruling, the defendant has to pay a specific amount with certainty to the defendant.

5.7 EXAMPLES

5.7.1 Compensation: Evidence

In the setting considered here in which externality victims are represented by a collective actor, that is, the environmental group, it is not clear whether compensation payments to the group will be redistributed to the actual externality victims. Clearly, within nature conservation cases or other complex environmental externalities, it may be prohibitively costly to organize the transfer to all affected persons.

From an efficiency perspective, compensating the victims is not necessary, as long as the optimal spending level S^* is realized.[14] Then, transfers may also take the form of a bribe aimed at the organization's leadership. From a political perspective, however, this may be an unsatisfactory outcome.

Empirical evidence from the US suggests that the fear of appearing bribable makes environmental groups highly reluctant to accept unconditional transfers in cash (Bacow and Wheeler 1984, 54, 345; Field and Susskind 1996). This is explained by the fact that negotiated agreements may be scrutinized by the interested public and the mass media. As environmental organizations' funding crucially depends on reputation, they have an interest in avoiding any suspicion of accepting true side-payments.

Instead, they may be ready to accept compensation in kind: 'For example, if a development is going to destroy a highly valuable piece of forest, the

---

[14]Legally guaranteeing total compensation of the remaining environmental damage will have adverse effects on efficiency, when externality victims also have opportunities to avoid the damages (by relocating or other defensive activities). Guaranteeing total compensation, under a liability rule, would destroy the incentives to engage in avoidance, and would disturb location decisions (Browning 1977; Butler and Maher 1986; Baumol and Oates 1988, 23ff.). In the present setting, however, compensation is not legally guaranteed; instead, a specific transfer level results endogenously from the bargaining constellation and the value of the investor's outside option. As the affected persons reap all the gains from trade, $D(S)$ will also incorporate defensive activities undertaken by externality victims, but financed by the investor.

developer as compensation might offer to purchase comparable land for the creation of a perpetual wildlife preserve'. (Bacow and Wheeler 1984, 54).[15]

Conditional payments, for example, the creation of trust funds for specific environmental purposes, is another possibility. Susskind and Field (1996, 151) note that, as a general rule:

> It is crucial that the nexus between compensation or contingent offers and the injury or harm being addressed be made explicit. The better the compensation fits the cost or suffering in question, the more likely the outcome will be perceived as fair to the public, and the more likely the company or agency will be able to regain its credibility. ... The more the compensation veers from the complaint, the more it will be seen as a payoff or bribe.

In the two examples presented here to illustrate the theoretical analysis, the creation of such funds were an important part of the negotiated agreements. Both examples involve the construction of a dam; thus, they fit the assumption of an indivisible project, in which the environmental damage is site-specific and, hence, not taxable. Nature conservation was an important issue in the first, the exclusive issue in the second case. Both cases involved environmental groups. Furthermore, the documentation of both cases present the private parties as the relevant adversaries in the negotiations.

5.7.2   United States: Grayrocks Dam, Wyoming (1970–79)

The case is documented in Bacow and Wheeler (1984, 46–50). The project under dispute was a dam and reservoir on the Laramie river, Wyoming, intended to provide cooling for a coal-fired power plant planned by the Missouri Basin Power Project (MBPP), a utility consortium. Environmental damage resulted via the additional streamflow reduction and its repercussions on agriculture and wildlife. Downstream farmers were represented by the state of Nebraska. Environmental groups such as the National Audubon Society worried that streamflow reductions would damage the downstream habitat of the whooping crane, an endangered species.

After some unsuccessful settlement meetings, lawsuits were filed by Nebraska and the environmental groups against the issuance of a 404 permit, charging an inadequate Environmental Impact Assessment and violation of

---

[15]This corresponds to the mitigation/compensation requirements in the US wetlands regulation and in the German nature conservation law. The analysis, however, makes clear that the incentives to implement compensation as part of a bargained solution crucially differ between environmental groups and welfare-maximizing agencies.

the Endangered Species Act. Bacow and Wheeler (1984, 48) argue that the negotiations were not successful because each party was overly optimistic about prevailing in court.

Ultimately, successful settlement negotiations occurred only after the first trial, where the court ruled against MBPP. Future outcomes, however, were still uncertain. First, it was uncertain as to how the appeal courts would decide. Second, Congress intervened by passing a bill exempting Grayrocks dam from regulation, provided that a special body newly created under the Endangered Species Act, the so-called Endangered Species Committee, gave its approval. Hence, it was not clear how the committee would decide.

The first settlement offer by MBPP totalled $15m to purchase water rights in order to maintain appropriate streamflows. This total payment was not under dispute in the subsequent negotiations: 'The parties spent much time in discussing how much a settlement could be consummated and no time discussing the size of the settlement' (Bacow and Wheeler 1984, 50). The ultimate agreement included a set of guaranteed minimum streamflows for different seasons and the creation of a trust fund for the preservation of the whooping crane and its habitat. The agreement was concluded by a formal, binding contract in January 1979.

Apparently, the information generated during the first trial corrected the parties' overly optimistic beliefs concerning the strength of their case, which made successful bargaining possible. In the light of the theoretical analysis, the total payment of $15m can be readily interpreted as MBPP's expected spending level under its outside option. The introduction of streamflow guarantees means technical avoidance depicted, in the model, by $D(S)$. The problem of MBPP's adversaries in the negotiations was to find the 'right mixture' of those technical measures and compensation.[16]

5.7.3   Germany: Goldisthal, Thüringen (1994–97).

The project under dispute was a pumped storage work planned by the *Vereinigte Energiewerke AG* (VEAG), one of the major German power utilities. The project was challenged by the Thüringen section of the *Bund für Umwelt und Naturschutz Deutschland* (BUND), which feared negative impacts on aquatic wildlife and, more importantly, on a nearby nature reserve protecting the habitat of a rare species of capercaillies. Given the poor

---

[16]Adversaries of MBPP also worried about reputation losses when accepting cash payments and about possible legal obstacles (it was not clear whether water rights could be purchased for conservation purposes) (Bacow and Wheeler 1984, 50).

economic conditions in the former GDR, public authorities were quite enthusiastic about the project. Political resistance against the works, by the interested public or mass media, was virtually absent. Residents from the nearby town of Goldisthal were in favor of the project. Also, backing from the federal BUND to its *Länder* section was rather moderate. This was not a high-profile environmental conflict.

During the formal hearings, the BUND was able to push through additional technical measures to avoid environmental damages (for example, construction changes to ensure fish migration, restrictions on construction periods) as well as mitigation measures in the form of additional areas for the wildlife reserve.

Despite these successes, the BUND took action under the Thüringen Nature Conservation Act which grants associational standing against projects impairing nature reserves. Again, it was uncertain how the court would decide. First, the project was not sited within, but only near the capercaillie reserve. Thus, it was possible that the court would dismiss the complaint outright for lack of standing. Second, given the fact that the organization was active during the formal procedure and was able to push through substantial measures, BUND representatives perceived the chances of ultimately prevailing in court as rather low. Still, they were able to delay execution of the project via an ongoing court battle.

The dispute was settled six months after the BUND filed suit. The settlement agreement stipulated the creation of a trust fund totalling DM7m of nature conservation purposes and the promotion of renewable energy. The agreement was concluded by a formal settlement contract (*Vergleich*) (BUND 1997a, b).

As part of the agreement (over the level of site-specific protective activities) was made before suit was filed, the case makes clear that it is not necessary to actually take legal action in order to improve environmental regulation. Furthermore, as Goldisthal was not a politicized environmental dispute, the BUND did not have the option of mobilizing political pressure against the project. Hence, the case points to the role of legal standing for gaining bargaining power during negotiations over permit conditions.[17]

---

[17]Interestingly, the dispute gained profile in the media after the settlement, because negotiated settlements with environmental groups involving cash payments are rare exceptions in Germany. Also, the settlement led to a vivid discussion within the BUND concerning the legitimacy of such compensation payments (BUND 1997b). Insofar, the settlement was, for Germany, highly innovative.

5.8 LITIGATION COSTS

Symmetrical reimbursement.   Litigation   costs   can   be   introduced
analogously to the analysis of Section 4.4.2. Assume again the British cost
allocation rule, where the winner of the case has his litigation costs
reimbursed by the loser. The private parties' incentives to contest a permit
negotiated without their respective participation are given by conditions (5.1)
and (5.2); under positive costs of trial C_t, they turn into

$$C_t < \frac{p_I}{1 - p_I} S^B \tag{5.13}$$

for the investor and

$$C_t < \frac{p_E}{1 - p_E} D^B \tag{5.14}$$

for the environmental group. Clearly, for adequately high litigation costs, no
party has an interest to contest a permit over S^*.

In the analysis under asymmetrical standing (Section 4.4.2), it was shown
that, for some level of litigation costs, the agency has an incentive to issue a
permit over an inefficiently low spending level, which the investor will not
contest (proposition 4.2 (ii)). This incentive may not exist for an identical
level of court costs under symmetrical standing: as $D(S)$ is monotonically
decreasing in S, lowering the prescribed spending level increases
environmental damage, which, according to (5.14), may induce the
environmental group to file suit even when it does not have an incentive to do
so for D^*.

Note, however, that (5.14) is a necessary, but not a sufficient condition to
file suit for a larger environmental group which has a restricted budget. Such
an environmental organization usually disputes different projects with
environmental externalities concurrently and has to decide which cases to
prioritize. One possible solution is their ranking with respect to the expected
surplus each generates for the organization, according to (5.14). The
organization would prioritize those cases generating the highest surplus.
Consequently, a threat to sue in a case with a lower surplus may not be
credible for the other parties, even when (5.14) holds.

Asymmetric reimbursement and the US rule. The organization's incentive to file suit will be higher under the asymmetric reimbursement rule specified in the US citizen suit provisions.[18] Citizen suits give environmental groups the possibility to charge administrators for the violation of non-discretionary duties. In cases where it is not clear a priori whether the administrator has leeway in his decision-making or not, the court ruling will be uncertain, and the setting formalized here will apply.

Asymmetric reimbursement means that, while the environmental group gets reimbursed its court costs and attorney's fees in the case of winning the trial,[19] this will not be so for investors challenging the project permit. Investors, under the usual US rule, will always be forced to bear their legal costs. Denote the investor's and the environmental group's legal costs by C_I and C_E, respectively.

The private parties' incentives to contest the permit negotiated without their respective participation are then given by

$$C_I < p_I S^B \tag{5.15}$$

for the investor and

$$C_E < \frac{p_E}{1-p_E} D^B \tag{5.16}$$

for the environmental group. Should the usual US allocation rule also apply to environmental groups, (5.16) would transform into

$$C_E < p_E D^B. \tag{5.16a}$$

Comparing (5.13) with (5.15) and (5.14) with (5.16a) shows that the effect of changing the allocation rule from the British to the US one on private parties' incentive to sue is ambiguous. However, introducing asymmetric reimbursement improves the environmental group's incentive both with respect to the British and to the usual US rule. In this sense, US

---

[18]Asymmetric reimbursement is also studied by Baik and Shogren (1994). They use a contest model to show that asymmetric reimbursement increases the equilibrium probability of prevailing for the environmental group, whereas rent dissipation is lower.

[19]Baik and Shogren (1994, 1) note that, while the reimbursement rule could include court costs as well as the cost for discovery, investigation and support staff, only attorney's fees are usually repaid.

environmental groups are more privileged than their German counterparts, which yields an additional explanation for their more important role within environmental negotiations.

5.9 INFORMAL AGREEMENTS AND SYMMETRICAL STANDING

This section will reconsider self-enforcing informal agreements between agencies and investors. It will explore the incentive of environmental organizations to sue permits issued under such informal arrangements and, hence, the stability of these agreements under symmetrical standing. It will analyze the two settings presented in Section 4.5, where

- The agency issues a permit over the negotiated spending level S^{Ba}, or
- The agency issues a permit over S^*, but agrees to tolerate a lower spending level S^{Ba}.

The analysis will only consider negotiations within the licensing of a new project. Thus, the subscript n will be omitted.

5.9.1 Negotiated Permits

Consider first the case where S^{Ba} is stipulated in the permit issued by the agency. The investor did not waive its right to sue: as long as the legal deadline for filing suit has not expired, the investor is free to take action against the negotiated permit. When the environmental group does not have standing, the permit is enforced by repeated interaction of the agency and the investor. Assume that the legal deadlines for taking action are identical for both investors and environmental groups.

Consequently, the environmental group does not have an incentive to fight any permit negotiated without its participation because its expected payoff from suing is no longer given by (5.1). The group will sue, if

$$-D(S^{Ba}) < -(p_I D_0 + p_A D(S^{Ba})) , \qquad (5.17)$$

When the environmental organization takes action against the permit, the investor will defend its stake in court as well, whereas the agency will defend the permit over S^{Ba}.

Consider now the investor's incentive to sue a non-negotiated permit over S^*. When the investor goes to court, the environmental organization will also present its case, that is, will also sue the permit over S^*, because

$$-[p_I D_0 + (1 - p_I)D(S^*)] < -[p_I D_0 + p_A D(S^*)]$$

for $p_E > 0$. Consequently, the expected profit from trial is no longer given by (4.1), but by (5.5). The investor will sue, when

$$\Pi^* < p_I \Pi_0 + p_A \Pi^*, \tag{5.18}$$

Depending on whether conditions (5.17) and (5.18) hold or not, different constellations result. The following proposition summarizes.

Proposition 5.2. Consider the impact of associational standing on the stability and outcome of an informal agreement between the investor and the agency.

(i)   When both conditions (5.17) and (5.18) do not hold, the agency can issue an efficient permit over S^*.

(ii)   When (5.17) holds and (5.18) does not, an efficient outcome will be implemented under private bargaining.

(iii) When (5.17) does not hold and (5.18) does, bargaining between the agency and the investor results.
  - When $\Pi^{ca} > \Pi^{Na}$, , associational standing increases welfare.
  - When $\Pi^{ca} \leq \Pi^{Na}$ and $W^{ca} \leq \Pi^{Na}$, , associational standing has no impact.
  - When $W^{ca} > \Pi^{Na}$, associational standing decreases welfare.

Proof. Note that, when (5.17) holds, it does so for a spending level S^*. When (5.16) holds, it does so for any spending level.
(i) and (ii): This corresponds to part (ii) of lemma 5.1.
(iii): The group would not sue a negotiated permit issued without its participation, whereas the investor would sue any non-negotiated permit. Consequently, the group does not have bargaining power. Bargaining between the investor and the agency results. When one of those parties quits bargaining and thus triggers a trial, the group would also plead in court. Both parties' expected values from trial are reduced. Welfare implications immediately result from lemma 4.1, parts (iii) and (i). ∎

This analysis makes clear that the impact of introducing standing for environmental groups is twofold:

- its reduces the parties' outside option values in negotiations between the investor and the agency,
- it may provide an incentive to the environmental organization to sue against any permit negotiated without its participation, which induces the organization to enter environmental negotiations as an active bargaining party.

When the investor does not waive its right to sue in the case of an informal agreement with the agency, only the former impact channel may exist. Then, the impact on welfare is ambiguous. As the introduction of standing may reduce the expected welfare from trial, it will induce a lower negotiated spending level when the agency's threat to opt out is credible in bargaining with the investor.

This ambiguity may be avoided by granting longer legal deadlines for action to persons affected by environmental externalities and their representatives. Then, the environmental organization can file suit at a point in time in which the investor is already committed to the negotiated permit, and condition (5.1) applies again: the group has an incentive to contest every permit negotiated without its participation, and will always enter the negotiations.

5.9.2 Toleration and Citizen Suits

Consider now the case in which the spending level S^{Ba} negotiated between the agency and the investor is implemented by on account of toleration; that is, while issuing a permit over S^*, the agency tolerates the lower spending level S^{Ba}. Consider the situation in which the agency and the investor are not yet legally committed. When the environmental group decides to fight, it will plead against the optimal permit S^*. It will have an incentive to do so, when

$$- D(S^{Ba}) < -[p_I D_0 + p_A D(S^*)].$$

When compared to the constellation where the informal agreement between the agency and the investor is stipulated in the permit, the group's incentive to sue is higher, because

$$-[p_I D_0 + p_A D(S^*)] > -[p_I D_0 + p_A D(S^{Ba})]$$

for any $S^{Ba} < S^*$. In this sense, informal agreements between investors and agencies implemented on account of toleration react more sensitively to the introduction of associational standing. Proposition 5.2 applies accordingly.

However, the environmental group has an additional opportunity for legal action under the citizen suit provisions of most US environmental laws. For instance, the US Clean Air Act (CAA) not only entitles 'any person' to take action against administrators for violations of 'nondiscretionary duties', but also against 'any person' alleged to be in violation of an 'emission standard or limitation' (Rodgers (1994, 154, 177)). The environmental group may directly sue the investor for violating the permit requirements.

Consider the situation in which the environmental organization is legally entitled to sue the investor for violation of the official permit over S^*. Assume that enough time has elapsed under the toleration, so that the operator has lost his standing against the formal permit due to the statutory deadline.[20] Thus, all the operator can do is to defend S^{Ba}. The environmental organization, in this case, cannot plead for a rejection of the project, but merely for enforcement of the permit S^*. The repercussions of citizen suit provisions on the informal agreement are straightforward.

Corollary 5.1. When environmental organizations are entitled to act as private attorneys-general (citizen suits), informal agreements between investors and the agencies cannot be implemented via toleration.

Proof. Given commitment by the agency, the environmental group has an incentive to sue, as, for any $p_E > 0$,

$$-[p_E D^* + (p_A + p_I)D(S^{Ba})] > -D(S^{Ba})$$

When the agency is not committed to S^{Ba}; it will also plead for S^*, when the environmental group takes action. Again, the group has an incentive to sue, because, for any $p_E > 0$,

---

[20] 'If a standard is overly stringent, the regulated entity has the right to appeal the permit. But once the permit is final, the regulated party may not challenge the underlying standard in a defense to an enforcement action.' (Babich 1996, 10147).

$$-[(p_E + p_A)D^* + p_I D(S^{Ba})] > -D(S^{Ba}). \quad \blacksquare$$

This proposition has to be qualified when taking into consideration that, in reality, the monitoring of agencies' regulatory activities and of firms' compliance therewith will be costly for environmental organizations. This means that they have to concentrate on the most significant environmental damages. Thus, arrangements between industry and agencies may not be contested by environmental groups, even when such groups would have an incentive to do so under absence of monitoring costs.

Chapter 2 described how environmental organizations were able to effectively sue against violations of the permit program belonging to the National Pollutant Discharge Elimination System (NPDES) because of the citizen suit provision in the Clean Water Act (CWA). In the eighties, a sharp increase in citizen suits under CWA was observed. Corresponding to a study of the Environmental Law Institute, known notices and suits were less than 20 per year prior to 1983, whereas 108 suits were filed in 1983, and 87 in the first quarter of 1984 (ELI 1984). In such enforcement cases, the probability of winning is high.[21]

It is often argued that this increase in citizen suits can be explained primarily by the decline in the federal EPA's enforcement activity during this period, due to sharp budget cuts under the first years of the Reagan administration (Naysnerski and Tietenberg 1992, Mashaw et al. 1992, 1030–32). The intent here is not to contest this argument. However, the present analysis offers a slightly different explanation: the citizen suit provisions gave an opportunity for environmental groups to fight tacit agreements *ex post* between the agency and operators that were implemented on account of toleration, which arose because of an uncertain legal setting.

When the violation is not caused by high enforcement costs, but by an agency tolerating the violation in order to implement an informal agreement with the operator, additional reactions by these parties should be expected. They could either choose another self-enforcement mechanism for their informal agreement, or, when the environmental group has an incentive to sue even under the other mechanism, they may accept the environmental organization as a bargaining partner. When the latter occurs, citizen suits,

---

[21]See Naysnerski and Tietenberg (1992), who found 503 court victories out of 507 considered cases.

beyond assuring the private enforcement of permits issued by regulating agencies, will also have a substantial impact on the stipulated regulation.

5.10 EXTORTION IN PRIVATE BARGAINING

Strategic choices at the pre-bargaining stage may enable a party to extort its adversary, that is, to extract additional rents within private negotiations. The strategic advantage of a specific choice may lead to a Pareto-inferior allocation.[22] This paragraph will re-examine the setting considered by Althammer (1995), Buchholz and Haslbeck (1997) and Richter and Stranlund (1997), in which a project operator can commit credibly to a specific production technology. This section will show that the investor's extortion possibilities and incentives will depend crucially on the bargaining constellation, that is, whether bargaining occurs when licensing a planned project or when regulating an existing facility.[23]

To undertake the comparison, characterize first the solution of private negotiations over the existing project. For reasons that are now familiar, the axiomatic characterization can be derived by shifting the status-quo payoffs from $(0, 0)$ to $(\Pi_0, -D_0)$, and applying the outside option principle.

Lemma 5.2. For a common discount factor δ^Λ and $\Lambda \to 0$, the unique solution of the bargaining game between the investor and the environmental group, when negotiating the regulation of an existing facility, is characterized as follows.

(i)   Bargaining incentives exist for p_I, p_A, $p_E > 0$.

(ii) The unique solution of the bargaining game is given by

$$(\Pi_e^{Bs}, Q_e^{Bs}) = (\Pi^*, -D^*), \text{ if } \Pi^{cs} \leq \Pi^* \text{ and } -D^{cs} \leq -D^*,$$

$$(\Pi_e^{Bs}, Q_e^{Bs}) = (\varphi_s^{-1}(-D^{cs}), -D^{cs}) \text{ else, where}$$

[22] Under the heading of extortion, this insight was first offered by Mumey (1971) and subsequently discussed in the *American Economic Review* (Jaffe 1975; Daly and Giertz 1975 and the comments from Bromley 1978; Demsetz 1978 and Daly and Giertz 1978).

[23] Buchholz and Haslbeck (1997), by exogenously allocating all bargaining power to one party, do not clearly characterize which status quo they assume. Althammer (1995) and Richter and Stranlund (1997) assume that operators commit by sunk investments and, hence, that the facility is under operation at the moment at which bargaining takes place.

$$\varphi_s^{-1}(-D^{cs}) = \begin{cases} \Pi_0 - S(D^{cs}) & \text{for } -D^{cs} < -D^*, \\ \Pi_0 - S(D^*) - C^{Bs} & \text{for } -D^{cs} \geq -D^*. \end{cases}$$

Proof. See the appendix. ∎

Again, the reasoning transpires from Figure 5.1. Part (ii) of lemma 5.2 is simpler, because the environmental group cannot pay compensation. Consequently, the group's threat to opt out will always be credible. In this case, it is the investor who profits from dragging out the negotiations and, consequently, reaps all gains from trade. When $-D^{cs} \geq -D^*$, the solution involves payment of compensation to the environmental group; however, it is the investor who reaps the efficiency gains from compensation.

Consider now the following setting borrowed from Buchholz and Haslbeck (1997). Assume the operator of a divisible project has two different production technologies at hand. Technology one, without additional avoidance activities, generates profit Π_0^1 and environmental damage D_0^l. Technology two yields a lower profit Π_0^2, which, however, is compatible with differing environmental damages $D_0 \in [D_0^l, D_0^h]$. The idea is that the same maximal profit may result under different output levels[24] which, in turn, imply different environmental damages. Denote the expected profit from trial by Π^{c1} and Π^{c2} under the respective technology; clearly, $\Pi^{c2} < \Pi^{c1}$.[25] Also, when the investor threatens to choose an output level leading to the environmental damage D_0^h, $D^{c2} > D^{c1}$.

For the following analysis, assume that, once a party opts out, at least one party has an incentive to sue the non-negotiated permit issued by the agency. Furthermore, assume that the commitment to use a specific technology is possible without cost. The following reasoning is depicted by Figure 5.2. To facilitate the presentation, it is assumed in the figure that $p_A = 0$.

Proposition 5.3. The investor's incentives to extort by technology choice are given by the underlying bargaining constellation.

---

[24]Such a result can be derived by assuming a cost function having a linear segment on profit-maximizing output levels.

[25]Note that $\Pi^{c1} < \Pi^{c1}$ even when assuming that the court will *not* dislike extortion attempts, meaning that it would rule against facility owners undertaking such attempts with higher probability.

(i) In bargaining over the license for a new project, the investor will never commit, during the a pre-bargaining stage, to a welfare-inferior technology.

(ii) In bargaining over the regulation of existing facilities, the facility owner may have an incentive to commit, during the pre-bargaining stage, to a welfare-inferior technology.

Proof.

(i) *The New Project.* Consider an investor who is committed to technology two (it will be discussed in a moment whether it is rational to do so). Its threat to plead, once in court, for an output level leading to a higher environmental damage D_0^h will clearly be credible (its profit is not reduced by such a threat). Note that a welfare-maximizing agency would plead for welfare-superior technology number one.

The investor's expected profit from trial does not depend on this pleading choice. Assume its threat to opt out is credible during negotiations. Trial would be triggered when the investor opts out. To settle, the environmental group still has to offer a negotiated solution yielding the same payoff Π^{c2} to the investor (possibly, the environmental group will pay an additional ε, ε being the smallest monetary unit). The investor will accept this offer because it cannot get more by opting out. Under such a bargaining outcome, however, a commitment to technology two is not rational, because $\Pi^{c1} > \Pi^{c2}$.

When the investor's threat to opt out is not credible, the parties would agree on the Nash solution and split the (private) surplus from executing the project under efficient regulation. As technology number two yields a lower surplus, it would not pay to commit to technology number two. The result is that the investor will never commit to technology two.

(ii) *The existing project.* Consider again the facility owner committed to technology two. The owner's threat to plead, once in court, in a way that leads to the higher environmental damage D_0^h is still credible. By pleading in such a way, it can strategically lower the environmental group's expected value of trial from $-D^{c1}$ to $-D^{c2}$. As shown by lemma 4.4, the group's threat to opt out will always be credible in the negotiations, and the owner has to make an offer guaranteeing the value of the outside option to the group. Hence, by strategically lowering the group's expected value of trial, the owner can push through a lower spending level.

Consider now the facility owner's decision whether to commit to technology two when investing in technology. Under technology one, the investor can only plead in a way such that D_0^l would result. The investor chooses technology two, if

$$\varphi_1^{-1}(D^{c1}) < \varphi_2^{-1}(D^{c2}),$$

where the left-hand side gives the investor's payoff in a bargained agreement under technology one and the right-hand side gives the investor's negotiated payoff under technology two, when credibly threatening with an output level leading to D_0^h. In Figure 5.2, $\Pi_e^{B1} = \varphi_1^{-1}(D^{c1})$ and $\Pi_e^{B1} = \varphi_2^{-1}(D^{c2})$. When technology two is chosen, a welfare-inferior situation results from bargaining: the same profit could be realized under technology one with lower environmental damage. ■

It may be objected that a regulating agency would reject installation of (welfare-inferior) technology two in the first place. Also, why should an environmental group not intervene when the operator makes the technology choice? At the moment the technology choice is made, one has again the bargaining constellation of a planned project, in which, as was shown before, extortion will not result.[26] Thus, the analysis applies when environmental regulation is absent (and environmental groups do not exist or are powerless) at the moment at which the operator chooses the technology. Hence, the analysis may be especially relevant for the early phase of environmental policy, in which wide areas were not yet or only poorly covered by environmental legislation and the corresponding regulatory institutions.

Schlicht (1996, 327) draws attention to a somewhat different extortion problem. Arguing in a Coasean context, he points to the extortion problem potentially arising after a sunk investment, whereby the neighboring community (owning a secure property right) 'may be tempted to exploit the specific investment made by the entrepreneur'. A similar problem may appear to arise in the present context of insecure property rights and standing for environmental organisations. In principle, a bargained agreement between

---

[26]This is a variant of Jaffe's 1975 critique, who argues that rational parties will have an incentive to extend the bargaining agenda to the technology choice.

the investor and an environmental group may not hinder other groups from showing up 'later' and raising additional claims.

The shortcoming of such an objection, however, is that it neglects the institutional setting in which real-world bargaining occurs:

- First, the group's threat relies on a possible suit against the administrative licensing action, and not directly against the activity of the investor. Hence, once a (bargained) permit is issued, deadlines for filing legal objections are short. Arguably, they are much shorter than construction

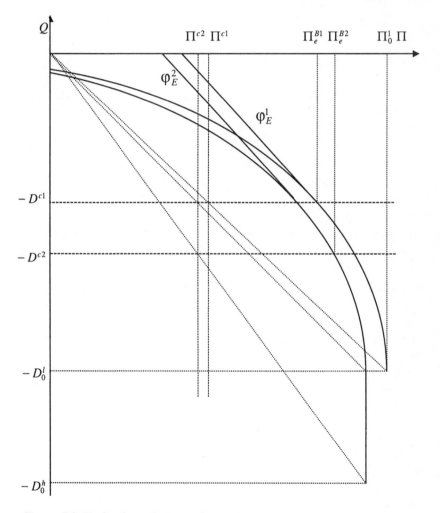

Figure 5.2 Technology choice and extortion

periods. Once the deadline has elapsed, the license, with respect to the permissible level of environmental damage, corresponds to a secure property right for the investor.

- Second, German procedures demand that, in order to obtain standing, parties must raise objections during the early stages of the permitting process. Such a procedural rule would be fruitful in the present context, because it also prevents parties showing up with new claims only after investments have been already made.

5.11 NEGOTIATED RULEMAKING: SOME DIFFERENCES

This section will discuss some crucial differences between environmental bargaining at the project level and negotiated rulemaking. First, remember from Chapter 2 that agency discretion in rulemaking is more difficult to defend in the first place: under complex environmental problems, even the elaboration of highly differentiated, detailed rules may not preclude case-to-case regulation and subsequent negotiations.[27] When, however, the underlying environmental problem is not complex, the introduction of standard economic instruments is possible and efficient. For instance, in order to regulate ubiquitous pollution problems, it is possible to introduce taxes on key pollutants by law. There is no necessity for regulatory discretion in implementation, either at the plant-specific, or at the rulemaking level.

Furthermore, the issuance of ever more specific rules, by overcharging agencies' capacities within licensing procedures, may even lead to higher discretion exerted at the project level. Due to restrictions in time and staff, agencies will then not be able to ensure that a specific project is in complete compliance, by issuing the subsequent set of additional requirements in a permit. In order to decide within a reasonable time period, these constraints will force agencies to ignore some rules or, at least, to be lenient in applying them. From a specific level of rule density, additional rules will not reduce agencies' *de facto* discretionary behavior, but only raise the contestability of agency permits.[28]

Notwithstanding these reservations, US agencies often have to define a set of regulatory rules in a situation in which those supposed to be regulated and

---

[27]Consequently, the US EPA is ready, under project XL, to circumvent its own rules to find more tailored, site-specific, and hence more efficient regulation.
[28]See also Caldart and Ashford (1999, 143–80) for a critique based on an extensive analysis of negotiated rulemaking cases.

other parties can fight the planned regulation. The possibly bargaining incentives that may emerge differ in several crucial aspects from environmental negotiations over the regulation of a single facility:

- In rulemaking negotiations, it is not only externality victims who are represented by a collective actor. Usually, industry's interests are defended by branch-specific associations. Then, additional compensation payments from industry as part of a negotiated agreement are improbable. To agree on compensation payments is beyond the competence of industry federations. Internal cost allocation of an industry-wide compensation scheme would be extremely difficult under heterogeneous firms and unenforceable when association membership is facultative.
- As rules usually address whole industries, they will affect market prices via the firms' output decisions. This will influence the incentives of industry representatives to contest the regulation, which, in turn, will shape possible incentives to negotiate in the first place.

The following analysis will address these issues in a setting in which the agency has to define a firm-specific standard for a specific industry. Firms are assumed to be identical; therefore, inefficiencies arising from the application of uniform standards to heterogeneous firms are not addressed.[29]

The analysis will show that the agency may be able to implement an efficient level of per-firm standards even when industry representatives have very similar opportunities to issue threats as in the analysis presented so far. The argument relies on the observation that the introduction of environmental standards may induce implicit cartelization of the regulated industry, with ambiguous impacts on firms' profits (Buchanan and Tullock 1975).

When this case holds, the involvement of environmental groups is not necessary to improve efficiency. On the contrary, as compensation payments from whole industries are not possible, additional involvement of environmental groups, via legal power, may lead to inefficiencies.[30] This contrasts with the situation at the project level.

Let m be the number of identical firms in a competitive industry emitting pollutants E_0 when regulation is absent. It is only this industry which emits E. The emissions of a firm are e; thus,

---

[29]See Section 4.4.5.

[30]Spulber (1989, 351–5) presents a model of private bargaining over industry-wide regulation, where property rights are certain, and also derives an inefficient result because compensation is not possible.

$$E_0 = \sum_{}^{m} e_0 .$$

Assume entry to be restricted:[31] $m = \overline{m}$. Industry output is $X = \overline{m}x$, and market demand $X = X(q)$, which is downward-sloping and linear. Denote inverse demand by $q = q(X)$ and a firm's strictly convex production costs by $c(x)$. Market price without environmental regulation is $q_0 = q(\overline{m}x_0)$, where x_0 solves $q_0 = c'(x_0)$. Without regulation, the profit of a firm is $\pi_0 = q_0 x_0 - c(x_0) > 0$. Denote industry's profit and costs of producing X by, respectively,

$$\Pi_0 = \sum_{}^{m} \pi_0 , \ C(X) = \overline{m}c\left(\frac{X}{\overline{m}}\right).$$

Clearly, industry profit is given by

$$\Pi(x, \overline{m}) = X \, q(X) - C(X) .$$

and environmental damage by $D_0 = D(E_0)$. The agency's objective is to maximize welfare

$$W(E, X) = \int_0^X q(X)dX - C(X) - D(E) ,$$

and W_0 is the welfare level under X_0, E_0 . Let $\varphi(\Pi)$ be the maximal welfare level for a given industry profit Π associated with a specific stringency of the standard. Under homogenous firms and restricted entry, the efficient welfare level is denoted by W^* . The corresponding industry's profit is Π^* ; assume $\Pi^* > 0$.[32]

Emissions are a byproduct of x , under a simple linear relationship $e = \beta x$, and, for notational convenience, $\beta = 1$. Assume for the moment that

---

[31]The analysis can be reformulated for the case of free entry, when assuming that the industry representative will contest any regulation inducing firm exit. It seems reasonable to assume that the industry federation represents the collective interests of actual, but to a far lesser extent of potential firms of a specific branch. See also footnote 34.

[32]For $\Pi^* < 0$, exit occurs under regulation, and the representative will contest the regulation.

technological measures to avoid emissions per output unit do not exist or are prohibitively costly. Then, regulation of the industry necessarily means a reduction in industry output.

Denote the per firm emission quota prescribed by the agency by $\bar{e}$ and the corresponding industry standard by $\bar{E} = \overline{me}$. When emissions reduction is possible only through a reduction of output, this amounts to the introduction of an upper limit on production per firm $\bar{x} = \bar{e}$ and, hence, on total output: $\bar{X} = \overline{mx}$. Then, the introduction of quota invokes an implicit cartelization of the industry, and the impact on industry's and, hence, firms' profits is ambiguous:

$$\frac{d\Pi(\bar{X})}{d\bar{X}} = q(\bar{X})(1 + \tfrac{1}{\eta}) - C'(\bar{X}) \lessgtr 0,$$

where η is the price elasticity of demand. Define

$$\bar{X}^M = \arg\max_{\bar{X}} \Pi(\bar{X});$$

this is the monopoly output. Denote the corresponding maximal profit level by $\Pi^M > \Pi_0$; under linear demand, the maximum is unique. Denote the welfare-maximizing output level by $\bar{X}^*$; thus, $\bar{X}^* = E^*$ solves $q(\bar{X}) = C'(\bar{X}) + D'(\bar{X})$. The efficient per firm emission standard is then

$$\bar{e}^* = \frac{\bar{X}^*}{m}.$$

Representatives of industry interest can contest the regulation through a legal or political intervention that is without costs. Again, the introduction of intervention costs is straightforward. Allow for two interpretations:

- According to the court model presented in this chapter, they may reach rejection of the regulation with a specific probability.
- By the intervention, they may not be able to effectively prevent, but only delay ultimate realization of the regulation over (W^*, Π^*). This corresponds to the analysis presented in Section 4.4.6.[33]

---

[33]Unlike in 4.4.6, a delay in regulation is not a potential bargaining outcome here, but the result of the legal intervention.

Denote the intervention's value for the industry by Π^c and the corresponding welfare by W^c. Under both interpretations, (W^c, Π^c) is a convex combination of (W^*, Π^*) and (W_0, Π_0). The subsequent analysis boils down to deriving $\varphi(\Pi)$ and comparing Π^c with Π^*. If $\Pi^c > \Pi^*$, the industry has an incentive to contest non-negotiated regulation analogously to the analysis presented in 4.3. Then, (W^c, Π^c) are the parties' outside options in a strategic bargaining game between the industry and the agency. If, however, $\Pi^c \leq \Pi^*$,, the agency will be able to implement an efficient level of standards with non-negotiated regulation.

Note that $\Pi^c > \Pi^*$ implies $\Pi_0 > \Pi^*$ and conversely. The industry representative's incentive to contest the intended regulation hinges on whether industry's profit under efficient regulation is higher or lower than without regulation. This, in turn, may be characterized partly by whether the output level maximizing industry's profit is above or below the output level under the efficient quota. Specifically, consider the following cases:

- $\overline{X}^M \leq \overline{X}^*$. Then, $\Pi^* > \Pi_0$ holds unambiguously. It follows that the industry representative has no incentive to fight efficient regulation. The agency is able to implement efficient per firm emission standards $\overline{e}^*$ even when a political or legal intervention is without cost.
- $\overline{X}^M > \overline{X}^*$. Then, $\Pi^* \gtrless \Pi_0$. The above case may still hold. However, when, $\Pi^* < \Pi_0$, the industry representative has an incentive to contest efficient regulation. Subsequent bargaining will lead to inefficiently low emission standards.

Thus, efficient[34] environmental regulation can be implemented even under constraints stemming from the legal or political system. This is because emissions quotas, unlike taxes, do not extract the rents arising from a reduction in output below the competitive level. It is well-known that this difference may induce industry to dislike taxes (Buchanan and Tullock 1975; Baumol and Oates 1988, 178). When higher industry profit results from cartelization under efficient environmental regulation, the industry representative will not contest the regulation.

---

[34]The result will also hold under free entry with respect to the mere environmental side of regulation, when the industry representative only contests regulation which does induce exit. However, the market structure will be inefficient under regulation by quota: too many firms will produce too little output (Buchanan and Tullock 1975; for a formal analysis: Spulber 1985 and 1989, 363).

As a consequence, the empowerment of environmental groups has a more ambiguous impact. In the case in which the industry will protest the regulation, it may have positive consequences, according to the analysis presented so far. However, as compensation payments from industry are not possible, overregulation may also result. In the case in which the industry will not fight the regulation in the first place, the empowerment of environmental interests will never improve efficiency, but may reduce it in the case in which the environmental group, *via* negotiations, can put through inefficient severe regulation.[35]

A similar result holds under the existence of technical abatement opportunities, unless such technical measures only raise fixed production costs. The following framework is borrowed from Spulber (1989, chap. 13.1). Consider a representative firm producing X under competition. Define the general cost function $C(X(q), E)$, where

$$\frac{\partial C}{\partial X} > 0, \ \frac{\partial^2 C}{\partial X^2} > 0, \ \frac{\partial C}{\partial \overline{E}} < 0 \ \text{and} \ \frac{\partial^2 C}{\partial X \partial \overline{E}} < 0.$$

Higher prescribed effluent levels, that is, more lenient environmental standards, decrease marginal production costs. Denote the market price resulting from the introduction of a given emission standard by $q(\overline{E})$. Under competition, $q(\overline{E})$ solves

$$q = \frac{\partial C(X(q), \overline{E})}{\partial X}$$

for any given $\overline{E}$. Then, the market price is reduced if the firm is permitted to discharge a higher amount of effluents, as

$$\frac{dq(\overline{E})}{d\overline{E}} = \frac{\dfrac{\partial^2 C}{\partial X \partial E}}{1 - \dfrac{\partial^2 C}{\partial X^2} \dfrac{dX}{dq}} < 0.$$

---

[35]The results casts some doubts on Rose-Ackerman's (1995) urge for a strengthening of third-party review within German rulemaking. Her comparison of German and US policy implementation does not consider emerging bargaining incentives. While she expresses clear reservations against US negotiated rulemaking (Rose-Ackerman 1994), she does not investigate how a specific system of judicial review shapes bargaining incentives and the subsequent regulatory outcomes.

Denote the representative firm's profit by

$$\Pi(\overline{E}) = q(\overline{E})X - C(X,\overline{E}),$$

and

$$\frac{d\Pi}{d\overline{E}} = X\frac{dq}{d\overline{E}} - \frac{\partial C}{\partial \overline{E}} \gtrless 0 .$$

Firm's profits are increasing/decreasing in higher emissions standards, that is, lower prescribed effluent levels, when the positive effect on revenues is greater/lower than the higher costs (Spulber 1989, 353).

5.12 SUMMARY

This chapter presented an analysis of bargaining under symmetrical standing and complete information. The most important policy results can be summarized as follows.

- Legal standing may allow the environmental group to enter the game as a bargaining party. The subsequent possibility of bargaining between the private parties over the project permit leads to an efficiency improvement or to an efficient solution, when compared to the situation in which the group does not have standing.
- Besides standing, asymmetrical reimbursement rules also privilege US environmental groups in comparison with their German counterparts.
- Even when granted standing, the environmental group may not enter the bargaining game when the agreement between the investor and the agency is only informally stated. The spending level agreed between the investor and the agency is possibly lower than under asymmetrical standing. This situation can be avoided by granting the investor a shorter legal deadline within which to take action against the permit conditions.
- The option of directly suing the investor for permit violations (as under the citizen suit provisions) prevents the implementation of informal agreements between investors and agencies by a toleration of permit violations.

- Positive effects stemming from associational standing do not carry over unambiguously to regulatory negotiations. First, compensation payments are usually not possible at this level. Second, because of implicit cartelization by regulation under standards, industry and environmental interests are not necessarily opposed in the first place. Hence, a balancing of legal power via associational standing may not be necessary in order to improve the bargaining outcome.

While not arguing from a welfare viewpoint, the general thrust of the analysis presented here is nicely put by Rodgers:

> [W]hen the game [between the operator and the agency] is played over time under the constraints of reciprocity, short-run pound-of-flesh strategies are abandoned in favor of more 'cooperative' strategies featuring compliance most of the time and enforcement only occasionally. Those outcomes that evolve to the advantage of the principals may coincide only approximately or not at all with formal legal obligations. A wayward citizen group introduced into this game would be likely to identify a 'best' strategy that would depart from the position taken by other players. Citizen organizations, too, may become cooperative players rather than isolated iconoclasts .... [T]he national environmental organizations like the Natural Resources Defense Council, the Environmental Defense Fund and the Sierra Club may be in pursuit of a comprehensive bargain that requires a strategy greatly different from the peripheral sniping that is the best course for an outsider who has no hope of cracking the inner circles. (Rodgers 1992, 211).

As theoretical results, the analysis demonstrated that

- Well-defined property rights are neither a prerequisite for the existence nor for the efficiency of a bargained solution between private parties, as some interpretations of the Coasean analysis suggest. The chapter presented a theory of private bargaining under uncertain rights, where the Coasean case of secure-rights bargaining emerges as a benchmark case.
- In a finite-offer bargaining game, a delayed agreement will generally not result, even when the environmental group has an incentive to settle as late, and the investor has an incentive to settle as early as possible. Spier's (1992) result only holds for zero-sum disputes.
- Investor's opportunities to extort additional transfers by strategically committing, at a pre-bargaining stage, to a specific technology crucially depend on the bargaining constellation. Incentives to commit will not arise within negotiations over the permit conditions for a planned project. They

may arise, however, when bargaining over the regulation of existing facilities.

A more complete discussion of the policy conclusions and of possible objections will be relegated to the concluding Chapter 7. For now, one may wonder whether the enumerated results, and particularly the conclusion that associational standing increases the welfare of the bargaining outcome, crucially hinge on the assumption of complete information. It is a shortcoming of bargaining models of complete information that negotiations are always successful in the equilibrium, when bargaining incentives exist *ex ante*. When parties are privately informed about relevant variables, they may have an incentive to strategically misrepresent their information, which may, in equilibrium, impair efficient bargaining. Specifically, the environmental group may be privately informed about the environmental damage resulting from execution of the project. During negotiations, it may then have an incentive to overstate the damage amount, to extract a higher settlement, that is, a higher spending level or a higher amount of compensation. Conversely, in the case of a planned project, the investor may be privately informed about the level of expected profit, which, in turn, may be decisive for its readiness to pay compensation. These issues of bargaining under private information will be considered in the next chapter.

5.13 APPENDIX

Proof of lemma 5.1

The bargaining game when outside options are not credible threats. Consider Figure 5A.1. Applying Shaked and Sutton's (1984) method yields as a condition for a subgame-perfect equilibrium

$$Q^+ = \varphi_E(\delta\varphi_E^{-1}(\delta Q^+))$$

or, equivalently

$$\varphi_E^{-1}(Q^+) = \delta\varphi_E^{-1}(\delta Q^+) \tag{5A.1}$$

As $\varphi_E(.)$ is decreasing in negotiated profit, $\varphi_E^{-1}(.)$ is decreasing in the environmental group's payoff. Assume $Q^+ < 0$. Then, $Q^+ < \delta Q^+$, and $\varphi_E^{-1}(Q^+) > \varphi_E^{-1}(\delta Q^+)$, implying that (5A.1) cannot hold for positive profit levels. Therefore, any bargaining solution of the game without outside options must yield a positive payoff for the environmental group, and, thus implies that $Q^+ > -D^* + C_{min} = 0$, or $\Pi^+ < \Pi_{min}$. In the bargaining solution, the investor at least spends S^* and totally compensates for the damage D^*. Denote the investor's compensation payment exceeding C_{min} by C^+; thus, $Q^+ = C^+$ and. The game simply consists of how to split the 'pie' Π_{min}:

$$\varphi_E^{-1}(Q^+) = \Pi_{min} - Q^+ \qquad (5A.2)$$

period	offer made by	env. group receives at most/at least	Investor receives at least/at most
$t = T - 2$	env. group	$\varphi(\delta\varphi^{-1}(\delta Q^{sup/inf}))$	$\delta\varphi^{-1}(\delta Q^{sup/inf})$
		$\varphi(\delta\varphi^{-1}(-D^{out}))$	$\delta\varphi^{-1}(-D^{out})$
		$\varphi(\Pi^{out})$	Π^{out}
$t = T - 1$	investor	$\delta Q^{sup/inf}$	$\varphi^{-1}(\delta Q^{sup/inf})$
		$-D^{out}$	$\varphi^{-1}(-D^{out})$
$t = T$	env. group	$Q^{sup/inf}$	

Figure 5A.1   Subgame payoffs and discounting: bargaining within licensing and symmetrical standing

Substituting (5A.2) into (5A.1) yields the usual solution for such a splitting-the-pie problem:

$$\Pi_{min} - Q^+ = \delta(\Pi_{min} - \delta Q^+) \quad \Leftrightarrow$$

$$Q^+ = \frac{1}{1+\delta}\Pi_{min}, \text{ and } \quad \Pi^+ = \frac{\delta}{1+\delta}\Pi_{min}.$$

For a discount factor δ^Λ and $\Lambda = 1$, the environmental organization has a first-mover advantage. This advantage disappears for $\Lambda \to 0$:

$$\lim_{\Lambda \to 0}\left(\frac{1}{1+\delta^\Lambda}\Pi_{min}\right) = 0.5\,\Pi_{min}, \text{ and } \lim_{\Lambda \to 0}\left(\frac{\delta^\Lambda}{1+\delta^\Lambda}\Pi_{min}\right) = 0.5\,\Pi_{min}.$$

These expressions correspond to the (symmetrical) Nash solution of a splitting-the-pie bargaining problem.

Credible threats to opt out. According to (5.8), the values of the parties' outside options are given by

$$(\Pi^{out}, -D^{out}) = \begin{cases} (\Pi^*, -D^*) & \text{iff } \Pi^{cs} \leq \Pi^* \text{ and } -D^{cs} \leq -D^*, \\ (\Pi^{cs}, -D^{cs}) & \text{else.} \end{cases}$$

The value of the group's outside option is negative in any case, whereas the outcome from the unconstrained bargaining is positive. Thus, the group's threat to opt out will never be credible.

The investor's threat will be credible, when $\delta\varphi_E^{-1}(\delta Q^+) = \Pi^+ < \Pi^{out}$. Inspection of table A.2 and (5.8) gives the bargaining solution of lemma 5.1.

Per.	Offer made by	env. group gets at most/at least	Investor gets at least/at most
$T-2$	investor	$\varphi^{-1}(\delta\varphi(\delta\Pi^{\text{sup/inf}} + \pi_0) - d_0)$ $\varphi^{-1}(\delta\varphi(\Pi^{out}) - d_0)$ $\varphi^{-1}(-D^{out})$	$\delta\varphi(\delta\Pi^{\text{sup/inf}} + \pi_0) - d_0$ $\delta\varphi(\Pi^{out}) - d_0$ $-D^{out}$
$T-1$	env. group	$\delta\Pi^{\text{sup/inf}} + \pi_0$ Π^{out}	$\varphi(\delta\Pi^{\text{sup/inf}} + \pi_0)$ $\varphi(\Pi^{out})$
T	investor	$\Pi^{\text{sup/inf}}$	

Figure 5A.2   Subgame payoffs and discounting: clean-up bargaining and symmetrical standing

Existence. Denote the set of possible bargaining solutions by Φ (the area on and below φ). The existence of outside options restricts this set, by defining a subset of Φ for which $\Pi^n \geq \Pi^{out}$ and $Q^n \geq -D^{out}$. Thus, the condition for (possibly degenerate) bargaining incentives to exist under outside options is $(\Pi^{out}, -D^{out}) \in \Phi$. This is clearly fulfilled for $(\Pi^{out}, -D^{out}) = (\Pi^*, -D^*)$. Thus, it has to be investigated whether $(\Pi^c, -D^c) \in \Phi$.

Consider the benchmark case in which $p_E \to 0$. In this case, $(\Pi^c, -D^c)$ approximates a convex combination of $(\Pi^*, -D^*)$ and $(\Pi_0, -D_0)$, where $(\Pi^*, -D^*) \in \Phi$ and $(\Pi_0, -D_0) \in \Phi$. As $\varphi_E(.)$ is concave, any $(\Pi^c, -D^c)$ will be an element of Φ in this benchmark case.

This argument may be restated for the cases in which $p_A \to 0$, and where $p_I \to 0$. Thus, bargaining incentives exist for any $p_E, p_I, p_A > 0$.

Consider Figure 5.1 for a graphical presentation. The benchmark cases construct a triangular area with the corner points $(\Pi_0, -D_0)$, $(\Pi^*, -D^*)$ and $(0,0)$. Any $(\Pi^c, -D^c)$ with $p_E, p_I, p_A > 0$ lies within this area. ∎

Proof of lemma 5.2

Periodical status-quo payoffs $-d_0$ and π_0 are integrated into Figure A5.2. Analogous to the reasoning of lemma 4.2, the fixpoint condition is

$$\Pi^+ = \varphi^{-1}(\delta\varphi(\delta\Pi^+ + (1-\delta)\Pi_0) - (1-\delta)D_0) \tag{5A.3}$$

Again, it is clear that $\Pi^+ = \Pi_0$ solves (5A.3). Any offer $Q^n > -D_0$ implies $\Pi^n < \Pi_0$, and

$$\varphi^{-1}(\delta\varphi(\delta\Pi^n + (1-\delta)\Pi_0) - (1-\delta)D_0) < \Pi_0 \, ;$$

hence, it would not be rational for the investor to submit such an offer. Thus, $(\Pi^+, Q^+) = (\Pi_0, -D_0)$ uniquely solves (5A.3).

As $\Pi^c < \Pi_0$, the investor's threat to opt out will never be credible, while the environmental organization's threat will always be credible ($-D^c > D_0$). Consequently, the bargaining solution is

$$(\Pi^{Bs}, Q^{Bs}) = (\varphi^{-1}(-D^c), -D^c)$$

for $p_I \in (0,1)$. The existence of the solution is proved according to the proof of lemma 5.1. ∎

6. Negotiations under Uncertain Court Outcomes: Incomplete Information

6.1 INTRODUCTION

Relaxing the assumption of complete information may typically lead to inefficient bargaining outcomes.[1] This chapter will re-examine bargaining over the conditions for a new project under one-sided incomplete information. To picture bargaining in the shadow of the law, it will be assumed throughout the chapter that the investor's threat to opt out is credible in private bargaining.

Negotiations under incomplete information were widely addressed in the literature on litigation and settlement. The analyses presented now differ in two ways from most of these contributions.

- First, bargaining is often modeled by a procedure in which one party is exogenously given the opportunity to submit a take-it-or-leave-it offer. When its adversary rejects the offer, the case proceeds to court. As a consequence, the former party would, in the complete-information benchmark case, reap all gains from trade.[2] In contrast, the approach presented here comes close to Wang et al. (1994), who analyze offer/counter-offer bargaining under one-sided incomplete information. In their model, it is only the privately informed party that has the outside

---

[1] In general seller–buyer bargaining, delay in the infinitely repeated offer/counter-offer game under one-sided incomplete information is derived in Rubinstein (1985), Grossman and Perry (1986), Admati and Perry (1987), Gul and Sonnenschein (1988), Ausubel and Deneckere (1989). Bargaining can break down under a finite version of the game (Fudenberg and Tirole 1983) or when the uninformed party has an outside opportunity (Fudenberg et al. 1987). Under two-sided incomplete information, no bargaining procedure can ensure the efficient bargaining solution (Myerson and Satterthwaite 1983).

[2] Specifically, within single-offer models, Bebchuk (1984), Nalebuff (1987), Katz (1990), Spier (1994) assume that it is the uninformed party which submits the offer, and P'ng (1983) and Reinganum and Wilde (1986) assume the informed party submits the offer. Spier (1992, 97–103) presents a model of finitely repeated offers where the uninformed party submits all offers. Schweizer (1989) presents a model of two-sided incomplete information, where the defendant submits a single offer.

option of going to court, whereas the following sections will analyse cases where both the informed and the uninformed party can exert the outside option. Their analysis corresponds to the case presented in Section 6.3.

- Second, the models usually feature common values by assuming that the (expected) value of trial, for both parties, depends on the information privately held by one party. Specifically, in two-party disputes and a stochastic court outcome, the party's private information is directly represented by its probability of winning in court (Bebchuk 1984; Schweizer 1989; Katz 1990; Spier 1992, 1994).[3] However, the underlying assumptions as to why legal outcomes are stochastic in the first place are usually not elucidated explicitly.[4]

The next section will address this latter issue and give a rationale for the assumption of private values used in the subsequent sections. In contrast to the private liability disputes usually depicted by the literature, environmental disputes have specific features, that is, legal formalisms stemming from administrative law. Consequently, the impact of the private information on the probability of prevailing in court may only be comparatively small. The assumption of private values represents the benchmark case where this impact is nil. This assumption merely simplifies presentation within the analysis of Section 6.3; however, it will be crucial for the result of Section 6.4. The sections present two settings of one-sided private information:

- First, it will be assumed that the investor is privately informed about the expected profit of its project. A unique, perfect Bayesian equilibrium will be derived in which negotiations break down with a positive probability. It will then be investigated whether a mediator can improve the bargaining outcome.
- Second, it will be assumed that the environmental group is privately informed about the environmental damage occurring under construction of the project and specific avoidance activities. This setting will be used to

---

[3]In contrast, seller–buyer bargaining occurs under private values. Once the negotiations break down (for example, the seller decides to consume the goods himself, or to negotiate with another buyer), the uninformed seller is no longer interested in the buyer's private information (that is, the buyer's valuation of the object that was under sale). See Spier (1992, 94–5) for a short discussion.

[4]Other models (P'ng 1983; Nalebuff 1987) assume that the private information is verifiable: the court finds out the information and decides accordingly. Common values result because, in liability disputes, the indemnity to be paid from the defendant to the uninformed plaintiff is type-contingent.

re-investigate Farrell's (1987) analysis of bargaining under incomplete information with second-best centralized regulation by a 'bumbling bureaucrat'.

6.2 THE COURT'S OUTCOME: COMMON OR PRIVATE VALUES?

Reconsider the stochastic legal setting used in the preceding chapters. Assume for illustration of the argument that the environmental group has private information on the environmental damage (this will be the assumption of Section 6.4). Under private and non-verifiable information, common values result when the environmental group has the opportunity to influence its probability of prevailing in court, and when incentives to do so are contingent on type. Then, the investor's expected payoff from going to court, via the probability of winning, will depend on the group type.[5]

These conditions are fulfilled when the trial is modeled as a contest in which parties can influence the probability of winning by choosing their respective effort level. Consider the following setting adapted from Heyes (1997). For presentation of the argument, assume that the contest takes place exclusively between the private parties; hence, normalize $p_A = 0$. The investor's probability of winning $p_I = p_I(c_I, c_E)$, where $c_I > 0$ and $c_E > 0$ are the parties' respective legal expenditures, is given by a unit-logit function (Dixit 1987; Hirshleifer 1988, 1989):

$$p_I = \frac{c_I}{c_I + c_E}, \qquad (6.1)$$

and $p_E = 1 - p_I$. Assume that, when bargaining breaks down, it will be the investor who sues the non-negotiated permit. The private parties now play a Stackelberg game in which the (uninformed) investor decides first how much effort to put into the case. The group follows by choosing its own effort level.[6] The group's problem is

---

[5] That common values may result via probabilities is also stressed by Maskin and Tirole (1990, 381, fn. 4).
[6] The analysis can be suitably adapted to the case where the environmental group moves first, and to the case where both parties decide simultaneously. Such a Cournot game is used by Baik and Shogren (1994).

$$Min_{c_E \geq 0} [p_I(c_I, c_E) D_{0i} + c_E].$$ (6.2)

where D_{0i} is the type-specific damage level, $i \in \{l, h\}$. Deriving and solving for c_E gives the type-specific reaction function of the environmental group:

$$c_E(c_I | D_{0i}) = \begin{cases} \sqrt{D_{0i}\, c_I} - c_I & \text{for } D_{0i} \geq c_I, \\ 0 & \text{for } D_{0i} < c_I. \end{cases}$$

For any effort level of the investor, the type with the higher damage will spend more to defend the environment, which accords with intuition. The uninformed investor, as the Stackelberg leader, will take the reaction of the environmental group into account when choosing its effort. Its problem is to maximize expected profits

$$Max_{c_I \geq 0} [(q\, p_I(c_I, c_E(c_I | D_{0l})) + (1 - q) p_I(c_I, c_E(c_I | D_{0h}))) \Pi_0 - c_I],$$ (6.3)

where q is the investor's prior belief of opposing the low type. The investor, irrespective of the group type it actually confronts, will always choose the same level of legal expenditures. As the group with high damage spends more than the group with low damage, the investor's equilibrium probability of winning will be lower when being confronted with the high type:

$$p_I(c_I^*, c_E(c_I^* | D_{0l})) > p_I(c_I^*, c_E(c_I^* | D_{0h})).$$

Consequently, the investor's expected payoff from trial will depend on the environmental group's private information, via the group's type-specific legal expenditures, and the outside options of the bargaining parties feature common values.

The general thrust of the argument can also be applied to the court variant presented in Section 5.4, in which the group can only delay trial. When delay depends on the group's type-specific efforts, the investor's expected payoff from trial will depend on the group type.

The contest function implies that the marginal return of legal expenditures (in terms of an increase in the probability of winning) is decreasing, but strictly positive for any level of expenditures. With respect to the group's probability of winning,

$$\frac{\partial p_E}{\partial c_E} = \frac{c_I}{(c_E + c_I)^2} > 0$$

for any $c_I > 0$. One may wonder whether this property correctly depicts why court outcomes are stochastic in the first place. It surely seems reasonable to assume that, within some limits, the parties can increase their probability of prevailing in court by spending more on the case, for instance by hiring a better, but more expensive attorney or scientific expert. In turn, the decision whether to hire an attorney or expert of a given quality or not, may be type-contingent. The present reasoning, however, focuses on these limitations. It is argued here that, beyond a specific level of expenditures, further effort will no longer increase the probability of winning for a given level of effort by the adversary. These expenditure levels implicitly define a probability of prevailing which reflects 'pure' legal uncertainty. A substantive reason for such a model shall be given now.

Subjective assessments and expert witnesses. Remember that D was assumed to represent the aggregate of true individual valuations of environmental damages. Even while D itself is not verifiable, the group could gather evidence supporting its case. The high type is ready to spend more on finding favorable evidence. Furthermore, were D objective information on the true state of the world, it would be reasonable to assume that the type with high damages will find favorable evidence at lower costs than a low type who only claims to have high damage. In the contest equilibrium, the high type would then show up with better evidence, for example by presenting an expensive expert with a good reputation. When courts base their decision on the quality of the evidence presented, and the quality of the evidence presented is correlated with the type, the expected court ruling would also be type-specific, and common values would result.

In reality, however, D will not be objective information, but will merely represent the subjective assessments of externality victims. Scientific evidence in the court is typically given by expert witnesses. From the viewpoint of the court, the quality of the expert is given by his/her reputation. Experts do not report on the victims' subjective valuations, but give another assessment of the (physical) environmental damages. This raises two questions:

- Will the high type spend more on the expert?
- Will the high type present the expert with the better reputation?

It may seem reasonable to assume that experts with a good reputation are more expensive. However, the connection between the expert's reputation and the group type is blurred, for two reasons:

- To obtain a favorable report of a given quality will depend crucially on the experts' opinions (unless experts simply write the report desired by the victim in the first place, in which case their reputation would suffer in the long run). Hence, spending more money is limited by the necessity of obtaining a favorable report in the first place.
- Usually, experts have differing opinions, which are not necessarily correlated with the group types in the sense that the high type more often finds an expert with a good reputation to support its case. For instance, when conservationists form their subjective assessment by believing in scientific outsiders rather than in mainstream scientists, and when outsiders have a lesser reputation, the converse may also be true. Hence, from an economic viewpoint, it is the individual preferences that should count, not the opinions of experts with a high reputation.

Consequently, the high type will not necessarily choose an expert with a better reputation than the lower type. In equilibrium, both types may hire the same expert, who, for the substantial case being given, delivers the same report on the physical damages. Even then, however, the legal outcome may be uncertain, for reasons beyond the taking of evidence:

Legal formalisms. In the framework of private liability disputes usually considered in the literature on settlement negotiations, courts are required by law to find out who is liable, and will therefore consider the related evidence. In contrast, in disputes over environmental regulation, courts may not consider evidence related to the welfare of intended regulation in the first place. Instead, legal decisions under complex and inconsistent environmental acts often hinge on legal formalisms. Consequently, parties may find it useful to argue on mere formal grounds. Consider the following points.

- The court may conclude that welfare is not the issue in the first place. This was exactly the reasoning in the often-cited US case *Citizen to Preserve Overton Park Inc. vs. Volpe*, in which the US Supreme Court gave the following ruling:

[Respondents] argue that the Secretary should weigh the detriment resulting from the destruction of parkland against the cost of other routes, safety considerations, and other factors, and determine on the basis of the importance that he attaches to these other factors whether, on balance, alternative feasible routes would be prudent. *But no such wide-ranging endeavor was intended.* ... Such factors are common to substantially all highway construction. Thus, if congress intended these factors to be on an equal footing with preservation of parkland there would be no need for the statutes. (401 U.S. 402 (1971), cit. after Mashaw et al. 1992, 710–11: italics added)

- As another example, consider the following case also widely discussed in the United States. In *Gwaltney of Smithfield vs Chesapeake Foundation* (484 U.S. 49 (1987)), a citizen suit under the Clean Water Act was dismissed because the Supreme Court interpreted literally the citizen suit provision in the Act. As the corresponding passage used the present tense, the court restricted standing under the Clean Water Act to 'ongoing permit violations', at the moment a suit was filed.[7]
- Still another example is the restrictive Supreme court decision of *Lujan vs Defenders of Wildlife* presented in Chapter 2, according to which environmental groups, to gain standing, have to present affidavits by members which 'establish "concreteness" at a place certain and "actuality" or "imminence" at a time certain' concerning their injury-in-fact. (McElfish 1993, 100026–7)

It is difficult to conceive how the group could reduce the probability of such decisions via additional legal expenditures, or how the probability of such rulings depends in another respect on privately known information.

The reasoning also applies to the variant of the court model presented in Section 5.5, in which the group can only delay the date of trial. When delay can be increased by (costly) motions of the environmental group, it will depend on the group's effort, and the common values analysis applies. However, as the number of motions and possible tactical maneuvers in court is limited, the group cannot boundlessly delay the case by exerting additional effort.

How can these considerations be illustrated within the contest function presented above? It is argued here that the legal uncertainty can be influenced

---

[7]The 1990 amendment of the Clean Air Act considered the *Gwaltney* decision by explicitly stating that administrative penalties can be assessed upon a finding that a person 'has violated or is in violation' and that actions can be brought against any person who is alleged 'to have violated (if there is evidence that the alleged violation has been repeated) or to be in violation' (U.S.C. §7604(a)(1),(3)) (Leonard 1995, 556; Rodgers 1994, 154).

by the litigants up to a specific effort level, at which marginal returns of legal expenditures become zero. Below this specific level, expenditure choice will be type-contingent; however, all group types may have an incentive to spend up to the critical level. The critical level is not type-dependent because it is induced by the very nature of legal uncertainty within environmental disputes (note that there is nothing type-specific in the contest function itself). The argument may be captured by the following variant of the contest function (6.1):

$$p_I = \frac{\min[c_I, c^c]}{\min[c_I, c^c] + \min[c_E, c^c]},$$

where c^c is the parties' critical spending level beyond which pure legal uncertainty applies.[8] The optimization problems (6.2) and (6.3) are additionally constrained by the requirements

$$c_I^{**} \le c^c \tag{6.4}$$

for the investor and

$$c_E(c_I^{**}|D_{0i}) \le c^c \tag{6.5}$$

for the environmental group. Solutions under these additional constraints are denoted with two stars. When (6.5) does not bind, both group types will spend below c^c, and the higher type will spend more on the preparation of the case. Clearly, (6.5) may bind only for the type with high environmental damages. When, in contrast, (6.5) binds for all types, the uncertain court outcome, in equilibrium, is not influenced by type-specific expenditures, and values from trial will be private. Then, (6.2) and the type-specific reaction function yields the relevant condition:

$$D_{0i} \ge \frac{(c^c + c_I^{**})^2}{c_I^{**}}. \tag{6.6}$$

---

[8]The formalization is somewhat crude, because it implies that $p_I(c_I, c_E, c^c)$ is not differentiable at c^c. However, the formulation allows an immediate comparison of the outcomes in the contest.

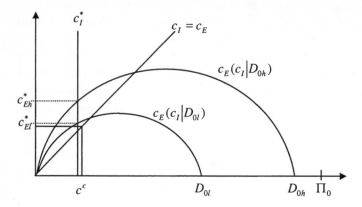

Figure 6.1 A court contest

Hence, when damage is large in the first place (irrespective of its specific amount), (6.6) holds, and $c_E^{**} = c^c$. When (6.4) does not bind in equilibrium, the investor's equilibrium spending is given by

$$c_I^{**} = \arg\max_{c_I \geq 0} \left[\frac{c_I}{c_I + c_E^c}\Pi_0 - c_I\right].$$

This case is illustrated in Figure 6.1, which is an adaptation from Heyes (1997, 415). In consequence, the analysis shall give a rationale for the following assumption.

Assumption 6.1. Probabilities of prevailing in court are not type-contingent. The trial features private values.

Remember that in the aforementioned literature on litigation and settlement, the impact channel from the private information actually held by the party to the probability of prevailing in court is usually not discussed (a party's private information is often directly represented by its (type-contingent) probability of winning the case). Therefore, the extent to which the private information influences the probability of a favorable court decision is not addressed. Then, assumption 6.1 represents the benchmark case in which the impact of private information on a party's probability of prevailing is very small.

6.3 BARGAINING AND MEDIATION

6.3.1 The Role of Environmental Mediation

This section will analyze private bargaining within the licensing procedure for a new project, in which the investor has private information on expected profit. Under the bargaining procedure used so far, a unique Bayesian equilibrium will be derived. The solution is inefficient for some distributions of investor types, that is, it will imply a positive probability of negotiations breaking down and parties going to court, even while it is known beforehand that gains from trade exist.

In a next step, it will be investigated whether the bargaining equilibrium is at least constrained efficient (Fudenberg and Tirole 1991, 427), that is, whether the parties, under the private information, could improve on the outcome through mediation or not. In contrast to an arbitrator, the mediator cannot impose a solution to the dispute, but can merely help the parties to find an agreement.

In the United States, mediation is now a widely accepted procedure for the settlement of environmental disputes, as part of the so-called Environmental or Alternative Dispute Resolution techniques. Institutions involved in the field are not only university-based institutes and consortia, but also business-oriented entities and specialized lawfirms (see RESOLVE 1994 for an overview).[9] In the nineties, the transferability of this concept to the German situation was also widely discussed by German scholars and administrators. Here, mediation is still on the experimental level and a rare exception.[10]

---

[9]See the contributions mentioned in footnote 3, Chapter 5. O'Leary (1995) or Elliott (1996) give an overview of the development and the discussion in the United States. Sander (1990) concisely summarizes and discusses the pro and cons forwarded in the literature.

[10]See, without claiming to be exhaustive, the contributions in Hoffmann-Riem and Schmidt-Aßmann (1990, vol. 2); also, Holznagel (1990), Claus and Wiedemann (1994), Weidner (1996), Holzinger and Weidner (1996). Claus (1996) counts some 30 German cases from 1990 and ironically notes that the number of scientific contributions and conferences on mediation by far exceeds this number. Furthermore, he observes that many of these cases are mediated policy dialogues, but not mediated negotiations (ibid. 54–5, 59). These empirical findings are consistent with the analysis given in Chapter 5, which depicts legal standing as an especially important means to gain bargaining power.

Reasons given as to why a mediator may be helpful are diverse.[11] This section will concentrate on the issue as to what extent the mediator, in a setting of private information, can help the parties overcome strategic behavior that leads, in equilibrium, to an inefficient outcome.

From a theoretical perspective, a mediator is usually depicted as designing a direct mechanism. He aims to define a set of payoffs and settlement probabilities directly contingent on the parties' announcement of their private information, such that parties choose to participate in the mechanism and to truthfully reveal their information.[12] Any solution of a specific bargaining process can also be depicted by such a mechanism (Fudenberg and Tirole 1991, 290).[13] Therefore, the mechanism which maximizes expected welfare implicitly gives the possible efficiency improvement of the mediator with respect to this solution. As the bargaining game investigated here yields a unique Bayesian equilibrium, a welfare-maximizing mechanism may directly give the maximal potential beneficial impact of a mediator with respect to the strategic game without mediation.

6.3.2 The Setting

Consider again private bargaining over the realization of a planned project. As the project is not yet realized, Π_0 depicts the expected profit based on the investor's assessment of market data. The value of Π_0 is the private information of the investor. It is commonly known that the variable may take

---

[11]McCarthy and Shorett (1984) is a practitioners' guide on how a mediator may facilitate or improve a bargained agreement. They underline, for instance, the important role the mediator may play in bundling comparatively homogenous interests by coalition building (ibid. 2–3). The present analysis, by assuming that environmental interests, in the negotiations, are represented by a single player, does not formalize this point.

[12]See Myerson and Satterthwaite (1983, 267) or Ausubel and Deneckere (1989, 21–2). Fudenberg and Tirole (1991, 289–91) criticize the interpretation of the mechanism as a mediator. Under private information, the urge to use a mediator to solve the conflict, by one party, may reveal information to the other party. Then, the discussion of whether to use a mediator will be used to update probabilities, and the constraints used to design the mechanism may be mis-specified. This effect, however, may be prevented by mandatory mediation, which is an empirically relevant phenomenon in the United States (see Moberly 1994). Mandatory mediation means that parties cannot avoid the proposition of mediation; the mediator still does not have authority to prescribe an agreement.

[13]Fulfilled participation constraints reflect the fact that agreeing to negotiate is voluntary. Incentive-compatibility is fulfilled because of the so-called revelation principle: the mechanism implements the parties' (expected) payoffs under their equilibrium strategies in the strategic bargaining game. For instance, consider a bargaining outcome in which a given party does not reveal its private information in equilibrium, and subsequently realizes a specific payoff. When guaranteed this same payoff for truth-telling under a specific mechanism, however, the party will reveal its information, and the mechanism is incentive-compatible.

two values: $\Pi_0 \in \{\Pi_0^l, \Pi_0^h\}$ depicting, respectively, an investor expecting a low or a high profit. Assume that the total profitability condition holds for both types; thus,

$$\Pi_0^i - D(S^*) - S^* > 0$$

for $i \in \{l, h\}$. The marginal condition for the optimal spending level given by (3.2) is not influenced by the amount of expected profit. As a consequence, the agency still has the informational endowment necessary for the relevant decision: it can determine the optimal spending level for environmental protection, which it will defend in court when the conditional permit is sued by either of the private parties.

Denote by Π_l^{cs}, Π_h^{cs} the type-specific value of a trial for the investor:

$$\Pi_l^{cs} = (p_I + p_A)\Pi_0^l - p_A S^*,$$
$$\Pi_h^{cs} = (p_I + p_A)\Pi_0^h - p_A S^*,$$

clearly, $\Pi_l^{cs} < \Pi_h^{cs}$. Assume that the investor's threat to opt out is credible for the environmental group under both investor types. Assume also that a non-negotiated permit S^* would be challenged by at least one party. Then, under complete information, the following constellations may result:

- Both types would agree on an inefficiently low spending level, and the high-profit investor would have to agree on a higher spending level.
- The low type agrees on an inefficiently low spending level, and the high type agrees on the efficient spending level, plus an additional compensation payment.
- Both types agree an the efficient spending level plus an additional compensation payment, and the high type pays higher compensation.

Consequently, in a setting of incomplete information, the high investor type may have an incentive to hide its type, and hope that the group will be ready to settle for less.

To simplify notation, consider only the third constellation by assuming that under complete information, the parties would agree on payment of additional compensation for all investor types. Any offer is thus comprehensively described by a requested level of compensation, as the group will always require spending S^* on environmental protection. Denote by C_l^{Bs} and C_h^{Bs} the level of compensation on which the low and the high investor types would agree in negotiations under complete information. Let C^a be an offer, where a stands for the amount demanded. Denote by h_t a history of the bargaining game at the beginning of period $t > 0$; h_t is a sequence of offers C^a and rejections (denoted by r) leading to specific information set at the beginning of period $t > 0$. For every possible history h_t, define by $q_t(\Pi_0^h | h_t)$ the posterior belief of the environmental group that the investor is of the high type at the beginning of period $t > 0$. The group's prior belief is q_0, which may represent the fraction of high-profit investors in the economy.

Assume that the environmental group submits the first offer in the presented Rubinstein bargaining game, which will be solved for perfect Bayesian equilibria. As the present analysis will introduce an additional refinement to rule out implausible equilibria, reconsider shortly the definition of a perfect Bayesian equilibrium:[14]

1. *Existence of a belief system.* At each information set, the player with the move must possess a belief about which node in the information set has been reached by the play of the game. For a non-singleton information set, a belief is a probability distribution over the nodes of the information set.
2. *Sequential rationality.* Given their beliefs, at each information set, the strategy taken by the player with the move must be optimal given the other player's beliefs at that information set and his subsequent strategies.
3. *Consistency with Bayes' rule.* Whenever possible with respect to requirement one, the players' beliefs are consistent with the posterior probabilities determined by Bayes' rule and the player's equilibrium strategies.

Strategies and beliefs satisfying these requirements form a perfect Bayesian equilibrium. The following refinement will be used to rule out equilibria resulting from implausible beliefs off the equilibrium path.

4. *No belief in strictly dominated strategies.* If consistent with requirement one, each player's beliefs off the equilibrium path should place zero probability on nodes that are reached only when the other player plays a

---

[14]See Gibbons (1992, 177–8) for the following formulation.

strategy that is strictly dominated beginning at some information set.[15] A strategy is strictly dominated for a player if he has another strategy at hand yielding a higher payoff for every belief and every possible subsequent strategy of his adversary (Gibbons 1992, 235).

As will be shown, this additional requirement ensures uniqueness of the bargaining solution.

6.3.3 The Bargaining Equilibrium

The intuition for the following bargaining equilibrium is as follows. The group knows that the threats of all investor types to opt out are credible and that, in the complete information benchmark case, it could reap all gains from trade. When submitting an offer implying too high a compensation payment, the low investor type will prefer to go to court, whereas the high type would accept. When the group submits an offer over low compensation, the group will not risk trial, but will obtain lower compensation. Hence, when submitting the first offer, the group has to weigh the probability of confronting the low type (and the subsequent risk of trial) against the possibility of higher compensation. By assumption, the environmental group prefers an out-of-court settlement when the relevant condition holds as an equation.

Lemma 6.1. In the bargaining game in which the investor is privately informed about the project's expected profits and the investor's outside option is credible for every type, a unique equilibrium results, in which the game ends in the first period.[16]

---

[15]Gibbons (1992, 235). This is a weaker version of Cho and Kreps's (1987) intuitive criterion. The intuitive criterion requires that, if possible, each player's beliefs off the equilibrium path should place zero probability on nodes that are reached only when the other player plays an *equilibrium*-dominated strategy, that is, a strategy yielding lower payoff than its *equilibrium* payoff for every belief and every possible subsequent strategy of his adversary. See Gibbons (1992, 239).

[16]Uniqueness of the solution contrasts with the literature referred to under footnote 1, which typically features a multiplicity of equilibria. Uniqueness does not hinge on the assumption that there are only two investor types. Wang et al. (1994) present a similar model where there are common values of trial and where the plaintiff's type is distributed with positive density over a specific support. They derive a unique equilibrium, where the group submits an offer which guarantees the reservation value to an investor with a specific profit level. All types above this profit level also accept the offer, whereas all types below this level go to court.

(i)   When

$$q_0 \leq \frac{D^c - D^* + C_l^{Bs}}{D^c - D^* + C_h^{Bs}},$$ (6.7)

an efficient equilibrium results where the environmental group offers C_l^{Bs}, which is accepted by both investor types. The group's off-equilibrium posterior belief in the second period is $q_1[\Pi_0^h|(C_l^{Bs}, r)] \in [0,1]$. The high-profit type's payoff is $\Pi_h^{cs} + C_h^{Bs} - C_l^{Bs}$; it additionally gains an information rent $C_h^{Bs} - C_l^{Bs}$.

(ii)   When

$$q_0 > \frac{D^c - D^* + C_l^{Bs}}{D^c - D^* + C_h^{Bs}},$$

an inefficient equilibrium applies in which the group offers C_h^{Bs}. This offer is accepted by the high-profit investor type, whereas the low-profit type rejects the offer and takes its outside option. The group's off-equilibrium posterior in the second period is $q_1[\Pi_0^h|(C_h^{Bs}, r)] = 0$. Expected bargaining losses are $(1 - q_0)(D^{cs} - \varphi_s(\Pi_l^{cs}))$. A welfare loss occurs with probability $(1 - q_0)(p_l + p_E)$, when litigation itself is costless.

Proof. Consider first the move of the investor after being faced with a specific offer C^a.

The low type. An offer $C^a = C_l^{Bs}$ will immediately be accepted by the low type. It cannot gain from opting out or making a counter-offer: Any counter-offer $C^a < C_l^{Bs}$ is not backed by the group's information on the set of possible investor types $\{\Pi_0^l, \Pi_0^h\}$ and will therefore always be rejected and countered with an offer C_l^{Bs}. The investor, however, does lose from dragging on the negotiations: the best it can realize then is a payoff Π_l^{cs} (corresponding to C_l^{Bs}) in a later period, either from the group making an offer C_l^{Bs} in a later period (and the investor accepting it), or from proposing C_l^{Bs} (and the group accepting it), or from opting out in a later period. All possibilities yield a lower payoff than when C_l^{Bs} is accepted immediately. Clearly, the low-profit investor would accept any offer $C^a < C_l^{Bs}$

immediately. However, it will reject any offer $C^a > C_l^{Bs}$ and take it outside option, thus realizing Π_l^{cs}. The best possible alternative is to reject and propose C_l^{Bs} in the next period. When this counter-offer is accepted by the group, the investor's payoff is $\delta\Pi_l^{cs} < \Pi_l^{cs}$. It can be concluded that to submit a counter-offer is a dominated strategy for the low-profit investor for all possible offers C^a.

The high type. For a similar reasoning, an offer $C^a = C_l^{Bs}$ will be immediately accepted by the high type. It cannot gain from opting out or making a counter-offer: Any counter-offer $C^a < C_l^{Bs}$ will be always rejected by the group. Then, the best thing that can happen for the high type investor is that the group counters with an offer C_l^{Bs}. The investor can at best realize $\Pi_h^{cs} + C_h^{Bs} - C_l^{Bs}$ (corresponding to C_l^{Bs}) in a later period, either from the group making an offer C_l^{Bs} in a later period (and the investor accepting it), or from proposing C_l^{Bs} (and the group accepting it), or from opting out in a later period. In consequence, it cannot gain from rejecting C_l^{Bs}. Also, the high-profit investor would immediately accept any offer $C^a < C_l^{Bs}$. It results that submitting a counter-offer is a dominated strategy for the high-profit investor, when being offered $C^a \leq C_l^{Bs}$.

Intermediate offers. Consider now an offer $C^a \in (C_l^{Bs}, C_h^{Bs}]$. The high-profit investor might gain from rejecting such an offer and proposing a lower compensation level, if the environmental group were prepared to accept this counter-offer. For instance, assume that the group has a posterior belief $q_1[\Pi_0^h|(C^a, r)] = 0$ for $C^a \in (C_l^{Bs}, C_h^{Bs}]$, meaning that, when observing a rejection of the offer and a subsequent counter-offer, the group assigns probability one of confronting the low-profit investor. Under such a belief, the group will be ready to accept a counter-offer C_l^{Bs}. However, such a belief is not consistent with the observation that presenting a counter-offer is a dominated strategy for the low-profit investor, for all offers. According to requirement four, the group should then assign $q_1[\Pi_0^h|(C^a, r)] = 1$. The investor, by merely deciding to submit a counter-offer (irrespective of its amount), sends a signal revealing its type. The group will infer from such a move that it is confronted with a high-profit investor, and would therefore always reject any offer $C^a < C_h^{Bs}$ and submit the offer $C^a = C_h^{Bs}$. The investor can only settle at C_h^{Bs} in a later period, which will generate a lower payoff than immediately accepting $C^a \in (C_l^{Bs}, C_h^{Bs}]$. It follows that the investor will immediately accept an offer $C^a \in (C_l^{Bs}, C_h^{Bs}]$. It also follows that the high-profit investor will reject any offer $C^a > C_h^{Bs}$ and opt out: by triggering a trial, the investor can immediately realize a payoff Π_h^{cs} corresponding to C_h^{Bs}, whereas, by submitting a counter-offer and thus sending the signal, it will realize the same payoff, but only in a later period.

These considerations imply the following restrictions on the set of possible offers by the environmental group.

- The group will never submit an offer $C^a \notin [C_l^{Bs}, C_h^{Bs}]$. An offer $C^a < C_l^{Bs}$ will be accepted immediately by both types, as will an offer $C^a = C_l^{Bs}$, which yields a higher payoff for the group. An offer $C^a > C_h^{Bs}$ will always trigger a trial (both investors opting out), whereas, for an offer $C^a \in (C_l^{Bs}, C_h^{Bs}]$, a trial results only when being confronted with a low type. A trial implies that the group would forego all gains from bargaining and realize only $-D^{cs}$.
- The group will never submit an offer $C^a \notin \{C_l^{Bs}, C_h^{Bs}\}$. To see this, consider an offer $C^a \in (C_l^{Bs}, C_h^{Bs}]$, which the low-profit investor will always reject and opt out. The incentive for the group to submit such an offer is to confront the high type with sufficiently high probability. The high type will always accept this offer. The group does not influence this decision by asking less than C_h^{Bs}, not does it influence the low type's decision to opt out by asking only a little bit more than C_l^{Bs}. In consequence, when the group decides to not ask for C_l^{Bs}, it will always ask for C_h^{Bs}.

Hence, the condition for the environmental group to submit an offer C_l^{Bs} is given by

$$-(1-q)D^{cs} + q(-D^* + C_h^{Bs}) \leq -D^* + C_l^{Bs}, \tag{6.8}$$

(6.7) is a reformulation of (6.8). ∎

The issue of updating beliefs is not relevant on the equilibrium path, because the game, in equilibrium, ends in the first period, either by the investor's immediate acceptance of the first offer or by its taking the outside option. Off the equilibrium path, the issue becomes relevant when the investor rejects the first offer, but does not opt out. As rejecting an offer is, in equilibrium, a zero-probability event for both investor types, it is not possible to derive the group's posterior belief by applying Bayes' rule. It is here that the refinement that was introduced becomes important. In the inefficient equilibrium, rejecting the offer C_h^{Bs} and submitting a counter-offer is dominated for the low-profit type, while it is not for the high-profit type. Requirement four applies accordingly to update the group's beliefs. In the efficient equilibrium, however, a rejection of an offer C_l^{Bs} is a dominated strategy for both investor types. Consequently, requirement four cannot be applied, or the group would have to assign zero probability to both investor types, which contradicts requirement one. Every posterior is then permissible and sustains the efficient equilibrium.

The inefficient equilibrium bears some resemblance to Bebchuk (1984), in whose model the uninformed party submits the only offer, and, in equilibrium, one type settles while the other triggers a trial. However, in his model, it is the uninformed party which credibly threatens (with trial), while in the present setting, it is the informed party's threat to opt out which is credible.[17]

6.3.4 The Scope for Mediation

In the inefficient equilibrium, both investor types realize their outside option value (the high-profit type by accepting the offer, and the low type by going to court), while the environmental group's expected payoff is $q_0(-D^* + C_h^{Bs}) + (1-q_0)(-D^{cs})$. It may be wondered whether the intervention of an external mediator can improve this bargaining outcome. Assume mediation to be free of charge. The following paragraph models mediation as a direct implementable mechanism, where the investor truthfully reveals its type, and explores whether the mechanism is feasible under the participation constraints of the parties.[18] These later constraints are relevant because mediation is voluntary.

To improve on the unmediated bargaining outcome, the mediator must reduce the equilibrium probability of going to trial. Hence, when the investor (truthfully or not) reveals itself to be of the low type, the mediated outcome should, with probability κ, not trigger a trial, but payment of compensation.

---

[17]Nalebuff (1987) considers a variant where the uninformed party updates its beliefs when its offer is rejected, and decides then whether to sue. This decision is not trivial, as the court features common values; hence, the uninformed party's expected outcome from trial is type-contingent. Then, the uninformed party will have to raise demands to ensure the credibility of its threat, which increases the probability that the case proceeds to court.

[18]This is an adaptation of Myerson and Satterthwaite (1983, 267); see also Ausubel and Deneckere (1989, 21–2). The difference, besides the by far simpler setting used here, is that they derive the mechanism maximizing expected social surplus to give the maximal surplus attainable under any strategic bargaining game. Here, in contrast, it is used to investigate whether the mediator can possibly improve on the (unique) outcome of a specific strategic bargaining game.

Denote by C_l^{Bm} and C_h^{Bm} the level of compensation to be paid dependent on the announced type, where m stands for mediation. A mechanism can then be described by $(C_h^{Bm}, (C_l^{Bm}, \kappa))$ and has to satisfy

$$\Pi_0^h - S^* - C_h^{Bm} \geq \Pi_h^{cs}, \tag{6.9}$$

$$\kappa(\Pi_0^l - S^* - C_l^{Bm}) + (1 - \kappa)\Pi_l^{cs} \geq \Pi_l^{cs}, \tag{6.10}$$

$$q_0(-D^* + C_h^{Bm}) + (1 - q_0)[\kappa(-D^* + C_l^{Bm}) + (1 - \kappa)(-D^{cs})] \geq$$
$$q_0(-D^* + C_h^{Bs}) + (1 - q_0)(-D^{cs}), \tag{6.11}$$

$$\Pi_0^h - S^* - C_h^{Bm} \geq \kappa(\Pi_0^h - S^* - C_l^{Bm}) + (1 - \kappa)\Pi_h^{cs}, \tag{6.12}$$

where (6.9)–(6.11) gives the participation constraints of the high, respectively, the low investor type and of the environmental group, and (6.12) is the incentive-compatibility constraint for the high-type investor. Note that for $\kappa = 0$ and $C_i^{Bm} = C_i^{Bs}$, the mechanism just implements the outcome of the unmediated game.

Proposition 6.1. There is no mechanism satisfying (6.9) to (6.12) that improves efficiency with respect to the inefficient bargaining outcome characterized by lemma 6.1, (ii).

Proof. Assume that $C_l^{Bm} = C_l^{Bs}$ (it will become clear in a moment that it is not rational to implement another level of compensation). Define $\Delta C = C_h^{Bs} - C_l^{Bs}$. According to (6.12), to induce truth-telling by the high investor type, it must be guaranteed a payoff of

$$\hat{\Pi}^h = \kappa(\Pi_h^{cs} + \Delta C) + (1 - \kappa)\Pi_h^{cs}, \tag{6.13}$$

for truthfully declaring its type. Clearly, $\hat{\Pi}^h > \Pi_h^{cs}$ for $\kappa > 0$; hence, according to (6.9), the high-type investor would agree on such a mechanism. The low-type still realizes Π_l^{cs}, by paying C_l^{Bs} with probability κ and by going to court with probability $(1-\kappa)$; thus (6.10) is fulfilled. Reformulating (6.13) gives $\hat{\Pi}^h = \Pi_h^{cs} + \kappa\Delta C$ and the corresponding level of compensation is $C_h^{Bm} = C_h^{Bs} - \kappa\Delta C$.

Consider the possibility of $C_l^{Bm} \neq C_l^{Bs}$. For $C_l^{Bm} > C_l^{Bs}$, the low-type investor would always go to court, and the mechanism does not improve on the non-mediated outcome. For $C_l^{Bm} < C_l^{Bs}$, the problem of inducing truth-telling, according to (6.12), is aggravated without improving efficiency.

It remains for us to ascertain whether the mechanism $(C_h^{Bs} - \kappa\Delta C, (C_l^{Bs}, \kappa))$ fulfills (6.12) for some κ. However,

$$q_0(-D^* + (C_h^{Bs} - \kappa\Delta C)) + (1 - q_0)[\kappa(-D^* + C_l^{Bs}) + (1 - \kappa)(-D^{cs})] \geq$$
$$q_0(-D^* + C_h^{Bs}) + (1 - q_0)(-D^{cs}) \Rightarrow$$
$$q_0 \leq \frac{D^c - D^* + C_l^{Bs}}{D^c - D^* + C_h^{Bs}},$$

which corresponds to (6.7) and, hence, violates the condition of having an inefficient equilibrium in the first place. ∎

Consequently, the intervention of the mediator cannot improve the efficiency of the bargaining outcome. Given the information asymmetry, the non-mediated bargaining procedure implements the most efficient outcome possible.[19]

The intuition behind this result is that, *in equilibrium*, the bargaining game corresponds to a procedure in which the uninformed party makes a take-it-or-leave-it offer. Thus, the environmental group will submit an offer maximizing its expected payoff. Because inefficiency stems from the equilibrium probability of trial, this is equivalent to an offer maximizing expected welfare. Consequently, external intervention by a mediator cannot further improve the expected group's payoff and, hence, expected welfare without violating the investor's participation or incentive-compatibility constraint.

External finance is necessary to further improve expected welfare. For

$$D^{cs} - \varphi_s(\Pi_l^{cs}) < p_l(W_l^* - W_0^h) + p_E W_l^*,$$

where the left-hand side depicts the group's loss from trial when being confronted with a low-type investor, and the right-hand side the social loss of trial, there will be room to compensate the environmental group for accepting a lower compensation amount to be paid by the high-type investor (which is necessary to induce it to tell the truth when compensation is sometimes paid

---

[19]Given the inefficiency of the bargaining result, this result relates to Myerson and Satterthwaite (1983), who show that under two-sided private information, no (bargaining) mechanism satisfying individual rationality, incentive-compatibility and budget-balance can exploit all gains from trade, even when positive gains from trade are common knowledge. See Schweizer (1989), 170–71, for a similar result within a legal setting under common values.

to the low investor type). However, this option is usually beyond the competence of a mediator.

6.3.5   Discussion

When external finance is ruled out, mediation cannot reduce the possibly inefficient result of private bargaining. Because of the positive probability of trial in equilibrium, the welfare-improving property of legal standing for environmental groups, derived in Chapter 5, does not simply carry over to this setting of incomplete information. This is so, because the expected welfare from trial was assumed to be reduced by the introduction of associational standing. On the other hand, inefficiencies may also arise during bargaining between the investor and the agency, when the agency is not informed as to the project's profit. As Φ_a is not symmetric, the equilibrium spending level associated with the Nash solution will depend on privately-known profit levels, and incentives to conceal the private information result when both parties' threats to opt out are not credible under some type(s).

Such a setting would not violate the assumption of Chapter 3 that the agency learns the firm's information during the licensing procedure. Chapter 3 addressed privately-known avoidance cost functions, which are relevant for the agency's regulatory decision. In contrast, the profit level is not relevant for efficient regulation: the agency still has the necessary information to reach an optimum decision even under privately-known profit.

In consequence, two inefficient bargaining constellations would have to be compared. This analysis will not delivered here. For incentives of the high-type to conceal the private information being rather small, the result of Chapter 5 will still hold. To see this, note that

$$\frac{D^c - D^* + C_l^{Bs}}{D^c - D^* + C_h^{Bs}} \to 1 \text{ for } C_h^{Bs} - C_l^{Bs} \to 0$$

and condition (6.7) for the efficient bargaining equilibrium will be fulfilled for $q_0 \in [0,1)$. The welfare comparison of the bargaining constellations would approach the complete-information comparison of chapter five.

The following section explores the case in which the investor is incompletely informed as to the environmental damage.

6.4 A RECONSIDERATION OF FARRELL'S BUMBLING BUREAUCRAT

6.4.1 Introduction

The following section compares the constellations of asymmetrical and symmetrical standing within the licensing of a new project whereby the environmental group is privately informed as to the extent of environmental damage. The analysis has strong ties with Farrell (1987); therefore, reconsider shortly the thrust of this contribution and the research it spurred.

After the challenge of the Pigovian tradition by Coase (1960), it was intensely debated in environmental economics whether the internalization of environmental externalities should be organized by a central authority, or whether it is sufficient to define property rights and rely on the subsequent bargaining between the concerned private parties. Indeed, Coase's contribution was often interpreted as a strong argument against a centralized governmental intervention. However, Farrell (1987) convincingly argued that the view of the Coase theorem as a *decentralization result* does not make sense in a world of complete information. In such a setting, both centralized regulation and decentralized bargaining lead to the efficient outcome; therefore, a superiority of the bargaining solution cannot be proven. Hence, Farrell uses a model of bilateral private information and compares the inefficiency resulting from Coasean bargaining under incomplete information with the inefficiency emerging from second-best centralized regulation. The agency, which seeks to maximize welfare, but which is also incompletely informed, uses a rule of thumb to maximize expected welfare.[20] The result of this comparison is ambiguous: depending on the distribution of types, Coasean negotiations may be more or less efficient on average than the 'bumbling bureaucrat'.

Farrell's approach was used by several authors to explore more specific, but related issues. Buchholz and Haslbeck (1991) and Haslbeck (1995) reformulate Farrell's analysis in a model of one-sided incomplete information, in which the damage function is privately known, and obtain a similar result. Illing (1992) and Demougin and Illing (1993) also use models

---

[20]As the analysis intends to focus on real-world, day-to-day policy implementation, it does not consider other methods to determine environmental valuations, like contingent valuation. For the same reason, mechanisms in the tradition of Clarke (1971), Groves (1973) and d'Aspremont and Gérard-Valet (1979) are not considered. See Haslbeck (1995, 119–50) for a thorough discussion and a critique within the context of environmental externalities.

of one-sided private information; they compare pure Coasean bargaining with a situation in which the bumbling bureaucrat sets an environmental standard, which serves as a threat point from which the private parties may renegotiate. They show that the introduction of an intermediate standard will improve welfare, when compared to the situation in which one of the parties exclusively owns the property right. A similar result was derived by Johnston (1995), where the intermediate standard is generated by an ex post nuisance test by the judicial system.

All of these analyses, as well as Farrell's, assume that the property right's structure in regard to environmental assets is a perfect policy instrument: the legislature can reallocate rights without limit and, specifically, may implement secure public rights for the agency or secure private property rights. This assumption will now be relaxed in order to explore the presented case of uncertain property rights, in which a private party can sue against a project permit, and the courts decide only with a specific probability in its favor. The setting considered, in which the environmental damage associated with a planned economic project is private information of the environmental group, corresponds to Buchholz and Haslbeck (1991).

6.4.2   The Setting

Take again the technical setting of the preceding parts and assume for now that the damage function $D = D(S)$ is private information of the environmental organization. The group will be one of two types: $D_i(.) \in \{D_l(.), D_h(.)\}$, where, for every S, $D_l(S) < D_h(S)$. The probability that $D_i(.) = D_l(.)$ is denoted by q. Assume that

$$D_l'(S) > D_h'(S) \qquad (6.14)$$

for every S. The optimal spending levels depend on the types and are denoted by $S^* \in \{S_l^*, S_h^*\}$. Assume an interior solution for both types: $S^* \in (0, \Pi_0)$. Conditions for the optimal level of environmental spending are:

$$D_i'(S_i^*) = -1, \qquad (6.15)$$

$$\Pi_0 - D_i(S_i^*) - S_i^* > 0. \qquad (6.16)$$

for $i \in \{l, h\}$. Again, condition (6.16) is met by assumption. Because of (6.14), $S_l^* < S_h^*$. Denote $D_i^* = D_i(S_i^*)$. Assume that $D_l^* < D_h^*$.

Furthermore, the spending level which would completely avoid environmental damage is higher than the private profit Π_0 for both types:

$$D_i^{-1}(0) > \Pi_0, \tag{6.17}$$

where $S = D_i^{-1}(D)$. Related welfare and profit levels are also denoted by the corresponding subscript.

An example. In Section 6.4.4, a specific representation of $D(S)$ will be used to simplify the presentation of a proposition. No loss of generality will be incurred. Let damage costs D and abatement costs S depend on a physical variable E, where E stands for a physical parameter. E_0 is the level of E when no environmental spending occurs. Assume a constant marginal damage and quadratic abatement costs. Thus,

$$D_i = D_i(E) = d_i E$$

where $d_l < d_h$, and

$$S = S(E) = (E_0 - E)^2$$

which, by assumption, is defined for $E \in [0, E_0]$. Taking the inverse function $E(S) = S^{-1}(E)$ and substituting into the damage function yields

$$D_i(S) = d_i(E_0 - \sqrt{S}), \tag{6.18}$$

which satisfies the above assumptions. Specifically, using (6.15) shows that S^* increases in the marginal damage: $S^* = 0.25 d_i^2$. Thus, $S_l^* < S_h^*$ if $d_l < d_h$.

The agency's objective. Following the tradition of Farrell (1987), the agency is assumed not to be biased. Hence, the administrator maximizes expected welfare

$$\tilde{W}(S) = \Pi_0 - q(D_l(S) + S) - (1 - q)(D_h(S) + S). \tag{6.19}$$

As (6.16) is met for every type, the agency will always accept the project. Under complete information ($q \in \{0,1\}$), the agency would simply prefer the 'right' spending level S_i^*. In a world of incomplete information, however, the agency will aim at a level $\tilde{S}^*$ maximizing expected welfare:

$$\tilde{S}^* = \arg\max_S[\Pi_0 - q(D_l(S) + S) - (1 - q)(D_h(s) + S)].$$

This is the 'bumbling bureaucrat'. Denote the corresponding welfare level by $\tilde{W}^*$. Under a constant marginal damage and quadratic avoidance costs, expected welfare is $\tilde{W}(S) = \Pi_0 - (qd_l + (1 - q)d_h)(E_o - \sqrt{S}) - S$. Thus, an agency maximizing expected welfare would use, as a rule of thumb, the weighted mean of the privately known marginal damage $\tilde{d} = qd_l + (1 - q)d_h$.

Consider first the situation of asymmetrical standing.

6.4.3   Asymmetrical Standing and the Bumbling Bureaucrat

In this case, both the investor and the agency are uninformed. When bargaining breaks down, the agency will issue a permit over $\tilde{S}^*$. The expected outcomes from trial are

$$\tilde{\Pi}^{ca} = \Pi_0 - (1 - p_l)\tilde{S}^* \tag{6.20}$$

for the investor and

$$\begin{aligned}\tilde{W}^{ca} = \Pi_0 &- (1 - p_l)[\tilde{S}^* + qD_l(\tilde{S}^*) + (1 - q)D_h(\tilde{S}^*)] \\ &- p_l[qD_{0l} + (1 - q)D_{0h}]\end{aligned} \tag{6.21}$$

for the agency. Assume that the stipulations of a negotiated permit are enforceable.

Under a secure public right, $p_l = 0$; thus, the investor does not have an incentive to file suit against a permit prescribing a positive level of protective activities.

Under incomplete information, the agency will prescribe the spending level $\tilde{S}*$ maximizing expected welfare, as specified by the agency's objective function. The expected inefficiency is

$$q[D_l(\tilde{S}^*) + \tilde{S}^* - D_l^* - S_l^*] + (1 - q)[\overline{D}(\tilde{S}^*) + \tilde{S}^* - D_h^* - S_h^*] \tag{6.22}$$

Thus, either uncertain rights or incomplete information give rise to inefficiencies:

- Under insecure rights and complete information, bargaining over S will result, with an inefficient outcome $S^{Ba} < S^*$. This result was derived in Chapter 4.
- Under incomplete information and a secure public right, the rule of thumb applied by an agency maximizing expected welfare – the bumbling bureaucrat – would lead to a spending level $\tilde{S}^*$. The resulting efficiency loss is given by (6.22).

Consequently, it results from a restatement of lemma 4.1 for $q \in (0,1)$ and the definition of $\tilde{S}^*$ that:

Proposition 6.2. Under incomplete information about environmental damage and insecure rights, bargaining incentives emerge between the investor and the bumbling bureaucrat. The bargained outcome will lead to a higher inefficiency when compared with a bumbling bureaucrat's regulation which has a secure public property right.

The bumbling bureaucrat under incomplete information, who has to bargain with an investor over an insecure public right, will not even be able to implement a spending level $\tilde{S}^*$ which maximizes expected welfare, but only a smaller $\tilde{S}^{Ba}$. Thus, the inefficiency arising under incomplete information will be higher in a setting of insecure public rights.

This result can be readily explained with Figure 4.2 by adding swung dashes, where necessary; thus, substitute $\varphi_a(.)$ by $\tilde{\varphi}_a(.)$, W^* by $\tilde{W}^*$, and so on. For the bumbling bureaucrat under secure public property rights, set $p_l = 0$. Bargaining would degenerate into the investor's immediate acceptance of $(\tilde{\Pi}^*, \tilde{W}^*)$, meaning that $\tilde{S}^*$ will be implemented.

6.4.4 Private Bargaining under Insecure Rights and Private Information

Consider now the case of symmetrical standing. (5.1) and (5.2) still hold. Again, bargaining occurs between the private parties. The agency will always accept the agreement, as can been seen by stating the incentives to negotiate for the investor, the low and the high group type, and the agency:

$$S \le p_A \tilde{S}^* + p_E \Pi_0,$$
$$D_l(S) \le p_A D_l(\tilde{S}^*) + p_l D_{0l},$$
$$D_h(S) \le p_A D_h(\tilde{S}^*) + p_l D_{0h}$$
$$S + q D_l(S) + (1-q) D_h(S) \le p_A [\tilde{S}^* + q D_l(\tilde{S}^* + (1-q) D_h(\tilde{S}^h)]$$
$$+ p_l [q D_{0l} + (1-q) D_{0h}]$$
$$+ p_E \Pi_0.$$

Again, the agency will be ready to accept any agreement between the private parties. Specify the assumption of a passive agency in the sense that the agency does not sit at the bargaining table, but will accept the negotiated outcome. This specification is crucial for the following result to hold, and thus allows one to state an additional institutional requirement for environmental bargaining under private information. This issue will be discussed below.

When negotiations break down, the bumbling bureaucracy will issue a permit over $\tilde{S}^*$, which the private parties may fight in court. Assume for presentational reasons that either both group types or no type has an incentive to challenge this permit; the assumption holds for the functional form of $D(S)$ introduced by (6.18).[21] Then, the parties' outside options are defined by

$$(\tilde{\Pi}^{out}, -D_i^{out}) = \begin{cases} (\tilde{\Pi}^*, -D_i(\tilde{S}^*)) & \text{if } \tilde{\Pi}^{cs} \le \tilde{\Pi}^* \text{ and } -D_i^{cs} \le -D_i(\tilde{S}^*), \\ (\tilde{\Pi}^{cs}, -D_i^{cs}) & \text{else,} \end{cases} \quad (6.23)$$

where

$$\tilde{\Pi}^{cs} = p_l \Pi_0 + p_A (\Pi_0 - \tilde{S}^*) \quad (6.24)$$
$$-D_i^{cs} = -(p_l D_{0i} + p_A D_i(\tilde{S}^*)) \quad (6.25)$$

Assume that the investor's threat to opt out is credible for all group types. Denote by Π_l^+, Π_n^+ the payoffs for the investor when bargaining with the low, respectively, the high type under complete information, when its threat is not credible (remember that, for $\Lambda \to 0$, $\Pi_i^+ \to \Pi_i^{Ns}$). As $\Pi_l^+ > \Pi_h^+$, credibility of the threat means $\tilde{\Pi}^{cs} \ge \Pi_l^+$. Also, note that $\Pi_l^* > \tilde{\Pi}^* > \Pi_h^*$.

---

[21] When, for example, only the low type has an incentive to challenge the permit, the expected value of the investor's outside option will be $q\tilde{\Pi}^{cs} + (1-q)\tilde{\Pi}^*$. The results to be derived will hold accordingly; no loss of generality is incurred.

Lemma 6.2. Under private information about the environmental damage and a credible threat of the investor to opt out, the unique solution of bargaining over the conditions for a new project between the investor and the environmental group is characterized as follows.

(i)   Bargaining incentives between the investor and the environmental group exist for $p_I, p_A, p_E > 0$.

(ii) The bargaining solution is given by

$$(\Pi^{Bs}, Q_i^{Bs}) = (\tilde{\Pi}^*, \varphi_{si}(\tilde{\Pi}^*)) \quad \text{if } \tilde{\Pi}^{cs} \leq \tilde{\Pi}^* \text{ and } -D_i^{cs} \leq \varphi_{si}(\tilde{\Pi}^*),$$

$$(\Pi^{Bs}, Q_i^{Bs}) = (\tilde{\Pi}^{cs}, \varphi_{si}(\tilde{\Pi}^{cs})) \quad \text{else, where}$$

$$\varphi_{si} = \begin{cases} -D_i(\Pi_0 - \tilde{\Pi}^{cs}) & \text{for } \tilde{\Pi}^{cs} > \Pi_i^*, \\ -D_i(S^*) + C_i^{Bs} & \text{for } \tilde{\Pi}^{cs} \leq \Pi_i^*, \end{cases}$$

and $C_i^{Bs} = \Pi_0 - S_i^* - \tilde{\Pi}^{cs}$.

Proof.

(i)   This is a restatement of the proof of (i) from lemma 5.1. Instead of $(\Pi^*, -D^*)$ and $(\Pi_0, -D_0)$, use $(\tilde{\Pi}^*, \varphi_{si}(\tilde{\Pi}^*))$, (Π_0, D_{0i}).

(ii) As the investor can credibly threaten to opt out irrespective of the type of group it confronts in the negotiations, it is guaranteed its outside option payoff as a bargaining outcome, according to lemma 4.1; thus, $\tilde{\Pi}^{Bs} = \tilde{\Pi}^{out}$. Consider the following cases.

- $\tilde{\Pi}^{cs} \leq \tilde{\Pi}^*$ and $-D_i^{cs} \leq -D_i(\tilde{S}^*)$.

  A permit over $\tilde{S}^*$ would not be challenged. Consequently, the parties agree on this spending level. The investor's payoff is $\tilde{\Pi}^{Bs} = \tilde{\Pi}^*$ in any case. Because of $\Pi_i^* > \tilde{\Pi}^* > \Pi_h^*$, $S_l^* < \tilde{S}^* < S_h^*$. Consequently, the high group type will prefer spending of $\tilde{S}^*$ on environmental avoidance, while the low type will prefer the investor to spend only up to S_i^* and to pay the difference $\tilde{S}^* - S_i^*$ as a compensation.

- $\tilde{\Pi}^{cs} \leq \Pi_h^*$ and $-D_i^{cs} > -D_i(\tilde{S}^*)$.

  The permit would be challenged by the environmental group, and both group types can extract compensation: $C_i^{Bs} \geq 0$. The investor's payoff is $\tilde{\Pi}^{Bs} = \tilde{\Pi}^{cs}$ in any case.

The group has an incentive to reveal its type, to obtain the optimal type-specific 'mixture' of environmental spending and compensation $S_i^* + C_i^{Bs} = \Pi_0 - \tilde{\Pi}^{cs}$ for $i \in \{l, h\}$:

$$-D_i(S_i^*) + C_i^{Bs} > -D_i(S_j^*) + C_j^{Bs} \text{ for } i, j \in \{l, h\}, \text{ and } i \neq j.$$

The bargaining outcome will realize the type-specific efficient spending level.

- $\tilde{\Pi}^{cs} > \Pi_l^*$.

  The permit would be challenged by the investor, and neither group type would be able to extract compensation. The investor spends $S^{Bs} = \Pi_0 - \tilde{\Pi}^{cs}$, which implies type-specific damage $D_i(S^{Bs})$. Revealing private information is irrelevant for the bargaining solution.

- $\Pi_h^* \leq \tilde{\Pi}^{cs} \leq \Pi_l^*$.

  Assume that the permit would be challenged, or the situation corresponds to the first point. The investor's payoff is $\tilde{\Pi}^{Bs} = \tilde{\Pi}^{cs}$. According to $\Pi_l^* > \tilde{\Pi}^* > \Pi_h^*$, $S_l^* < \tilde{S}^* < S_h^*$, and the low type has an incentive to extract additional compensation, while the high type prefers the entire amount $\Pi_0 - \tilde{\Pi}^{cs}$ being spent on protective activities. Again, the group types, in order to obtain that result, must reveal their private information. ∎

For lemma 6.2 to hold, it is crucial that the environmental group, by revealing its information, will not influence the agency's pleading and, hence, the value of the investor's outside option. The information transmitted to the investor has to be confidential. That is why it is important that the agency not be present at the bargaining table. Were this the case, the agency could adapt its intended regulation and its subsequent pleading in accordance with the information given by the group. Consequently, the low type will not have an incentive to reveal its type, when

$$\varphi_l(\tilde{\Pi}^*) + C_l^{Bs} > \varphi_l(\Pi_l^*) + C_l,$$

where $\tilde{\Pi}^* - C_l^{Bs} = \tilde{\Pi}^{cs}$; and $\Pi_l^{cs} = \Pi_l^* - C_l$ denotes the investor's outside option when the agency, in response to the low-type information, would correctly plead for a permit over S_l^*.

Again, the reasoning behind this result is that the citizen group has 'all the bargaining power' in the sense that the investor is guaranteed only its reservation payoff, that is, the value of its credible outside option, whereas the group reaps type-specific bargaining gains $\varphi_{si}(\Pi^{out}) - D_i^{out}$. Therefore, the situation is analogous to a bargaining protocol in which the informed group, by assumption, is the principal and makes a take-it-or-leave-it offer.[22] This observation relates the result to Maskin and Tirole (1990), who show that in such a contract-design problem, the principal's private information has no strategic value under quasi-linear utility functions (like the one used here for the environmental group) and private values of the outside option.

Compare now the bargaining between the private parties with bargaining involving the bumbling bureaucrat. Proposition 6.2 and lemma 6.2 immediately yield

Proposition 6.3. Under insecure property rights, the introduction of associational standing and the resulting private negotiations unambiguously improve welfare.

(i)   For $\tilde{\Pi}^{cs} \in [\Pi_l^{\dagger}, \Pi_h^*]$ and $-D_i^{cs} > -D_i(\tilde{S}^*)$, bargaining between the private parties will be first-best efficient.

(ii)   For $\tilde{\Pi}^{cs} \in [\Pi_h^*, \Pi_0]$, the outcome may be first-best efficient. At least an efficiency improvement will result when compared to the outcome negotiated between the bumbling bureaucrat and the investor.

(iii)   At least for $\Pi^{cs} \in [\Pi_l^{\dagger}, \tilde{\Pi}^*]$, the outcome will be more efficient than under a bumbling bureaucrat owning a sure public property right.

Proof.

(i)   This corresponds, in the proof of lemma 6.1, to the case in which both group types extract compensation $C_i^{Bs} \geq 0$. Consequently, the type-specific efficient spending level will be realized.

(ii)   For $\tilde{\Pi}^{cs} > \Pi_h^*$, the bargained agreement will be inefficiently low at least for the high type. Efficiency improvements, when compared to the setting of asymmetrical standing and insecure rights, will result,

---

[22]Under such a bargaining procedure, a similar result is derived in Schweizer's (1988, 259), investigation of Coasean bargaining under secure property rights.

because $\tilde{\Pi}^{cs} < \tilde{\Pi}^{ca}$, and the proof of proposition 5.1 applies accordingly.

(iii)   This is clear for $\tilde{\Pi}^{cs} \in [\Pi_l^+, \Pi_h^*]$, where private bargaining is first-best efficient. Assume $\tilde{\Pi}^{cs} \in (\Pi_h^*, \tilde{\Pi}^*]$. Consider the benchmark case where $\tilde{\Pi}^{Bs} = \tilde{\Pi}^{cs} = \tilde{\Pi}^*$. In the bargained solution, the investor spends the same amount as under a bumbling bureaucrat owning a secure public right. The spending level for the high type will be inefficiently low, leading to a welfare loss of

$$(1-q)(D_h(\bar{S}^*) + \bar{S}^* - D_h^* - S_h^*) \tag{6.26}$$

However, the low type will agree on an efficient spending level plus additional compensation. An increase in the bargained spending level ($\tilde{\Pi}^{Bs} = \tilde{\Pi}^{cs} < \tilde{\Pi}^*$) will decrease (6.26). For $\tilde{\Pi}^{Bs} = \tilde{\Pi}^{cs} \leq \Pi_h^*$, (6.26) equals zero. A comparison of (6.26) with (6.22) completes the proof. ∎

Hence, when rights are insecure and $\tilde{\Pi}^{cs} \geq \Pi_l^+$, the ambiguity between regulation by a bumbling bureaucracy and private bargaining, which was derived by Farrell (1987) and confirmed under one-sided incomplete information by Buchholz and Haslbeck (1991), simply vanishes.

When $\tilde{\Pi}^{cs} < \Pi_l^+$, the ambiguity result holds, but is shifted in favor of private bargaining. This is so because proposition 6.2 is valid even when the property right for the citizen group is secure enough to yield Coasean bargaining under incomplete information, where the low type may have a strategic incentive to misrepresent private information.

Resulting bargaining inefficiencies under private information were widely analyzed in the literature (see the cited references for analyses within environmental regulation). The substantial reason for not reiterating this issue within the present setting is that, to generate almost secure property rights for the environmental organization, p_A and p_I need to be rather small. Empirically, however, it could be argued that, while public rights may be insecure, they will not be very insecure in the sense that courts will very often confirm legal challenges against agency activities by environmental groups.

Because of part (iii), proposition 6.2 is stronger than proposition 5.1 with respect to the assumed court model. To see this, assume for the moment that the group can also pay compensation. In the case in which the negotiated payment from the investor $\Pi_0 - \tilde{\Pi}^{cs}$ implies too low a spending level, this means that the group would co-finance protective activities up to the efficient level. Consider the case in which public rights are almost secure; hence, $p_A \to 1$ and $\tilde{W}^{Ba} \to \tilde{W}^*$. Under complete information, any welfare difference between asymmetrical and symmetrical standing would then vanish. This is not so, however, under incomplete information.

Corollary 6.1. Assume $(\Pi^{cs}, Q_i^{cs}) \in \Phi_{si}$. Under $p_A \to 1$ and unrestricted possibilities to compensate, private bargaining will never perform worse than the bumbling bureaucrat, as long as the investor's threat to opt out is credible for every group type.

Proof. For $p_A \to 1$, the investor's threat to opt out, in private bargaining, will always be credible. Assume that at least one party has an incentive to sue the non-negotiated permit. Consider the case $\tilde{\Pi}^{cs} \in (\Pi_h^*, \Pi_0]$. When compensation is not restricted, the high type alone ($\tilde{\Pi}^{cs} \in (\Pi_h^*, \Pi_l^*]$) or both types ($\tilde{\Pi}^{cs} \in (\Pi_l^*, \Pi_0]$) will offer compensation. The reasoning is exactly analogous to the proof of lemma 6.2: as the efficient spending levels are type-specific and compensation has to ensure that $\tilde{\Pi}^{Bs} = \tilde{\Pi}^{cs}$, the group will reveal its information by submitting a type-specific compensation offer to the investor for additional spending on protective activities.

When no party will sue against the non-negotiated permit, private bargaining yields the same outcome as that for the bumbling bureaucrat. ■

6.4.5 Comments

The analysis under privately-known environmental damage confirms and strengthens the result of chapter five with respect to the efficiency-improving property of associational standing. Specifically, the following conclusions can be stated.

- *The court model.* Unambiguous superiority of private bargaining under private information may be derived for a more general court model. The only requirements on the parties' expected payoffs of going to court that remain to be relevant are $\tilde{\Pi}^{cs} \geq \Pi_l^*$ (credibility of the investor's threat to opt out for every group type), $(\Pi^{cs}, Q_i^{cs}) \in \Phi_{si}$ (bargaining incentives exist in the first place), and private values of trial. Specifically, bargaining between the investor and the bumbling bureaucrat, under asymmetrical standing, may or may not happen.

- *Secure property rights.* In Chapter 5, it was pointed out that well-defined property rights are not a prerequisite for efficient private bargaining. This result is confirmed under one-sided incomplete information, as long as the aforementioned conditions hold. Moreover, it is strengthened insofar as, under these conditions, insecure private property rights perform better than a secure public property right, independent of type distribution.

- *Agency participation.* The privately-informed party may have an incentive to reveal its information to its private adversary, but not to the agency, because of the subsequent adaptation of the agency's pleading in court. Hence, it may improve the (expected) bargaining outcome when the agency does not participate in the negotiations. Thus, in bipolar environmental conflicts, a restrained behavior by the administration in the settlement negotiations, by giving leeway to the private parties in making the deal, may have its merits.

Note that the model can be reformulated for a continuous, instead of a discrete, distribution of D_i, where types are distributed on the support $[D_l, D_h]$. The qualitative results of the analysis would not change. Using a bumbling rule would still be inefficient; bargaining under insecure public rights would increase this inefficiency. If the investor's outside option is credible in private bargaining, every group type still has an incentive to reveal its true marginal damage.

6.5   SUMMARY AND DISCUSSION

This chapter reconsidered bargaining over a new project under private information. It assumed private values of trial and a credible threat to opt out by all investor types. Two results were derived with respect to the relative efficiency of private bargaining induced by legal standing for the environmental group.

- When the project's profit is private investor's information, an inefficient bargaining outcome may result. Furthermore, this bargaining outcome will be constrained efficient, in the sense that it implements the highest possible (expected) welfare given the privacy of information. Hence, it cannot be improved by the intervention of a mediator. Mediation is not a panacea. Because of this result, the welfare-improving property of a legal standing for environmental groups, derived in Chapter 5, does not simply carry over to this setting of incomplete information. It will, however, also apply for most type distributions when the investor stands to gain little by concealing its private information.

- In contrast, the environmental group's private information on the extent of the environmental damage will have no strategic value in the negotiations, under the assumptions made. Consequently, a trial will never result in equilibrium, and the bargaining outcome may be first-efficient even in this setting of private information. As the bargaining constellation under asymmetrical standing performs worse when the group is privately informed about the environmental damage, the result of Chapter 5 concerning the welfare-improving property of standing is strengthened in this setting of incomplete information.

As a consequence, the policy conclusion of Chapter 5 should primarily apply to cases in which firm-specific information is fairly well known, and where privately known environmental damages are the decisive informational bottleneck. At least to some extent, this condition may be fulfilled for large facilities. These are usually planned by existing companies of major importance which have reporting obligations to stockholders with respect to their future activities. Such information, however, is publicly available. Even when the expected profit may not be known exactly, its (commonly known) support may be arguably rather small.

A possible limitation of the analysis under privately-known environmental damage is that D_i was assumed to represent the aggregate of the true individual damage functions. Hence, the group is assumed to know perfectly the individual damage caused. This assumption may seem reasonable when the environmental group is a local or regional citizen group and D_i is the damage borne by these citizens.[23] Thus, in Figure 2.1, the corresponding externality problem may be situated comparatively near the 'single neighbor' benchmark. Then, associational standing has a clear preference-revealing quality. When, in contrast, D_i is borne by a diffuse group of externality victims who are implicitly represented by an environmental organization of national importance, the assumption that this organization knows the exact amount of damage may seem more heroic. The local groups opposing the

---

[23]Remember that under narrowly defined individual rights, these citizens may not have standing under the German principle of individual rights' protection.

project, however, will not necessarily be interested in the possible losses of existence values borne by persons who do not live in the region.

The question is, whether there are mechanisms that prevent the major environmental organisations and their leaders from basing decision-making merely on their own subjective valuation of environmental damage. One such mechanism is the competition of environmental organizations, between each other and with other 'public interests' groups, for benevolent effort and for contributions from members' fees and donations. Hence, departures from the group's alleged assessment of victims' valuations from victims' actual valuations that are perceived as being too strong may be punished by losses in contributions and benevolent effort. Provided that this mechanism functions, the subsequent question is whether the group has the technical opportunities to establish the victims' true valuations of the environmental damage. In consequence, two possible limitations result.

- First, the punishment mechanism itself may not work. The group (or its leadership) will base decision-making on its own subjective valuation. In this case, the welfare implications derived in this section cannot be applied. Even then, however, the analysis of Section 6.4.4 shows that departures from efficiency under unknown environmental damages may not result from the collective actor's incentive to behave strategically in environmental negotiations:[24] the group leadership will still have an incentive to reveal its own valuation of the environmental damage.
- Second, while the punishment mechanism works in principle, the group may not have the technical opportunities to obtain better information from the externality victims than the regulating agency. Then, the best the group can do is to base its decisions on the expected environmental damage. Hence, with respect to the assessment of environmental damage, it will behave like the bumbling bureaucrat. While proposition 6.3 will no longer hold with respect to first-best efficiency, efficiency will still be improved. The analysis proceeds analogously to Chapter 5, with respect, however, to

---

[24]The assumption of a collective actor is one important difference to Rob's (1989) analysis. Rob considers negotiations between the operator of a planned pollution-generating plant and nearby residents, who are privately informed on their respective environmental damages. He shows that inefficient outcomes may result, in which the investor, in equilibrium, would have to pay too high a compensation, and decides not to build the plant even while it would improve welfare to do so. Furthermore, expected inefficiency increases in the number of residents. Rob points out that his results are not robust with respect to coalition formation between the residents (ibid. 319–20).

the expected environmental damage. Efficiency will be improved, possibly up to the expected welfare maximum.

The analysis considered bargaining within the licensing of a new project. It can suitably be adapted to the case of private negotiations over the regulation of an existing project, as will be sketched out now.

Informed investor. Consider the case in which the investor is privately informed about the profit generated by the project. In this case, the group's value of going to court, which is

$$- D^{cs} = -(p_I D_0 + p_A D_i(S^*)),$$

is not influenced by the investor type. When the facility already exists, it is the group's threat to opt out which will always be credible. The analysis of Section 6.4.4 applies accordingly. The privacy of information does not decrease efficiency.

Informed group. When, however, the group is privately informed about the environmental damage, its value of going to court is

$$- D_i^{cs} = -(p_I D_{0i} + p_A D_i(\tilde{S}^*))$$

and, hence, is type-specific. Analogously to the analysis of Section 6.3, the investor will screen the group; depending on the type distribution, an inefficient equilibrium with a positive probability of trial will result.

These observations relate the analysis presented here to Samuelson (1985), who analyses Coasean bargaining under secure rights and shows that the inefficiency of the agreement depends on the initial assignment of property rights and the bargaining procedure. Under insecure rights, a corresponding finding applies: for a given information structure and a given bargaining procedure, the inefficiency of the agreement depends on which status quo prevails as long as negotiations are ongoing.

7. Conclusions

7.1 SUMMARY

The book used game theory to analyze the bargaining incentives emerging in environmental policy implementation when agencies have discretion in decision-making. It focused on the role of judicial review of discretionary administrative acts; specifically, on the standing doctrine applied in Germany and the United States with respect to organized environmental interests. It departed from the common economic approach to analyze environmental negotiations within a Coasean setting in order to address some peculiarities of real-world bargaining within the licensing procedures of economic projects generating environmental externalities. Before summarizing the main outcomes concerning this application, consider two results of theoretical interest.

- The model in Chapter 5 presented a theory of private bargaining under insecure property rights, in which the Coasean case of bargaining under secure rights resulted as a benchmark case for specific values of the parties' outside options. As a consequence, complete property rights *ex ante* are not a prerequisite for the existence of bargaining incentives or for the efficiency of the negotiated agreement. A (possibly costly) institution which stochastically allocates such rights only *ex post*, that is, after failed negotiations, may be a sufficient condition for *ex ante* existence and efficiency. The right to call upon this institution can be interpreted as an attenuated, insecure property right. The role of compensation was also shown to be more limited: efficiency improvements or an efficient bargained solution will exist even under restricted compensation.
- As was shown in Chapter 4, the Rubinstein bargaining model with outside options allows one to endogenously derive the credibility of the parties' threat to opt out, *via* the probability of a specific party of prevailing in court. It results that the bargaining power of the respective parties is also endogenous. This approach allowed one to show, on different occasions, the limitations of simpler bargaining procedures that exogenously allocate

bargaining power to a specific party, that is, to the party which is assumed to make a take-it-or-leave-it offer. The present analysis suggests that, for a given status quo and given values of the parties' outside options, the modeler is not free to allocate exogenously all the bargaining power to any party he/she wishes. For instance, as was shown in Chapter 4, it would not make sense to allocate all the bargaining power to the agency when addressing negotiations with the investor over the regulation of an existing facility.

The main insights of the chapters with respect to real-world environmental bargaining and the role of different standing doctrines are summarized below:

- Chapter 3 investigated the legislators' decision as to whether to grant discretion in the first place in a setting in which investors hold private information on data relevant to efficient regulation, and in which better-informed agencies are open to collusion. It showed that combining agency discretion with legal standing for environmental groups, while implying regulatory costs and the possibility of court errors, may be a more efficient regulatory policy for some distributions of types than using direct regulation via uniform standards. Moreover, the analysis gave a rationale for simple legal decision rules and showed that extortion improves welfare when parties bid for preferred regulation under a strictly convex technology. Also, a more expansive standing doctrine was shown to possibly decrease the number of filed suits in equilibrium, because a legally empowered watchdog organization deters agencies from collusive bargaining with investors.
- Chapter 4 analyzed the bargaining incentives emerging in the framework of a stochastic court outcome, in which only the investor or project operator can fight environmental regulation in court. By comparing regulatory bargaining over new and over existing projects, it was shown that the grandfathering of existing facilities cannot always be explained by bargaining-inherent advantages of operators of existing facilities. Furthermore, the chapter addressed the role of specific features of German administrative practice. Specifically, it showed that conservation offset duties, the practice of grading permits and the toleration of permit violations have strategic importance in environmental negotiations: they may improve welfare in regards to the bargaining outcome and ensure self-enforcement of informal agreements.

- Chapter 5 focused on the case of licensing new projects. It introduced standing for the environmental group into the bargaining model presented in Chapter 4 and derived a welfare-improving property of such a legal standing *via* the emerging bargaining incentives between the private parties, even while the expected welfare from trial is reduced. Furthermore, it investigated the impact of associational standing on informal agreements between investors and agencies. In such a setting, the welfare effect was shown to be more ambiguous; however, the efficiency-improving property can be restored by granting shorter legal deadlines to the investor for filing suit against the permit conditions. Moreover, the chapter analyzed the possible incentives of the investor for extortion by committing, at a pre-bargaining stage, to technology that is inferior in terms of welfare, and showed that such incentives do not exist in the context of regulatory negotiations over new projects. Also, the analysis addressed some crucial differences between regulatory bargaining at the project and industry level, which limit the derived results to the former case.
- Chapter 6 reconsidered the setting of Chapter 5 under incomplete information. It investigated two settings of one-sided incomplete information, where either the investor or the environmental group possesses private information. In the former case, private bargaining was shown to possibly lead to an inefficient outcome, where trials are initiated with positive probability in equilibrium. This inefficiency cannot be reduced by the intervention of an external mediator. The finding in Chapter 5 that legal standing for environmental groups will improve regulatory efficiency had to be qualified for such a setting of private information. However, the finding was shown to be transferable when privately known environmental damage is the relevant informational constraint, and the environmental group, compared with the other actors, has superior information on environmental damage. This result holds when the court outcome features private values. Furthermore, a rationale was given as to why an agency should take a passive role in environmental negotiations within bipolar environmental conflicts.

7.2 THE POLICY CONCLUSION

The main policy conclusion of this study is that, under the possible qualifications given in Chapter 6, a more expansive standing for environmental groups may have its merits from the viewpoint of economic efficiency. This result is relevant for Germany, where administrative law traditionally has been very reluctant to extend legal standing beyond persons who are affected in their individual rights. But the result also bears a lesson for the United States, where the standing issue is far from moot. Recent Supreme Court jurisdiction, which tightened the standing requirements, led to harsh commentaries by legal scholars and minority opinion justices: Rodgers (1994, 106) speaks of a 'recent judicial war against standing' and, in a now famous formulation, Justice Blackmun expressed his dissent in the Lujan v. Defenders of Wildlife decision by characterizing the Supreme Court ruling as 'a slash-and-burn-expedition through the law of environmental standing' (cit. in Rodgers 1994, 108–9).

Notwithstanding these recent restrictions, standing barriers are still lower in the United States. Therefore, it may be wondered whether the US case might serve as a role model for possible reforms of German policy implementation procedures. Several qualifications can be made in this respect.[1]

The class of externality problems. The only departure, in German law, from the principle of individual rights' protection is to be found in the nature conservation acts. Even here, associational standing is restricted. While the theoretical analysis suggests that liberalizing associational standing under these statutes may have positive consequences on welfare, it also gives a rationale as to why associational standing should be restricted to nature conservation issues. As was explained when introducing the taxonomy of Chapter 2, these are environmental problems in which case-to-case regulation by discretionary agencies cannot be avoided in the first place. For problems in which direct regulation *via* taxes or tradable permits is possible, the normative conclusion may be rather to abolish agency discretion in the first place and to introduce these instruments.

The scope of standing rights. The analysis restricted attention to standing for organized environmental interests in a setting of environmental externalities borne by persons beyond neighbors. Hence, it carefully avoided speaking of

---

[1] It is for the following reasons that the policy conclusion cannot be tested by comparing the actual performance of German and US environmental policy. Furthermore, the impact of standing on efficiency in project-specific regulation is clearly restricted by the quality of the underlying environmental law. For example, when the law prescribes lax regulation with little agency discretion, standing for environmental groups will not improve the outcome.

standing for affected 'third parties' *in general* (beyond the subject of regulation and the agency). The reason for this procedure is that environmental externalities are technical externalities which are important from the viewpoint of welfare efficiency. In contrast, positive or negative pecuniary externalities of the project under dispute, resulting from a change in relative prices, do not constitute an allocation problem from the outset. Hence, granting standing to parties affected by pecuniary externalities would give rise exclusively to rent-seeking activities. For this reason, the German principle to extend standing only for organized environmental interests has some rationality.

The level of agency discretion. The analysis focused on policy implementation at the project level. It did consider implementation of environmental statutes via rulemaking, in Section 5.11, only to present some crucial differences with respect to the efficiency of negotiated agreements. The role of legal standing for environmental groups was shown to be ambiguous within negotiated rulemaking even under complete information. In consequence, the German principle of mainly providing for an indirect control of administrative procedures, within their application to specific regulatory cases, has its merits.

7.3 OBJECTIONS AND CAVEATS

Chapters 4 to 6 focused on the emerging bargaining incentives in a stochastic legal setting. Consider now some possible objections from a political perspective.

The search for legal precedents. Clearly, parties may not be ready to settle when actually aiming for a legal precedent. For instance, an administrator may not be sure how to interpret the statute in a given regulatory case and may therefore be interested merely in a court decision of general principle which may serve as a guideline for future cases. Such a situation, however, presupposes that the administrator, in this specific case, is indifferent between the different regulatory alternatives covered by the statute. While realistic, such a situation is beyond the scope of the model, which depicts an agency which knows perfectly which level of environmental spending it mostly prefers.

Project-specific or policy issues? Environmental groups may not be inclined to negotiate when primarily concerned with related policy questions, rather than project-specific externalities. For instance, consider a dispute over a planned power plant. Here, the issue of overriding importance for the group may not be the site- and plant-specific externalities, but the underlying energy policy. However, such policy questions are formally addressed neither during administrative licensing procedures nor during subsequent legal disputes. This mismatch between what can be addressed during formal procedures and what is actually at stake may lead environmental groups to use the formal procedures (possible trials included) only in a tactical sense. Hence, they may merely aim to inflict additional costs on the other parties and delay project realization, with the hope of ultimately preventing not only project execution, but also implementation of the policy. Conversely, 'making a deal' in such a situation, even while improving the project-specific payoffs, may have severe negative ramifications on the group's position in the overarching policy struggle.

Environmental groups and political power. The present analysis focuses on the bargaining power stemming from a standing to sue. This focus should not be misunderstood. It is not argued here that German environmental groups, while more restricted with respect to their legal options, are powerless actors within environmental policy implementation.

- Within formal licensing procedures, rights to comment and object extend beyond those legally affected by the project. Environmental groups will then also have a voice during the public hearing.
- As was described in Chapter 2, environmental groups, even when not entitled to sue, can support neighbors of the project in filing suit. Also, they may acquire land near the project and thus gain standing as a legally affected party.
- They can also try to impede execution of the project *via* the political mobilization of objections. As every person raising an objection has to be invited to the hearing, and as the agency has to give a comment on every objection, environmental groups, even while ultimately not stopping the project, can use these requirements to raise the costs of the procedure or delay issuance of the permit.
- Besides using the formal procedural requirements in this tactical sense, they can also make efforts – by mass mobilization or lobbying – for direct political intervention. Within the German discussion, it is frequently

pointed to this option, to underline that granting legal power to organized environmental interests is actually not necessary (see, for example, Kloepfer 1998, 523).

Consider each of these points in turn.

- With respect to procedural rights, a right to comment to a specific decision-making institution is clearly different from, and arguably weaker than, a right to fight the decision itself within another institution designed to control the decision-making institution.
- The possibility of a so-called 'improper associational standing' (*unechte Verbandsklage*) is clearly restricted to cases in which there are neighbors ready to file suit or areas of land to acquire. In nature conservation cases, this is not so natural an assumption, as it might appear at first glance, as the example presented in Section 5.7 made clear. Even when this possibility exists, a formal stake in court will be restricted to the damage to the neighbor's property or the harm done to the specific area of land. Then, the issue for which the group is really striving (the loss of total existence and indirect use values) is again not addressed in court. Consequently, possible bargaining power emerging from such an improper associational standing will be weaker.
- When political mobilization is possible in such a setting, the group may indeed prefer to prioritize this alternative instrument and use formal procedures only to support the political struggle. Such a decision, however, may restrict possibilities for a bargained solution in the first place, as will be argued in the next point.
- While it is clear that successful political mobilization generates power, it is questionable as to what extent it can be turned into *bargaining* power. While the logic of political mobilization calls for confrontation, all-or-nothing objectives and ideologization, the logic of bargaining calls for cooperation, compromise and pragmatism. Political mobilization then cuts both ways in heated political conflicts: the organization of political resistance against a project may actually impede a bargained solution. An environmental group which, in order to mobilize the public, first issues apocalyptic visions concerning the project's environmental impact, and afterwards decides to 'make a deal with the enemy of the environment' would clearly run into severe trouble with its constituency. In this sense, the logic of a *court* battle may be closer to the logic of negotiations within administrative procedures than a political fight.

Greve (1989, 242) suggests that the driving force behind the traditional German reluctance to extend associational standing is 'the wish to separate law from politics and prevent the politicization of law'. Indeed, this argument applies to the aforementioned constellation in which policy, not specific project issues, are actually relevant. It is here that environmental groups, because of the mismatch between the policy issue actually at stake and the characteristics of the project which can be addressed in court, may use legal procedures solely for tactical reasons. However, for the class of externality problems analyzed in this book, the latter comparison of legal standing with political mobilization suggests rather that extending associational standing may actually depoliticize the administrative process of environmental policy implementation. It may do so without necessarily putting further stress on the judiciary system because of the emerging bargaining incentives. Furthermore, as was shown in Chapter 3, even when possible bargaining incentives are not taken into account, an extension of standing may also lower the number of filed suits in equilibrium.

References

Admati, A. R. and M. Perry (1987): 'Strategic Delay in Bargaining'. *Review of Economic Studies 54*, 345–64.

Althammer, W. (1995): 'Bargaining and the Coase Theorem'. *Jahrbuch für Nationalökonomie und Statistik 214*, 641–62.

Amacher, G. S. and A. S. Malik (1996): 'Bargaining in Environmental Regulation and the Ideal Regulator'. *Journal of Environmental Economics and Management 30*, 233–53.

Amacher, G. S. and A. S. Malik (1998): 'Instrument Choice When Regulators and Firms Bargain'. *Journal of Environmental Economics and Management 35*, 225–41.

Aman, A. C. Jr.; W. T. Mayton (1998): Adminstrative Law. St. Paul, Minn.: West Group.

Amy, D. J. (1990): 'Environmental Dispute Resolution: The Promise and the Pitfalls'. in: Vig, N. J. and M. E. Kraft (eds): *Environmental Policy in the 1990s*. Washington, DC: CQ Press, 211–34.

Arndt, H. W. and W. Rudolf (1992): *Öffentliches Recht*. 9th edn, München: Franz Vahlen.

Asimov, M. (1994): 'On Pressing McNollgast to the Limits: The Problem of Regulatory Costs. *Law and Contemporary Problems 57*, 127–37.

Aspen Institute (1996): *The Alternative Path. A Cleaner, Cheaper Way to Protect and Enhance the Environment*. The Aspen Institute Series on the Environment in the 21st Century, Washington, DC: Aspen.

d'Aspremont, C. and L. A. Gérard-Varet (1979): 'Incentives and Incomplete Information'. *Journal of Public Economics 11*, 25–45.

Aumann, R. (1987): 'Correlated Equilibrium as an Expression of Bayesian Rationality'. *Econometrica 55*, 1–18.

Ausubel, L. M. and R. J. Deneckere (1989): 'A Direct Mechanism Characterization of Sequential Bargaining with One-Sided Incomplete Information'. *Journal of Economic Theory 48*, 18–46.

Babich, A. (1995): 'Citizen Suits: The Teeth in Public Participation'. *Environmental Law Reporter 25*, 10141–51.

Bacow, L. and M. Wheeler (1984): *Environmental Dispute Resolution*. New York: Plenum Press.

Baik, K. H. and J. T. Shogren (1994): 'Environmental Conflicts with Reimbursement for Citizen Suits'. *Journal of Environmental Economics and Management 27*, 1–20.

Banks, J. and B. Weingast (1992): 'Political Control of Agencies Under Asymmetric Information'. *American Journal of Political Science 36*, 509–24.

Baumol, W. J. and W. E. Oates (1988): *The Theory of Environmental Policy*. Cambridge, Mass., New York: Cambridge University Press.

Bebchuk, L. A. (1984): 'Litigation and Settlement under Imperfect Information'. *Rand Journal of Economics 15*, 404–15.

Bebchuk, L. A. (1988): 'Suing Solely to Extract a Settlement Offer'. *Journal of Legal Studies 17*, 437–50.

Beck, R. E. (1994): 'The Movement in the United States to Restoration and Creation of Wetlands'. *Natural Resources Journal 34*, 781–822.

Benz, A. (1990). 'Verhandlungen, Verträge und Absprachen in der öffentlichen Verwaltung'. *Die Verwaltung 23*, 83–98.

Benz, A. (1992): 'Normanpassung und Normverletzung im Verwaltungshandeln'. in: Benz, A. and W. Seibel (eds), loc cit., 31–58.

Benz, A. and W. Seibel (eds) (1992): *Zwischen Kooperation und Korruption: Abweichendes Verhalten in der Verwaltung*. Baden-Baden.

Bergstrom, Th., L. Blume and H. Varian (1986): 'On the Private Provision of Public Goods'. *Journal of Public Economics 29*, 25–49.

Bernholz, P. and F. Breyer (1984): *Grundlagen der Politischen Ökonomie*. 2nd edn, Tübingen: J. C. B. Mohr.

Bingham, G. (1986): *Resolving Environmental Disputes. A Decade of Experience*. Washington, DC: Conservation Foundation.

Binmore, K., A. Rubinstein and A. Wolinski (1986): 'The Nash Bargaining Solution in Economic Modeling'. *Rand Journal of Economics 17*, 176–88.

Binmore, K., A. Shaked; J. Sutton (1989): 'An Outside Option Experiment'. *Quarterly Journal of Economics 104*, 753–70.

Bizer, J., T. Ormond and U. Riedel (1990): *Die Verbandsklage im Naturschutzrecht*. Taunusstein: Blottner.

Bohne, E. (1981): *Der informale Rechtsstaat*. Berlin: Duncker & Humblot.

Bohne, E. (1984): 'Informales Verwaltungs- und Regierungshandeln als Instrument des Umweltschutzes'. *Verwaltungs-Archiv 75*, 343–73.

Bohne, E. (1990): 'Recent Trends in Informal Environmental Conflict Resolution'. in: Hoffmann-Riem, W. and E. Schmidt-Aßmann (eds), loc cit., vol. 1, 217–29.

Boyer, M. and J. J. Laffont (1999): 'Towards a Political Theory of the Emergence of Environmental Incentive Regulation'. *Rand Journal of Economics 30*, 137–57.

Breuer, R. (1990): 'Verhandlungslösungen aus der Sicht des deutschen Umweltschutzrechts'. in: Hoffmann-Riem, W. and E. Schmidt-Aßmann (eds), loc cit., vol. 1, 231–52.

Brohm, W. (1986): 'Die staatliche Verwaltung als eigenständige Gewalt und die Grenzen der Verwaltungsgerichtsbarkeit'. *Deutsches Verwaltungsblatt 101*, 321–30.

Brohm, W. (1987): 'Verwaltung und Verwaltungsgerichtsbarkeit in einem polyzentrischen System der Rechtserzeugung'. *Die öffentliche Verwaltung 40*, 265–71.

Bromley, D. (1978): 'Externalities, Extortion, and Efficiency: Comment'. *American Economic Review 68*, 730–35.

Browning, E. K. (1977): 'External Diseconomies, Compensation, and the Measure of Damage'. *Southern Economic Journal 43*, 1279–87.

Buchanan, J. M. and G. Tullock (1975): 'Polluters' Profits and Political Response: Direct Control versus Taxes'. *American Economic Review 65*, 139–47.

Buchholz, W. and C. Haslbeck (1991): 'Private Verhandlungen und staatliche Regulierung bei asymmetrischer Information: Ein Wohlfahrtsvergleich'. *Finanzarchiv 49*, 167–80.

Buchholz, W. and C. Haslbeck (1997): 'Strategic Manipulation of Property Rights in Coasean Bargaining'. *Journal of Institutional and Theoretical Economics 153*, 630–40.

Buchholz, W. and K. A. Konrad (1995): 'Strategic Transfers and Private Provision of Public Goods' *Journal of Public Economics 57*, 489–505.

Bulling, M. (1989): 'Kooperatives Verwaltungshandeln (Vorverhandlungen, Arrangements, Agreements und Verträge) in der Verwaltungspraxis'. *Die öffentliche Verwaltung 42*, 277–89.

Bund für Umwelt und Naturschutz Deutschland (BUND), Landesverband Thüringen (1997a): *Bewegung im Rechtsstreit um geplantes Pumpspeicherwerk Goldisthal: BUND Thüringen und VEAG schließen Vergleich*. Press release, 13.3.97, Eisenach.

Bund für Umwelt und Naturschutz Deutschland (BUND) (1997b): *Goldisthal*. dossier (mimeo), Bonn: BUND.

Burmeister, J. H. and G. Winter (1990): 'Akteneinsicht in der Bundesrepublik'. in: Winter, G. (ed.): loc cit., 87–128.

Burt, C. T. (1994): 'Procedural Injury Standing after *Lujan v. Defenders of Wildlife*'. *The University of Chicago Law Review 62*, 275–99.

Butler, R. V. and M. D. Maher (1986): 'The Control of Externalities: Abatement vs. Damage Prevention'. *Southern Economic Journal 52*, 1088–102.

Caldart, C. C. and N. A. Ashford (1999): 'Negotations as a Means of Developing and Implementing Environmental and Occupational Health and Safety Policy'. *Harvard Environmental Law Review 23*, 141–202.

Che, Y.-K. and D. Earnhart (1997): 'Optimal Use of Information in Litigation: Should Regulatory Information be withheld to Deter Frivolous Suits'. *Rand Journal of Economics 28*, 120–34.

Cheung, R. (1988): *A Bargaining Model of Pretrial Negotiation*. John M. Olin Program in Law and Economics Working Paper 49, Stanford Law School.

Chiang, A. (1984): *Fundamental Methods of Mathematical Economics*. 3rd edn, New York etc.: McGraw-Hill.

Cho, I.-K. and D. Kreps (1987): 'Signaling Games and Stable Equilibria'. *Quarterly Journal of Economics 102*, 179–222.

Clarke, E. H. (1971): 'Multipart Pricing of Public Goods'. *Public Choice 8*, 19–33.

Claus, F. (1996): 'Überblick über Fragen der Konfliktmittlung – Neun Fragen zu den Perspektiven in Deutschland'. in: Holzinger, K. and H. Weidner (eds), loc cit., 53–62.

Claus, F. and P. M. Wiedemann (eds) (1994): *Umweltkonflikte. Vermittlungsverfahren zu ihrer Lösung*. Taunusstein: E. Blottner.

Coase, R. (1937): 'The Nature of the Firm'. *Econometrica 4*, 386–405.

Coase, R. (1960): 'The Problem of Social Cost'. *Journal of Law and Economics 3*, 1–44.

Commission of The European Communities (EC) (1996): *On Environmental Agreements*. Communication from the Commission to the Council and the European Parliament. Brussels.

Cooter, R. D. and D. L. Rubinfeld (1989): 'Economic Analysis of Legal Disputes and Their Resolution'. *Journal of Economic Literature 26*, 1067–97.

Cooter, R. D. and T. Ulen (1988): *Law and Economics*. Glenview, London: Scott, Foresman & Co.

Cornes, R. and T. Sandler (1996): *The Theory of Externalities, Public Goods and Club Goods*. Cambridge: Cambridge University Press.

Coursen, D. (1996): 'Property Rights Legislation: A Survey of Federal and State Assessment and Compensation Measures'. *Environmental Law Reporter 26*, 10239–51.

Crowfoot, J. and J. Wollondeck (1990): *Environmental Disputes. Community Involvement in Conflict Resolution*. Washington, DC: Island Press.

Dalton, D. S. (1993): 'The Negotiated Rulemaking Process – Creating a New Legitimacy in Regulation'. *Review of European Community and International Environmental Law 2*, 35460.

Daly, G. and J. F. Giertz (1975): 'Externalities, Extortion, and Efficiency'. *American Economic Review 65*, 997–1001.

Daly, G. and J. F. Giertz (1978): 'Externalities, Extortion, and Efficiency: Reply'. *American Economic Review 68*, 736–8.

Damme, E. v. (1989): 'Renegotiation-Proof Equilibria in Repeated Prisoners' Dilemma'. *Journal of Economic Theory 47*, 206–17.

Deily, M. E. and W. B. Gray (1991): 'Enforcement of Pollution Regulations in a Declining Industry'. *Journal of Environmental Economics and Management 21*, 260–74.

Demougin, D. and G. Illing (1993): 'Property Rights and Regulation of Environmental Quality under Asymmetric Information'. *Jahrbuch für Nationalökonomie und Statistik 211*, 385–402.

Demsetz, H. (1978): 'On Extortion: Reply'. *American Economic Review 68*, 417–18.

Dixit, A. (1987): 'Strategic Behavior in Contests'. *American Economic Review 77*, 891–98.

Dose, N. (1989): 'Normanpassung durch Verhandlung mit der Ordnungs-verwaltung'. in: Benz, A. and W. Seibel (eds), loc cit., 87–112.

Dose, N. (1997): *Die verhandelnde Verwaltung: eine empirische Untersuchung über den Vollzug des Immissionsschutzrechts*. Baden-Baden: Nomos.

Eberle, C.-E. (1984): 'Arrangements im Verwaltungsverfahren'. *Die Verwaltung 17*, 439–64.

Elliott, M. (1996): 'The Use of Alternative Dispute Resolution in Environmental Decision Making: Status Report on the United States Experience'. in: Holzinger, K. and H. Weidner (eds): loc cit., 31–40.

Environmental Law Institute (ELI) (1984): *Citizen Suits: An Analysis of Citizen Enforcement Actions under EPA-Administered Statutes*. Washington, DC: Environmental Law Institute.

Epstein, D. and S. O'Halloran (1995): 'A Theory of Strategic Oversight: Congress, Lobbyists, and the Bureaucracy'. *Journal of Law, Economics, and Organization 11*, 233–54.

Farber, D. A. (1992): 'Politics and Procedure in Environmental Law'. *Journal of Law, Economics, and Organization 8*, 59–81.

Farber, D. A. and P. P. Frickey (1991): *Law and Public Choice. A Critical Introduction*. Chicago, London: University of Chicago.

Farrell, J. (1987): 'Information and the Coase Theorem'. *Journal of Economic Perspectives 1*, 113–29.

Farrell, J. and E. Maskin (1989): 'Renegotiation in Repeated Games'. *Games and Economic Behavior 1*, 327–60.

Fenn, P. and C. G. Veljanovski (1988): 'A Positive Economic Theory of Regulatory Enforcement'. *The Economic Journal 98*, 1055–70.

Fershtman, C. and S. Nitzan (1991): 'Dynamic Voluntary Provision of Public Goods'. *European Economic Review 35*, 1057–67.

Froeb, L. M. and B. H. Kobayashi (1996): 'Naive, Biased, yet Bayesian: Can Juries Interpret Selectively Produced Evidence?' *Journal of Law, Economics, and Organization 12*, 257–76.

Fudenberg, D. and J. Tirole (1983): 'Sequential Bargaining with Incomplete Information'. *Review of Economic Studies 50*, 221–47.

Fudenberg, D. and J. Tirole (1991). *Game Theory*. Cambridge, Mass., London: MIT Press.

Fudenberg, D., D. K. Levine and J. Tirole (1987): 'Incomplete Information Bargaining with Outside Opportunities'. *Quarterly Journal of Economics 102*, 37–50.

Führ, M. (1989): *Sanierung von Industrieanlagen am Beispiel der Änderungsgenehmigungsverfahren nach §15 BImSchG*. Düsseldorf: Werner.

Führ, M. (1990): 'Umweltinformationen in Genehmigungsverfahren. Eine Fallstudie', in: Winter, G. (ed.), loc cit., 129–58.

Führ, M. and G. Roller (eds) (1991): *Participation and Litigation Rights of Environmental Associations in Europe. Current Legal Situation and Practical Experience*. Frankfurt am Main etc.: Peter Lang.

Funke, R. (1990): 'Konfliktbewältiging aus Anlaß von Genehmigungsverfahren'. in: Hoffmann-Riem, W. and E. Schmidt-Aßmann (eds), loc cit., vol. 2, 209–20.

Galanter, M. and M. Cahill (1994): '"Most Cases Settle": Judicial Promotion and Regulation of Settlements'. *Stanford Law Review 46*, 1339–91.

Gardner, R. C. (1996): 'Federal Wetland Mitigation Banking Guidance: Missed Opportunities'. *Environmental Law Reporter 26*, 10075–9.

Garrett, T. L. (1991): 'Citizen Suits'. in: Kole, J. S. and L. D. Espel (eds), *Environmental Litigation*. Chicago: American Bar Association.

Gibbons, R. (1992): *Game Theory for Applied Economists*. Princeton: Princeton University Press.

Gould, J. (1973): 'The Economics of Legal Conflicts'. *Journal of Legal Studies 2*, 279–300.

Gradstein, M. (1992): 'Time Dynamics and Incomplete Information in the Private Provision of Public Goods'. *Journal of Political Economy 100*, 581–97.

Greve, M. S. (1989): 'The Non-Reformation of Administrative Law: Standing to Sue and Public Interest Litigation in West German Environmental Law'. *Cornell International Law Journal 22*, 199–244.

Greve, M. S. (1990): 'The Private Enforcement of Environmental Law'. *Tulane Law Review 65*, 339–95.

Greve, M. S. (1996): *The Demise of Environmentalism in American Law*. Washington, DC: American Enterprise Institute.

Grossman, S. J. and O. D. Hart (1986): 'The Costs and Benefits of Ownership: A Theory of Lateral and Vertical Integration'. *Journal of Political Economy 94*, 691–719.

Grossman, S. J. and M. Perry (1986): 'Sequential Bargaining under Asymmetric Information'. *Journal of Economic Theory 39*, 120–54.

Groves, T. (1973): 'Incentives in Teams'. *Econometrica 41*, 617–31.

Gul, F. and H. Sonnenschein (1988): 'On Delay in Bargaining with One-Sided Uncertainty'. *Econometrica 56*, 601–11.

Gurlit, E. (1990): 'Akteneinsicht in den Vereinigten Staaten'. in: Winter, G. (ed.), loc cit., 511–52.

Habicht II, F. H. and T. E. Hunt et al. (1999): 'Negotiated Settlement of EPA Enforcement Cases', in: Novick, S. et al. (eds), loc cit., vol. 1, 8.152–232.

Harter, P. J. (1982): 'Negotiating Regulations: A Cure for Malaise'. *Georgetown Law Journal 71*, 1–113.

Haslbeck, C. (1995): *Zentrale versus dezentrale Internalisierung externer Effekte bei unvollständiger Information*. Frankfurt/Main: Peter Lang.

Hennecke, H.-G. (1991): 'Informelles Verwaltungshandeln im Wirtschafts-verwaltungs- und Umweltrecht'. *Natur und Recht 13*, 267–75.

Hermes, G. and J. Wieland (1988): *Die staatliche Duldung rechtswidrigen Verhaltens. Dogmatische Folgen behördlicher Untätigkeit im Umwelt- und Steuerrecht*. Heidelberg: Müller.

Heyes, A. G. (1997): 'Environmental Regulation by Private Contest'. *Journal of Public Economics 63*, 407–28.

Hirshleifer, J. (1988): 'The Analytics of Continuing Conflict'. *Synthese 76*, 201–33.

Hirshleifer, J. (1989): 'Conflict and Rent-Seeking Success Functions: Relative versus Difference Models of Relative Success'. *Public Choice 63*, 101–12.

Hoffmann-Riem, W. and E. Schmidt-Aßmann (eds) (1990): *Konflikt-bewältigung durch Verhandlungen – informelle und mittlerunterstützte Verhandlungen in Verwaltungsverfahren.* 2 vols, Baden-Baden: Nomos.

Holzinger, K. (1987): *Umweltpolitische Instrumente aus der Sicht der staat-lichen Bürokratie. Versuch einer Anwendung der 'ökonomischen Theorie der Bürokratie'.* München: Ifo-Institut für Wirtschaftsforschung.

Holzinger, K. and Weidner, H. (eds) (1996): *Alternative Konfliktregelungsverfahren bei der Planung und Implementation großtechnischer Anlagen.* Wissenschaftszentrum Berlin (WZB) papers, FS II 96-301, Berlin: WZB.

Holznagel, B. (1990): *Konfliktlösung durch Verhandlungen.* Baden-Baden: Nomos.

Horbach, J. (1992): *Neue Politische Ökonomie und Umweltpolitik.* Frankfurt/Main, New York: Campus.

Horbach, J. (1996): 'Ökonomische Bürokratie- und Vollzugstheorien – Lehren für die Umweltpolitik', in: Gawel, E. (ed.), *Institutionelle Pro-bleme der Umweltpolitik. Zeitschrift für angewandte Umweltforschung, Sonderheft 8*, Berlin.

Illing, G. (1992): 'Private Information as Transaction Costs: The Coase Theorem Revisited'. *Journal of Institutional and Theoretical Economics 148*, 558–76.

Jaffe, J. F. (1975). 'The "Coase-Theorem": A Reexamination – Comment'. *Quarterly Journal of Economics 89*, 660–61.

Jarass, H. D. (1990): 'Basic Approach to and Examples of Negotiations in Resolving Environmental Disputes'. in: Hoffmann-Riem, W. and E. Schmidt-Aßmann (eds), vol. 1, loc cit., 259–62.

Jarass, H. D. (1993a): 'Strukturelemente des amerikanischen Umweltrechts im Vergleich'. *Natur und Recht 15*, 49–54.

Jarass, H. D. (1993b): 'Der Vollzug von Umweltrecht in den USA'. *Natur und Recht 15*, 197–202.

Jarass, H. D. and J. DiMento (1993): 'Through Comparative Lawyers' Goggles: A Primer on German Environmental Law'. *The Georgetown International Law Review 6*, 47–72.

Jensen, M. C., W. H. Meckling and C. G. Holderness (1986): 'Analysis of Alternative Standing Doctrines'. *International Review of Law and Economics 6*, 205–16.

Johnston, J. S. (1995): 'Bargaining Under Rules versus Standards'. *The Journal of Law, Economics, and Organization, 11*, 256–81.

Kahneman, D. and A. Tversky (1995): 'Conflict Resolution: A Cognitive Perspective'. in: Arrow, K. et al. (eds): *Barriers to Conflict Resolution*. New York, London: W. W. Norton.

Kalt, J. and M. Zupan (1984): 'Capture and Ideology in the Economic Theory of Politics'. *American Economic Review 74*, 279–300.

Katz, A. (1990): 'The Effect of Frivolous Lawsuits on the Settlement of Litigation'. *International Review of Law and Economics 10*, 3–27.

Khalil, F. and J. Lawarrée (1995): 'Collusive Auditors'. *American Economic Review (Papers and Proceedings) 85*, 442–7.

Kippes, St. (1995): *Bargaining. Informales Verwaltungshandeln und Kooperation zwischen Verwaltungen, Bürgern und Unternehmen*. Köln, Berlin, etc.: C. Heymanns.

Klein, B., R. G. Crawford and A. A. Alchian (1978): 'Vertical Integration, Appropriable Rents, and the Competitive Contracting Process', *Journal of Law and Economics 28*, 297–326.

Kloepfer, M. (1998): *Umweltrecht*. 2nd edn, München: C.H. Beck.

Kofman, F. and J. Lawarrée (1993): 'Collusion in Hierarchical Agency'. *Econometrica 61*, 629–56.

Komesar, N. (1990): 'Injuries and Institutions: Tort Reform, Tort Theory, and Beyond'. *New York University Law Review 65*, 23–77.

Kritzner, H. M. (1986): 'Adjudication to Settlement: Shading in the Gray', *Judicature 70*, 161.

Laffont, J.-J. and J. Tirole (1990): 'The Politics of Government Decision Making: Regulatory Institutions'. *Journal of Law, Economics, and Organization 6*, 1–32.

Laffont, J.-J. and J. Tirole (1991): 'The Politics of Government Decision Making: A Theory of Regulatory Capture'. *Quarterly Journal of Economics 106*, 1089–127.

Laffont, J.-J. and J. Tirole (1993): *A Theory of Incentives in Procurement and Regulation*. Cambridge, Mass., London: MIT Press.

Lahl, U. (1993): 'Das programmierte Vollzugsdefizit'. *Zeitschrift für Umweltrecht 6/93*, 249–56.

Lahl, U., K. Frank and B. Zeschmar-Lahl (1992): 'Die Eingriffsregelung in der Bauleitplanung und in der Baugenehmigung'. *Natur und Landschaft 67/12*, 580–85.

Landes, W. (1971): 'An Economic Analysis of the Courts'. *Journal of Law and Economics 14*, 61–107.

Lawrence, B. (1996): 'Supplemental Environmental Projects: A New Approach for EPA Enforcement'. *Environmental Law Reporter 26*, 10174–81.

Lehmann, M. (1996): *Bargaining in Environmental Policy Implementation. An Economic Analysis.* Freie Universität Berlin, discussion paper 26/96, Berlin.

Lehmann, M. (1997): 'Umweltrechtliche Genehmigungsverfahren und Verbandsklage: Eine verhandlungstheoretische Analyse'. in: Feser, H.-D. and M. v. Hauff (eds), *Neuere Entwicklungen in der Umweltökonomie und -politik*. Regensburg: transfer.

Leonard, A. R. (1995): 'When Should an Administrative Enforcement Action Preclude a Citizen Suit Under the Clean Water Act'. *Natural Resources Journal 35*, 555–624.

Leveque, F. (1995): 'Environmental European Policies. A Firm's Involvement in the Regulatory Process', draft report, Centre d'Economie Industrielle (CERNA), Ecole des Mines, Paris.

Levine, M. E. and J. L. Forrence (1990): 'Regulatory Capture, Public Interest, and the Public Agenda: Towards a Synthesis'. *Journal of Law, Economics, and Organization 6*, 167–98.

Lewis, T. and M. Poitevin (1997): 'Disclosure of Information in Regulatory Proceedings'. *Journal of Law, Economics, and Organization 13*, 50–73.

Lübbe-Wolff, G. (1993): 'Vollzugsprobleme der Umweltverwaltung'. *Natur und Recht 15*, 217–29.

Lupia, A. and M. D. McCubbins (1994). 'Learning from Oversight: Fire Alarms and Police Patrols Reconstructed'. *Journal of Law, Economics, and Organization 10*, 96–125.

Malik, A. S. (1993): 'Self-reporting and the Design of Policies for Regulating Stochastic Pollution'. *Journal of Environmental Economics and Management 24*, 241–57.

Mansfield, M. E. (1993): 'The "New" Old Law of Judicial Access'. *Administrative Law Review 45*, 65–106.

Mashaw, J. L., R. A. Merrill and P. M. Shane (1992): *Administrative Law. The American Public Law System*. St. Paul, Minn.: West.

Maskin, E. and J. Tirole (1990): 'The Principal–Agent Relationship with an Informed Principal: The Case of Private Values'. *Econometrica 58*, 379–409.

Maurer, H. (1988): 'Kontinuitätsgewähr und Vertrauensschutz'. in: Isensee, J. and P. Kirchhof (eds): *Handbuch des Staatsrechts der Bundesrepublik Deutschland*. vol. 3, Heidelberg: C.F. Müller, 211–71.

Mayntz, R. (1987): 'Politische Steuerung und gesellschaftliche Steuerungsprobleme'. Mayntz, R. (1997): *Soziale Dynamik und politische Steuerung. Theoretische und methodologische Überlegungen*. Frankfurt/New York: Campus.

Mayntz, R., E. Bohne, J. Hesse, J. Hucke and A. Müller (1978): *Vollzugsprobleme der Umweltpolitik. Empirische Implementation von Gesetzen im Bereich der Luftreinhaltung und des Gewässerschutzes*. Stuttgart: Kohlhammer.

McCarthy, J. and A. Shorett (1984): *Negotiating Settlements. A Guide to Environmental Mediation*. New York: American Arbitration Association.

McCubbins, M. and T. Schwartz (1984): 'Congressional Oversight Overlooked: Police Patrols versus Fire Alarms'. *American Journal of Political Science 2*, 165–79.

McCubbins, M., R. Noll and B. Weingast (1987): 'Administrative Procedures as Instruments of Political Control'. *Journal of Law, Economics, and Organization 3*, 243–77.

McElfish, J. M. (1993): 'Drafting Standing Affidavits After Defenders: In the Courts' Own Words'. *Environmental Law Reporter 23*, 10026–30.

McGrath et al. (1991): State Judicial Review of Administrative Action. *Administrative Law Review 43*, 571–812.

McKelvey, R. D. and T. R. Palfrey (1997): 'Endogeneity of Alternating Offers in a Bargaining Game'. *Journal of Economic Theory 73*, 425–37.

McKenna, C. J. and V. Sadanand (1995): 'The Timing of Arbitration and Sequential Bargaining'. *Canadian Journal of Economics 28*, 1180–93.

McSpadden Wenner, L. (1990): *U.S. Energy and Environmental Interest Groups. Institutional Profiles*. New York etc.: Greenwood.

McSwain, T. R. (1991): 'The Sun Rises on the Florida Legislature: The Constitutional Amendment on Open Legislative Meetings'. *Florida State University Law Review 19*, 307–68.

Melnick, R. S. (1992): 'Administrative Law and Bureaucratic Reality'. *Administrative Law Review 44*, 245. reprinted in Schuck. P. H. (ed.) (1994), loc cit., 200–11.

Migue, J.-L. and G. Belanger (1974): 'Toward a General Theory of Managerial Discretion'. *Public Choice 17*, 27–43.

Milgrom, P. R. and J. Roberts (1986): 'Relying on the Information of Interested Parties'. *Rand Journal of Economics 17*, 18–32.

Moberly, R. B. (1994): 'Ethical Standards for Court-Appointed Mediators and Florida's Mandatory Mediation Experiment'. *Florida State University Review 21*, 702–27.

Moe, T. (1989): 'The Politics of Bureaucratic Structure'. in: Chubb, J. and P. Peterson (eds): *Can the Government Govern?* Washington, DC: Brookings.

Mohr, E. (1990): 'Courts of Appeal, Bureaucracies and Conditional Project Permit: The Role of Negotiating Non-exclusive Property Rights over the Environment'. *Journal of Institutional and Theoretical Economics 146*, 601–16.

Mumey, G. A. (1971): 'The "Coase Theorem": A Reexamination'. *Quarterly Journal of Economics 85*, 718–23.

Muthoo, A. (1995): 'Bargaining in a Long-Term Relationship with Endogenous Termination'. *Journal of Economic Theory 66*, 590–98.

Myerson, R. and M. A. Satterthwaite (1983): 'Efficient Mechanisms for Bilateral Trading'. *Journal of Economic Theory 29*, 265–81.

Nash, J. F. (1950): 'The Bargaining Problem'. *Econometrica 18*, 155–62.

Naysnerski, W. and T. Tietenberg (1992): 'Private Enforcement of Federal Environmental Law'. *Land Economics 69*, 28–48.

Nalebuff, B. (1987): 'Credible Pretrial Negotiation'. *Rand Journal of Economics 18*, 198–210.

Niskanen, W. A., Jr. (1971): *Bureaucracy and Representative Government.* Chicago, New York: Aldine-Atherton.

Niskanen, W. A., Jr. (1973): *Bureaucracy: Servant or Master. Lessons from America.* London: Institute of Economic Affairs.

Nitzan, S. and R. E. Romano (1990): 'Private Provision of a Discrete Public Good with Uncertain Cost'. *Journal of Public Economics 42*, 357–70.

Novick, S. M. and R. V. Percival (1999): 'The Methods of Environmental Protection'. in: Novik, S. M. et al. (eds), loc cit., vol. 1, chap. 3.

Novick, S. M., D. W. Stever and M. G. Mellon (eds) (1999): *Law of Environmental Protection.* Environmental Law Institute, Release 22, 6/99, St. Paul, Minn.: West.

Oates, W. E. and R. M. Schwab (1988): 'Economic Competition among Jurisdictions: Efficiency Enhancing or Distortion Inducing?'. *Journal of Public Economics 35*, 333–54.

O'Hare, M., L. Bacow and D. Sanderson (1983): *Facility Siting and Public Opposition*. New York: Van Nostrand Reinhold.

O'Leary, R. (1993): *Environmental Change. Federal Courts and the EPA*. Philadelphia: Temple University.

O'Leary, R. (1995): 'Environmental Mediation: What Do We Know and How Do We Know It?' in: Blackburn, J. W. and W. M. Bruce (eds): *Mediating Environmental Conflicts. Theory and Practice*. Westport, Conn., London: Quorum Books.

Olson, M. (1965): *The Logic of Collective Action*. Cambridge, MA: Cambridge University Press.

Olson, M. (1969): 'The Principle of "Fiscalic Equivalence": The Division of Responsibilities among Different Levels of Government'. *American Economic Review, Papers and Proceedings 59*, 479–87.

Openchowski, C. (1990): *A Guide to Environmental Law in Washington, D.C.,* Washington, DC: Environmental Law Institute.

Ormond, T. A. (1991): 'Environmental Group Actions in Germany'. in: Führ, M. and G. Roller (eds), loc cit., 77–92.

Osborne, M. J. and A. Rubinstein (1990): *Bargaining and Markets*. San Diego, New York etc.: Academic Press.

Ossenbühl, F. (1987): 'Informelles Hoheitshandeln im Gesundheits- und Umweltschutz'. *Jahrbuch des Technik- und Umweltrechts 3*, 27–48.

Palfrey, Th. R. and H. Rosenthal (1984): 'Participation and the Provision of Discrete Public Goods: A Strategic Analysis'. *Journal of Public Economics 24*, 171–93.

Peacock, A. (1984): *The Regulation Game: How British and West German Companies Bargain with Government*. Oxford, New York: Basil Blackwell.

Pearce, D. W. and R. K. Turner (1990): *Economics of Natural Resources and the Environment*. Baltimore: John Hopkins.

Pedersen, W. F. (1999): 'EPA's Administrative Procedure', in: Novick, S. M. et al. (eds), loc cit., vol. 1., 4.7–20.

Peltzman, S. and T. N. Tiedeman (1972): 'Local versus National Pollution Control: Note'. *American Economic Review 62*, 959–63.

P'ng, I. P. (1983): 'Strategic Behavior in Suit, Settlement, and Trial'. *Bell Journal of Economics 14*, 539–50.

Porter, R. (1988): 'Environmental Negotiation: Its Potential and Its Economic Efficiency'. *Journal of Environmental Economics and Management 15*, 129–42.

Posner, R. (1973): 'An Economic Approach to Legal Procedure and Judicial Administration'. *Journal of Legal Studies 2*, 399–458.

Priest, G. L. and B. Klein (1984): 'The Selection of Disputes for Litigation'. *Journal of Legal Studies 13*, 1–55.

Pritzker, D. M. and D. S. Dalton (1995): *Negotiated Rulemaking Sourcebook.* Administrative Conference of the United States, Office of the Chairman, Washington, DC.

Randelzhofer, A. and D. Wilke (1981): *Die Duldung als Form flexiblen Verwaltungshandelns.* Berlin: Duncker & Humblot.

Rasmusen, E. (1995): 'Predictable and Unpredictable Error in Tort Awards: The Effect of Plaintiff Self-Selection and Signaling'. *International Review of Law and Economics 15*, 323–45.

Rehbinder, E. (1972): *Bürgerklage im Umweltrecht.* Berlin: E. Schmidt.

Reinganum, J. F. and L. L. Wilde (1986): 'Settlement, Litigation and the Allocation of Legal Costs'. *Rand Journal of Economics 17*, 557–66.

RESOLVE (1994): *The Cutting Edge. Environmental Dispute Resolution for the Nineties.* Symposium Summary. Institute for Environmental Negotiation, RESOLVE: Center for Environmental Dispute Resolution, Washington, DC.

Richter, J. and J. K. Stranlund (1997): 'Threat Positions and the Resolution of Environmental Conflicts'. *Land Economics 73*, 58–71.

Ricketts, M. and A. Peacock (1986): 'Bargaining and the Regulatory System'. *International Review of Law and Economics 6*, 3–16.

Rob, R. (1989): 'Pollution Claim Settlements under Private Information'. *Journal of Economic Theory 47*, 307–33.

Rodgers, W. H., Jr. (1994): *Environmental Law.* 2nd edn, St. Paul, Minn.: West.

Rose-Ackerman, S. (1994): 'American Administrative Law Under Siege: Is Germany a Model?'. *Harvard Law Review 107*, 1279–302.

Rose-Ackerman, S. (1995): *Controlling Environmental Policy. The Limits of Public Law in Germany and the United States.* New Haven, London: Yale University Press.

Roth, A. E. (ed.) (1985): *Game-theoretic Models of Bargaining.* Cambridge, Mass., New York, etc: Cambridge University Press.

Rubin, E. (1991): 'Beyond Public Choice: Comprehensive Rationality in the Writing and Reading of Statutes'. *New York University Law Review 66*, 1–64.

Rubinstein, A. (1982): 'Perfect Equilibrium in a Bargaining Model'. *Econometrica 50*, 97–109.

Rubinstein, A. (1985): 'A Bargaining Model with Incomplete Information about Time Preferences'. *Econometrica 53*, 1151–72.

Russell, I. S. (1993): 'The Role of Public Opinion, Public Interest Groups, and Political Parties in Creating and Implementing Environmental Policy'. *Environmental Law Reporter 23*, 10665–74.

Samuelson, W. (1985): 'A Comment on the Coase Theorem'. in: Roth, A. E. (ed.), loc cit., 321–39.

Sander, F. (1990): 'Alternative Methods of Conflict Resolution: A U.S. Perspective', in: Hoffman-Riem, W. and E. Schmidt-Aßmann (eds), vol. 1, loc cit., 141–50.

Schapman, C. (1997): *Der Sanierungsvertrag: Altlastensanierung und Verwaltungsvertrag.* Baden-Baden: Nomos.

Scherer, J. (1991): 'Rechtsprobleme normersetzender "Absprachen" zwischen Staat und Wirtschaft am Beispiel des Umweltrechts'. *Die öffentliche Verwaltung 44*, 1–7.

Schlicht, E. (1996): 'Exploiting the Coase Mechanism: The Extortion Problem'. *Kyklos 49*, 319–30.

Schmidt-Aßmann, E. (1978): 'Institute gestufter Verwaltungsverfahren: Vorbescheid und Teilgenehmigung'. *Festschrift aus Anlaß des 25-jährigen Bestehens des Bundesverwaltungsgerichts*, 569–84.

Schneider, J. P. (1996): 'Kooperative und konsensuale Formen administrativer Entscheidungsprozesse', in: Schenk, K. E., D. Schmidtchen and M. E. Streit (eds): *Vom Hoheitsstaat zum Konsensualstaat. Neue Formen der Kooperation zwischen Staat und Privaten. Jahrbuch für Neue Politische Ökonomie, Bd. 15*, Tübingen: J. C. B. Mohr.

Schuck, P. H. (ed.) (1994): *Foundations of Administrative Law.* New York, Oxford: Oxford University Press.

Schuck, P. H. and E. D. Elliott, (1990): 'To the Chevron Station: An Empirical Study of Administrative Law', reprinted in: Schuck, P. H. (ed.) (1994), loc cit., 212–17.

Schulze, W. and R. C. d'Arge (1974): 'The Coase Proposition, Information Constraints, and Long-Run Equilibrium'. *American Economic Review 64*, 763–72.

Schweizer, U. (1988): 'Externalities and the Coase Theorem: Hypothesis or Result?'. *Journal of Institutional and Theoretical Economics 144*, 245–66.

Schweizer, U. (1989): 'Litigation and Settlement under Two-Sided Incomplete Information' *Review of Economic Studies 56*, 163–78.

Schweizer, U. (1992): *Politische Regeln als unvollständige Verträge: Ursache von Staatsversagen.* Universität Bonn, discussion paper A-372, Bonn.

Schweizer, U. (1993): 'Institutional Choice: A Contract-Theoretical Approach'. *Journal of Institutional and Theoretical Economics 144*, 246–66.

Segerson, K. and T. J. Miceli (1998): 'Voluntary Environmental Agreements: Good or Bad News for Environmental Protection?'. *Journal of Environmental Economics and Management 36*, 109–30.

Segerson, K. and T. Tietenberg (1992): 'The Structure of Penalties in Environmental Enforcement: An Economic Analysis'. *Journal of Environmental Economics and Management 23*, 179–201.

Senate Committee on the Judiciary (1978): *Freedom of Information: A Compilation of State Laws.* 95th Congr. 2nd Sess. Washington, DC: Committee Print.

Shaked, A. (1994): 'Opting Out: Bazaars versus "High Tech" Markets'. *Investigaciones Económicas 18*, 421–32.

Shaked, A. and J. Sutton (1984): 'Involuntary Unemployment as a Perfect Equilibrium in a Bargaining Game'. *Econometrica 52*, 1351–64.

Shavell, S. (1982): 'Suit, Settlement, and Trial: A Theoretical Analysis under Alternative Methods for the Allocation of Legal Costs'. *Journal of Legal Studies 11*, 55–81.

Shavell, S. (1985): 'Uncertainty over Causation and the Determination of Civil Liability'. *Journal of Law, Economics, and Organization 28*, 587–609.

Sheldon, K. P. (1993): 'Lujan v. Defenders of Wildlife: The Supreme Court's Slash and Burn Approach to Environmental Standing'. *Environmental Law Reporter 23*, 10031–43.

Silverstein, J. (1994): 'Taking Wetlands to the Bank: The Role of Wetland Mitigation Banking in a Comprehensive Approach to Wetlands Protection'. *Environmental Affairs 22*, 129–61.

Sobel, J. (1985): 'Disclosure of Evidence and Resolution of Disputes: Who should bear the Burden of Proof?', in: Roth, A. E. (ed.), loc cit., 341–61.

Spier, K. A. (1992): 'The Dynamics of Pretrial Negotiation'. *Review of Economic Studies 59*, 93–108.

Spier, K. E. (1994): 'Settlement Bargaining and the Design of Damage Awards'. *Journal of Law, Economics, and Organization 10*, 84–97.

Spulber, D. F. (1985): 'Effluent Regulation and Long-Run Optimality'. *Journal of Environmental Economics and Management 12*, 103–16.

Spulber, D. F. (1989): *Regulation and Markets*. Cambridge, Mass., London: MIT Press.

Stähler, F. (1998): *Economic Games and Strategic Behavior. Theory and Application*. Cheltenham, Northampton, Mass.: Edward Elgar.

Stigler, G. (1974): 'Free Riders and Collective Action: An Appendix'. *Bell Journal of Economics 5*, 359–65.

Sunstein, C. R. (1992): 'What's Standing after Lujan? Of Citizen Suits, "Injuries", and Article III'. *Michigan Law Review 91*, 163–236.

Susskind, L. and J. Cruikshank (1987): *Breaking the Impasse. Consensual Approaches to Resolving Environmental Disputes*. New York: Basic Books.

Susskind, L. and P. Field (1996): *Dealing with an Angry Public: the Mutual Gains Approach to Resolving Disputes*. New York: Free Press.

Susskind, L. and D. Madigan (1984): 'New Approaches to Resolving Conflicts in the Public Sector'. *The Justice Systems Journal 9*, 179–203.

Susskind, L. and G. McMahon (1985): 'The Theory and Practice of Negotiated Rulemaking'. *Yale Journal on Regulation 3*, 133–65.

Sutton, J. (1986): 'Non-Cooperative Bargaining Theory: An Introduction'. *Review of Economic Studies 53*, 709–24.

Telser, L. G. (1980): 'A Theory of Self-Enforcing Agreements', *Journal of Business 53*, 27–44.

Tirole, J. (1986): 'Hierarchies and Bureaucracies: On the Role of Collusion in Organizations'. *Journal of Law, Economics, and Organization 2*, 181–214.

Tirole, J. (1988): *The Theory of Industrial Organization*. Cambridge, MA, London: MIT Press.

Tirole, J. (1992): 'Collusion and the Theory of Organization', in: Laffont, J.-J. (ed.), *Advances in Economic Theory*. Sixth World Congress of the Econometric Society. Cambridge, New York: Cambridge University Press.

Tomerius, S. (1995): *Informelle Absprachen im Umweltrecht. Möglichkeiten und Grenzen im kooperativen Normenvollzug aus verfassungsrechtlicher Sicht*. Baden-Baden: Nomos.

Treiber, H. (1990): 'Über mittlerunterstützte Verhandlungen bei umstrittenen Standortentscheidungen', in: Hoffmann-Riem, W. and E. Schmidt-Aßmann (eds), loc cit., vol. 1, 267–82.

Usher, D. (1998): 'The Coase Theorem is Tautological, Incoherent or Wrong'. *Economics Letters 61*, 3–11.

Varian, H. (1994): 'Sequential Contributions to Public Goods'. *Journal of Public Economics 53*, 165–86.

Vickrey, W. (1991): 'Counterspeculation, Auctions and Competitive Sealed Tenders'. *Journal of Finance 16*, 8–37.

Wang, G. H., J. Kim and J. Yi (1994): 'Litigation and Pretrial Negotiation under Incomplete Information'. *Journal of Law, Economics, and Organization 10*, 187–200.

Weidner, H. (1996): 'Freiwillige Kooperationen und alternative Konfliktregelungsverfahren in der Umweltpolitik. Auf dem Weg zum ökologisch erweiterten Neokorporatismus?'. in: van den Daele, W. and F. Neidhardt (eds), *Kommunikation und Entscheidung. Politische Funktionen öffentlicher Meinungsbildung und diskursiver Verfahren*. WZB Jahrbuch. Berlin: Rainer Bohn.

Weyreuther, F. (1975): *Verwaltungskontrolle durch Verbände?* Düsseldorf: Werner.

Williamson, O. (1975): *Market and Hierarchies: Analysis and Antitrust Implications*. New York: Free Press.

Winter, G. (1990) (ed.): *Öffentlichkeit von Umweltinformationen. Europäische und nordamerikanische Rechte und Erfahrungen*. Baden-Baden: Nomos.

Wolf, R. (1994): 'Zur Entwicklung der Verbandsklage im Umweltrecht'. *Zeitschrift für Umweltrecht 1*, 1–12.

Index

administration
administrators' objectives 23–5
collusion with environmental groups
67–70
informal agreements *see* informal
agreements
levels of administrative decision-making
18–20
reconsideration of 'bumbling bureaucrat'
201–12
Administrative Procedure Act (Germany)
21, 37
Administrative Procedure Acts (US) 32
agencies
collusion 3, 24, 41
legal standing as deterrent to 43
control 23–9
administrators' objectives 23–5
bargaining incentives 25–6
information rights 35–7
oversight and judicial review 26–9
courts and 82–5
discretion 2, 26, 41–2, 217, 220
with asymmetrical legal standing
82–5, 89–91
choice of regulatory regime 60–63
complexity and 13–18
court's decision rule in model and
63–5
levels of decision-making and
18–20
model 48, 49, 54–60
green 105–6
in model 48–50
with asymmetrical legal standing
82–5, 89–91
monitoring 26–9
participation by 212
air pollution 13–14, 15
alternative dispute resolution 1, 8, 110,
136–7
bargaining with incomplete

information and 189–200, 218
see also mediation
Alternative Dispute Resolution Act (US)
137
alternative regulatory pathway 19
Althammer, W. 163
Amacher, G.S. 105, 106
Arndt, H.W. 18, 29
Ashford, N.A. 20, 136
Asimov, M. 37
Aspen Institute 19
associational standing *see* legal standing,
symmetrical
asymmetrical information 10, 16–17, 23
asymmetrical legal standing *see* legal
standing, asymmetrical
axiomatic game theory 10

Babich, A. 34
Bacow, L. 110, 152, 153, 154
Baik, K.H. 86
bankruptcy, fallacy of 95–6
Banks, J. 43
bargaining 1–4, 16, 39
with asymmetrical legal standing 79–
134, 217
agencies and the courts 82–5
'bumbling bureaucrat' and 204–5
commitment 109–11, 126–7
compared with symmetrical
standing 147–9
conservation offset duties 111–14,
217
cost-efficiency and differentiated
norms 114–16
discussion 105–17
environmental bargaining in
Germany 79–82
graded permits 124–6, 217
litigation costs 106–9
model framework 87–96

243